Mariana M. Tallman

Pleasant Places in Rhode Island, and How to Reach Them

Mariana M. Tallman

Pleasant Places in Rhode Island, and How to Reach Them

ISBN/EAN: 9783337380489

Printed in Europe, USA, Canada, Australia, Japan

Cover: Foto ©Andreas Hilbeck / pixelio.de

More available books at **www.hansebooks.com**

PLEASANT PLACES

IN

RHODE ISLAND,

AND HOW TO REACH THEM.

By MARIANA M. TALLMAN,

AUTHOR OF "TENT V., CHAUTAUQUA," "THE FAIRHAVEN FOURTEEN."

PROVIDENCE:
The Providence Journal Company,
1896.

TO MY FRIEND ALICE,

Whose companionship in many of these rambles has made their memory doubly pleasant.

CONTENTS.

PART I.—ALONG SHORE.

NEWPORT.
NARRAGANSETT PIER AND POINT JUDITH.
WATCH HILL.
BLOCK ISLAND.
QUONOCONTAUG BEACH.
CHARLESTOWN AND MATUNUCK.
CONANICUT PARK AND JAMESTOWN.
PRUDENCE PARK AND PRUDENCE ISLAND.
BRISTOL FERRY.

BRISTOL NECK AND LITTLE'S NARROWS.
SAUNDERSTOWN AND NARRAGANSETT FERRY.
TIVERTON HEIGHTS AND STONE BRIDGE VILLAGE.
SAKONNET POINT AND LITTLE COMPTON.
PAWTUXET, OLD AND NEW.
FIELD'S POINT.
NARRAGANSETT BAY.

PART II.—INLAND AND UPLAND.

IN AND ABOUT PROVIDENCE.
WEST GREENWICH, COVENTRY, EXETER AND BEACH POND.
THE PAWTUXET RIVER.
CUMBERLAND HILL AND SNEACH POND.
THROUGH THE NORTHERN TOWNSHIPS.

DIAMOND HILL.
QUINSNICKET.
FOSTER AND SCITUATE.
LINCOLN AND NORTH SMITHFIELD.
BURRILLVILLE AND HERRING POND.
LIME ROCK.

INTRODUCTION.

IN preparing this little book for a summer public, in quest of pleasant places to be found within our boundary lines, the writer is only too conscious how insufficient it is as a representative of even our own small State. It would be hard to find elsewhere on our coast an equally limited amount of territory in which are found so many phases of life, so great variety of scenery and so large a fund of legend and history as lie latent or discovered within our own borders. Aristocratic South County, with its wealth of legendary lore, traditions of slave days and Indian occupancy, the bleak hills and shores of Charlestown where the last of the Narragansetts still abide; the craggy hills of Cumberland, breeze-swept and bracing of air as true mountain regions; the limestone crags and kilns of Lime Rock, sitting remotely on the Lincoln hills; the dreamy old town of Bristol, its quaint architecture and sleepy, green-arched streets like a bit out of a past century, and the teeming foreign factory villages of the Pawtuxet and Blackstone valleys; all these have their own peculiar life and atmosphere; and on the remote and desolate shores of Quonocontaug or the rocky point of sea-beaten Sakonnet are counterparts of the bleak Maine coast that dawn like a revelation on Rhode Islanders who know only the familiar shores of our fair bay.

By no means a complete or even comprehensive guide-book of the State is this volume of sketches to be considered, but merely as its name indicates, an index to a few of the "pleasant places" to which accident or design has led. No doubt many readers will aver, and justly, that they know within their own precincts, many spots fairer and more interesting than those pictured in these pages; but if one will but trouble himself to glance at the list of abiding places, small and great, in fair Rhode Island, he will realize that long years would be required, in visiting and familiarizing one's self with all. Only those most typical and most picturesque which have come under the writer's notice have been selected, while the field of exploration is practically limitless.

M. M. T.

PART FIRST.

Along Shore.

NEWPORT.

[Two hours from Providence by Continental Steamboat Co., fare 60 cents round trip, or by Old Colony Railroad.]

IT is wholly superfluous, at this late day, to attempt to say anything new concerning a watering place of not only national, but world-wide fame: it is sketched again briefly here simply because a Rhode Island guidebook without Newport would be quite too like the play of Hamlet with Hamlet left out. Newport has had the experience, unique in sea-faring towns, of rising, decaying, Only a jumble of wharves and warehouses, some green with moss and mouldering with age, a tangle of narrow and muddy streets with scant "elbow room" on the worn and uneven sidewalks; shabby old wooden houses edging as near the highway as possible, with old-fashioned door caps and fan lights, and a general look of discouragement and decay. These are what greet him, but let him take the

COTTAGES FROM EASTON POINT.

and rising again from the ashes of departed mercantile industry in a new and unparalleled splendor. It is this linking of its old by-gone and forgotten life of manufactories and commerce with its new one of wealth and fashion that gives Newport of to-day a double charm. To the stranger approaching the historic old town by water, the first sight of Newport proper is a sad blow. Where are the elegant villas, the magnificent drives, the citizens of wealth and fashion, of which he has so long and so often heard? cable car waiting by the Post Office at the head of the dock, and be whisked up the hill, past churches galore, and crossing Bellevue avenue with a transient, but bewildering glimpse of fairy land, past a few of the fine old mansions with ample, English-like grounds, and down a long incline again eastward to famous Easton's beach and the sea. Here, about the ample and commodious new building erected there with its accessories of cafe, piazzas and multitudinous bath houses is always a vast and changing throng of patricians and plebeians bathing or beholding. At the noon hour, the fashionable bathing time, resplendent are the equipages that grace the sand, awaiting my lady's daily dip; while wandering excursionists lunch and gaze, and stroll on to the wilder and lonelier attractions of the second beach, on to

WHERE BERKELEY LIVED.

the left, or follow to the right the famous "Cliff walk," past Newport's most magnificent summer homes southward to Ochre Point. The second beach claims Newport's grandest shore scenery; here lie those huge rent cliffs dubbed respectively Paradise and Purgatory rocks; though in point of beauty there seems very little to choose between them. Purgatory rock has, of course, the usual legend of a famous leap by a mythical hero across its yawning chasm, and he who would undertake it must be indeed a strong-hearted athlete. There is fascination in lingering here, watching the booming surf and flying feathers of spray on hidden reefs far out at sea. Beyond lies Sachuest Point, the hanging rocks and the fair shore scenery beloved by Bishop Berkeley of old. Turning in the other direction and following the beaten path leading over the Cliffs, rising momently higher from the ocean, the way grows fairer as one journeys, and as the velvety, well-kept grounds of the wealthy dwellers on this lovely coast, vie with each other in profusion of luxury, one has opportunity to see what gorgeous palatial abodes may rise in the name of cottages. Millionaires from all over the land have here their summer homes, and gay junketings and days of midsummer madness pass here that have

no counterpart elsewhere outside Ouida's novels. Still on to the southern point of Rhode Island, otherwise Land's End, where the gray rocks drop in lessening detached ranks to the water's edge, brilliant in gold and brown of wave-washed rock weed and barnacle, the coast turns sharply westward, and Bailey's beach, with the famed spouting rock, lies beyond. Visitors are plenty here after a wild southwester has been raging, for with a thunderous shock into the black caverns below, the wild swinging billows are driven with the force of the whole Atlantic at their backs, and up through the narrow rock tunnel they ascend and fly in a white fountain of spray forty feet in the sunny air. Again, one may listen and watch in vain, when old ocean is contrary, and will hear but a sullen gurgling wash somewhere down in the black spaces below. On this south shore is the dreaded Brenton's reef, off whose inhospitable rocks has swung night and day since mariners multiplied on these seas the staunch lightship, with its two signal lights faintly seen, rising and falling with the swell, away over at Narragansett Pier by night.

Rounding the point at Castle Hill—but

NEWPORT'S OLDEST.

one must have a carriage to come all this way at one trip—Conanicut Island lies across the harbor, with a white line always showing about the southern rocks where gray Beaver Tail light rises; and all the way between, the water is crowded with craft of every description, that make up the gayest harbor on the United States coast. Men-of-war, Government cruisers, pleasure yachts, great and small, from the king of floating pleasure craft—down to the butterfly bits of catboats. Excursion steamers, water boats, launches for Goat Island and the Torpedo Station, the great Wickford and Jamestown ferryboats, the Block Island and Pier steamers, lumber and coal schooners, and farthest up north the training ship with her scores of erect lings." On the farthest of the two Lime Rocks rises the square white lighthouse guarded by our heroine of Narragansett, Ida Lewis, now a middle aged woman. It is worth one's while, in visiting the Government station over on Goat Island—where the tiny steam launches take one for a trifling sum—to stroll out to the long northern breakwater there, and see the stranded collection of old and new buoys,

THE CASINO.

and athletic young lads aboard—and between these all the rowboats, flitting with their uniformed crews. Even Clark Russell would have a difficult task before him in describing in detail the effect of this astonishingly lively port. The long gray frontage of Fort Adams juts out into the bay from the island's southwest peninsula, and strives to meet that queer little round baby of a fort over on Conanicut's gray rocks—christened the "Dump- awaiting transplantation. Some are crusted thickly with eel-grass, sea-weed, shells and barnacles; and the bell-buoys show here for the huge things they are—not at all the flat-topped rafts they seem, rocking on the water.

Drives are of endless diversion in and about Newport, for one may traverse the island over and daily find something new to please and interest; the old island graveyards, the pleasant country homes inland, the ancient histories of Portsmouth and Middletown, as well as the gay society life in the heart of the town. Bellevue avenue is the grand rallying place for the resplendent turnouts, the fine saddle horses and the gay tallyhos that belong distinctively to Newport, and on a sunny afternoon they are out in full force. The many bazaars that line this Parisian-like avenue are dazzling with their showy fronts of exquisite and novel luxuries, from millinery to hothouse exotics; and the stranger who may not enter within its gates may yet behold the Newport aristocracy entering and emerging from the homesteads hidden in the heart of wooded parks, with a quaint little porter's lodge by the gate, all gray stone, pointed latticed slits of windows and ivy-shrouded sides. There are the two fine hotels, the Ocean House and Aquidneck, the imposing Rogers High School, and in pretty little Touro Park the Perry monument and, chief joy and treasure of Newport, the mysterious old stone tower, once green with riotous ivy, but now for its better preservation bare and gray, with the unbroken lines of its many arches, defying history and legend for its origin. Over its building historians and chroniclers

W. K. VANDERBILT'S MARBLE PALACE.

Casino here, which, attractive and beautiful as its interior is, compares but poorly in outer effect with Narragansett's and its gray springing arch by the ocean. Here in the white and gold ball-room assemble the belles and beaux in the full bravery of their elaborate raiment; and matrons and mammas who have outgrown gauze, solace themselves with diamonds. It is a glittering pageant. August sees the tennis tournaments, the fox hunts—elaborate travesties on the old English sport—and the gayest gatherings, yet the social season lasts well into Autumn. Outside the fashionable pageant, there is much of interest in the heart of the town—the fine old churches, the famous Redwood Library, the pleasant old have wrangled in vain; and no one may ever surely know whether it is a monument of the Vikings who have left scanty trace along our shores in an occasional carving or unaccountable skeleton, or only what Benedict Arnold too briefly describes of "my stone-built wind mill." Those of us poetically inclined will prefer the version that the "skeleton in armor" was obliging enough to give to Longfellow:

"So for my lady's bower
Built I this lofty tower,
Which to this very hour
   Stands looking seaward."

But of this and other historical spots in old Newport, guide books are full of legend and description, and to particularize farther would be needless.

NARRAGANSETT PIER.

[Thirty-five miles from Providence. By rail, New York, Providence and Boston Railroad to Kingston, Narragansett Pier Railroad to Pier, $1.50 round trip. Or by small steamer from Newport, 75 cents round trip. Largest and best hotels, Gladstone, Rockingham, Mathewson and Berwick. Massasoit best of lower priced.]

IN itself, Narragansett Pier is far from being such a show-place as Newport. Its attractions need time and familiarity to reveal, and it often happens that the one-day tourist departs without having seen any of these prime attractions—the rocks, the Casino, the Hazard castle, Canonchet, the Ocean Road cottages or Point Judith—and bears away, therefore, a very disappointing impression of this far-famed watering place. With a competent guide and a comfortable carriage, a great deal is to be seen in a single day, in the "off-hours," when it is not absolutely essential to be present at either the bathing beach or the Casino. One may turn northward, if he like, through the picturesque villages of Peace Dale, the home of the Hazards, and Wakefield, surrounded by the home of many weird, wild legends: wandering up to the lovely Manouna Lake near Wakefield, where among two or three other charming summer cottages, Mr. H. S. Bloodgood's most delightful house stands enshrined among the trees—the scene of the old Indian legend of the ghost of Manouna, the remorseful mother who murdered her babies in the "Crying Bog" across the way, and whose unappeased shade nightly flits and wails along the dark lake's surface. And there is the Hunnowill Hill down beneath the Tower Hill heights, a clustered rock hillock rising from the long salt marsh, where the old slave owner lashed his runaway slave to a tree, and left him naked through the night at the mercy of the myriad mosquitos that have infested the marsh from years remote, to find him stone dead in the morning. South County is fortunate in having bards to sing and chronicle her many old legends, and between Shepherd Tom, Miss Caroline Hazard and Miss Carpenter's graceful writings there is little left untold, and the glamour of well-written verse lies over all this legendary land.

The Pier is unique as a watering place on this account. Probably not another

CASINO FIRE PLACE.

favorite resort, in the whole country round, has so many nooks and byways quaint with story and legend, and though the tide of summer festivity may wane low, there is always something between the uplands and the ocean to reward the stroller and the lingerer as long as they may choose to tarry, or over nine of the adjustable miles peculiar to the South County, by a winding road, the traveller may journey from the Pier to the Rowland Robinson mansion and Gilbert Stuart birthplace, keeping the ocean in sight most of the time and winding in and out among scenery that, every inch of the way, is either picturesque or historic, and mainly both. It is a devious way, if one trusts to oral instruction, but we have hit on a simpler direction. Cross the Pettaquamscut bridge northward, turn to the left, pass a white schoolhouse numbered 22, and from thence—follow the telegraph poles. They will lead infallibly round all the corners to the very lane at the journey's end. But on the way, the old Rowland Robinson place, with quite as much, if not more, claim to distinction, is to be visited, and the prettiest part of the drive is on the hither side of it. Whale Rock light, dark red in the distance, is passed far out at sea. Bonnet Head, down beyond the high green pastures where sheep are grazing, where a long line of white runs far up into the tranquil harbor, leaping at the black ribs of an old wreck that lies there yet among the sand and harsh sea grass; Conanicut, with the long gray line of her ancient bluffs along the barren western shores, and away to the south Beaver Tail lighthouse, looming a darker gray above the pale gray of sea fog, and wild surges forever leaping and striving at its base; beyond all, the near, tranquil, blue sea; and, farthest of all, the white wings of the fleet that lie always in fair Newport's anchorage. Along the roadside, though dwelling houses be few and far between, there are the hundred and one little no-account things that make a country drive interesting, and an enjoyable visit to this most interesting part of North Kingstown ought to be granted a whole day.

South from the Pier to Point Judith is, however, the favorite drive; it is a short

THE CASINO.

six miles over a fine macadam highway, with the blue ocean always to the left, and passing the "rock cottages" which are soon to claim supremacy as the nucleus of Narragansett social life. Mrs. Cresson's lovely home, unpretending enough without, with its gray balconies and twining green vines, but full to overflowing with all manner of dainty luxuries within, Mr. Cook's, Mr. E. H. Sanford's, one of the most picturesque, and the David Stevenson place, one of the newest and finest, and of which a detailed description may not be out of place, as typical of a growing phase of luxurious summer life on our bay.

No longer is this last imposing erection a nameless child, for it has been christ-

Point Judith, advancing across the lawns and ascending to the family portals with joyous and easy confidence, in full faith that the butler is ushering them into the famous Casino! It is small wonder, indeed, nor would the delusion be at once dispelled, for the Casino hallway is a mere child beside this of the Suwanee villa. High, massive and echoing, the polished floor gleams with oak tiles, covered here and there with rugs; oaken chairs curiously carved and covered with embossed leather stand invitingly here and there; the great walls of tinted plasters have their bareness broken by engravings framed in shaded oak and hung in slanting lines with odd but picturesque effect. Everything in the great hall is oak, to

SEA VIEW OF SUWANEE VILLA.

ened "Suwanee Villa," in compliment to Mrs. Stevenson's maiden name. Coming upon the great gray mass, oval casements and Dutch doors screened with gold-brown shutters peeping out amid the massive battlements, huge granite steps leading up to the stone-pillared balconies, and the ruddy gold and red of nasturtiums in rich flame between the gray stone and green turf, and the whole rising stately before the clear sweep of the blue Atlantic background—seeing it thus, the word "cottage" rises in one's mind as a most ridiculous misnomer, and prepares one to hear without astonishment the story that is getting to be a stale joke to the dwellers within. That of frequent sojourners in the land, faring north, perhaps, from

the carved festoons that run about the frieze, and the broad stairways; and the crowning glory is the huge mantel with sombre-twisted pillars, all of black oak, that stretches to the ceiling, and whose dark and sombre beauty is relieved only by a single tall, slender vase, a dash of blue in the centre. When the ruddy flames are leaping in the fireplace and tingeing the great, dark crossbeams of the room, then it is simply perfect. Between hallway and parlor is a triangular space with high arched alcove on the left, and here on its pedestal, like a heathen god on its throne, stands in solitary state a huge Japanese vase, all black, red and gold, and big enough to have sheltered that luckless young lover who made himself historical by shutting himself into an ancient clock-case. The parlor is a long room looking southward, finished in white wood and furnished with crimson damask, with portieres of old gold and electric blue, in heavy hangings. A cushioned divan in gold brown plush, cosily fills the southern window recess, piled high with pale blue satin cushions. The mantel mirror carries out the design of the elaborate carved wood frieze in similar festoons garlanded about its edges in putty work directly on its face. Shaded oak frames, framing engravings and process reproductions, are hung everywhere through the house—the only exceptions being two bits of oil paintings reposing on the gold-brown mantel draping in easel frames. Out of the drawing room opens the music room, likewise with polished tiled floor, as are they all, and in shape a horseshoe, looking seaward. Rattan furniture reigns here, even to the music stool, upholstered with gay cretonne. Beyond, and opening from the hall, is the dining room, stately and spacious also, with its long polished table, ponderous leather chairs, and massive sideboards glittering with silver. Cabinets built in the walls give gleams of brightness from the many hued bits of dainty china, crystal and pottery. The seaward-looking balcony stretches before the dining room, the long glass doors stand open, and one dines in blissful contemplation of the dancing waves, the flitting yachts, the flying breakers, and the blue and white of sea and sky. The glossy table is extinguished beneath a cloth only at breakfast time; a half-dozen exquisitely wrought napkins, elaborate with embroidered margin of leaves and flowers, embellish it at the other meals, and electric lights heighten the gleam of silver, glass and napery. The great pantry lies just beyond, the lavatory across a smaller hall and down the steps, and the kitchens lie below in the basement. Farther north, with a smaller but no less delightful balcony of its own, whose arches are adorned with wooden points, is the billiard room, with its high chairs ranged in solemn expectancy about the table. On the second room are the sleeping apartments, nine in all, with broader views still of lawn and rocks and ocean, and over the billiard room, where they may romp to their heart's content, is the nursery of the half-dozen olive branches—the eldest but fourteen.

Still higher are the servants' quarters, comprising the whole third floor, and as the household staff numbers among its retainers a cook, a kitchen maid, a nurse, a laundress, a chambermaid, a waiting maid, a coachman, a butler and a few other modern conveniences, a whole floor is none too much. The house is furnished everywhere with exquisite harmony, and with a massive, luxuriant simplicity that carries out to completed perfection the promise of its stately exterior. Two sisters of Mr. Stevenson make the family ten, though Mr. Stevenson spends only Saturday and Sunday here. When one remembers that all this luxuriance and beauty is shut up in solitude here from October to June, as a mere superfluity to be dispensed with till the summer fitting, it sets one pondering upon the queer ways with which this world's goods seem to be divided; but it is nevertheless a small and sordid soul that cannot take an honest and unenvious pleasure in the contemplation of the goods that have fallen to a lucky winner in life's lottery.

DUNMERE.

Farther away from the road, quite down on the edge of the rough and surf beaten rocks, is the huge and imposing summer home "Dunmere," belonging to R. G. Dun, and notable as the scene of the most festive gatherings of a Pier summer, when Mrs. Dun gives her August reception, and young men and fair maidens come from over seas at Newport to grace the occasion, and the great mansion is ablaze with light and gayety almost till the gray morning breaks over the water. The very entrance to Dunmere, with its beautiful stone arch, cost the modest sum of $10,000. Farther beyond, in solitary state by itself, away down Point Judith way, is the queer gray and white stone cottage of Edmund Davis, known as Scarborough. "Scarborough Beach" is a new-fangled title which meets with scorn and derision among genuine old South County folk. On this subject a hoary-headed and hatless haymaker, looking much like a wild-eyed Father Time, held forth to us with righteous indignation as he pointed out the landscape from an exalted eminence on Tower Hill. "There's Stinkin' Beach down yender," he announced with indignant and wavering hand extended. "Folks hed t' go'n name it over Scarbry! Stinkin' Beach was plenty good enough for us!"

Past Scarborough, then, to go basely over to the modern majority, the road leads to Point Judith, name of ill-omen to mariners, with its blocky white lighthouse, its fog signal building, with its two huge horns, the life saving station, whose crew have jocularly nailed aloft over their door the legend washed ashore from a wrecked schooner, "Harry A. Barry." Fragments of rocks strew all this wild, stormy shore, and for a half mile out into the angry southern sea, the force of the breakers is spent on the sharp-tongued rocks of the hidden reefs that breed disaster. There is a constant seethe and foam like the Niagara rapids, but for all that, the ocean looks placid enough not to have sent high and dry up on the pebbly beach the two huge battered wrecks that have lain there now for years—one a framework open to the heavens and sea, half a mile down the coast, most affected by artists and photographs, because more picturesque; the other a huge four-masted schooner, looming up almost on her beam ends down on the shore directly before the fog signal house, now and then sadly diverting the sound to the misleading of

ENTRANCE TO DUNMERE.

passing craft. But it is a fascination to merely linger in the old wreck's aged timbers, to feel the shock of the sea's assault on her shattered frame—to see the green lifting billows shatter to foam on the sharp-toothed reefs that make the dreaded point a terror to mariners, or to venture out on the narrow and shaky fishing stand anchored to a rock that rises out in the boiling surf, hard by the well-known "old man's face" that stares stolidly up to the summer sky, unblinking in the fierce baptism of the waves.

From this sharp point the lonely shore stretches west, unbroken by settlements, away past Matunuck, Charlestown, Noyes's Beach and Quonocontaug till the

Rhode Island shore ceases with Watch Hill, and Little Narragansett Bay proclaims division from Long Island Sound.

Altogether, the Point Judith drive is prime favorite, and it is customary to pause in returning, before the Pier is quite reached, at "Sherry's," "Earlscourt," or "Casa Sherri," for the little isolated spa out on the reclaimed marsh is known indifferently by all three names. A half circle of seven gray cottages, with the cafe in the centre, it is the seat of the most select dinner parties and the gayest subscription balls of a Narragansett season. Sherry's fame needs no herald, as a caterer, and the seven cottages are invariably filled by satisfied sojourners. In its evening gala dress, with the half circle gay with pendant Japanese lanterns, the cafe and dance hall flower-entwined and green-festooned jardinieres with palms and ferns standing everywhere, the supper—itself a triumph of art—served in the midst of a floral bower, with a perfumed fountain of light musically dripping down a miniature ravine in a recess, and with the wild swirls and swells of the weird melodies played by the Royal Hungarian Band—then, indeed, is Sherry's a chief magnet of attraction to summer guests.

Between here and the Pier proper, in the heart of a dense jungle of woods, lies the queer freak of one of the Hazard family, known as the Hazard Castle, and with its seven-storied tower a landmark for many leagues of ocean. Built in 1842, for a purpose never yet defined, by Joseph Peace Hazard, both the tower and the queer little rambling house of twenty rooms at its base have been practically neglected for many years; but its latest change of hands has denied access to the tower and the grounds as well. It is almost a pity, for a bird's eye view like that from its summit is seldom granted a lover of nature. Its whole story is a very queer one, and almost equally queer is that of the great square stone house in the same grounds, a trifle farther down the road, known as the "Druid's Dream," and adjoining the Hazard graveyard with the memorial tablets to the memory of its founder, surrounded by the four stone posts with hollow caps for drinking fountains for the wild birds, and with the chiseled motto that reveals the kindliest side of the erratic builder's strange nature:

"Whate'er man's mode of faith, or creed,
Who feeds the wandering birds shall himself be fed."

No one has ever inhabited the Druid's Dream, either, but a care taker of the graveyard and the house, and within its walls music and dancing and merry making generally, are sternly forbidden.

HAZARD CASTLE.

The social life at Narragansett, though a cosmopolitan resort, yet is composed of on unvarying routine. One rises somewhere between eight and nine, breakfasts leisurely, and seeks the friendly "rocker" on the big hotel piazza, where a goodly community of rocking neighbors read their letters, gossip, work on the elaborate summer embroidery purchased for the pious purpose of astonishing and outshining the neighbor embroiderers, and contemplate the ocean and the passing yachts till it is time to join the line of march shoreward.

The ocean was presumably the prime magnet which resolved Narragansett into a unit. Its magnificent bathing beach, its long line of cliffs, the mildness of its sea air, and the goodly scenery on every hand; but the ocean would seem now but a mere excuse—a slighted object. Can it be the vast, wild Atlantic that tosses its spray up into the very streets where jaunty vehicles go bowling with stocky little steeds with tails more abbreviated than spaniels or fox terriers; dashing along in tandem profile, while jolly youths mounted aloft send the blast of the merry horn in wavering cadences along the echoing byways? One needs to look far out at sea to believe that this is indeed the same ocean that washes the wild Maine coast, or even the lonely shores and dunes of Quonocontaug, or the red rocks of Sakonnet. The real lover of sea and solitude must feel here as sadly bewildered as did the "princess of Thule" when she went with glad expectancy to see the ocean at Brighton. However, the Pier is cosmopolitan and independent, and if one wants to dress quietly, go bathing in the afternoon, and fishing in the early morning, he is welcome to, with no worse criticism than that of oddity.

An ephemeral summer population is composed by the many merchants and venders of dainty and expensive novelties, whose windows brighten the heart of the place, and adorn Beach Row. The cottagers are, in this as all else, the paying customers and the majority. It is the cottagers who make up the wealth and the patronage of the many Narragansett bazaars, though many of the hotel people can count their millions. Still, it is an open secret to those familiar with the Pier's denizens and their inner walks of life that two months at Narragansett Pier often means a lavish spread which is the reward of ten months pinching and scraping. These are the people at whom the rustic tourist stares and wonders, mistaking for true nobility. The real people are the quiet ones, and the pretenders or nouveaux riches are the snobs, almost without exception. No better instance can be shown of the quietly lavish expenditure of money than by a few samples of the articles that have gone into summer homes as summer luxuries, or shipped to Southern and Western cities; for it is the South and West that populate the Pier, as a Rhode Islander might easily guess by the almost foreign accent of a group at Casino, beach or tennis court. The caterers to luxurious tastes understood this fact; they know that rare importations, revived antiques and expensive bric-a-brac are not easily obtainable either south or west of us, and they prepare a gilded market accordingly. Rare Persian rugs, on either side of the $100 price, change hands readily for the assuagement of slippery hardwood floors; antique lamps, converted from old English wine coolers or tea urns, ranging from $50 to $75, may be found in dozens of the palatial "cottages," purchased from dealers here who make a specialty of genuine antiques; one massive and quaint silver candelabrum in spiral coils, valued at $75, is now for sale in such a bazaar, and the dealer says he has only to put it in the window to secure an immediate sale. Why? Well, because connoisseurs are plenty here at the Pier who are looking out for such things, and a connoisseur knows that candelabra for four candles, genuine antiques, are the rarest things in the world to find. They run to two, five, any number but four. The dealer was right, and the event fulfilled his sanguine prophecy. Curios in silver and handwrought gold frames sell dozens here in a summer's course at prices ranging from $25 to $50; and one has only to look around at an especial dress occasion, private ball or Casino hop to see the delicate carved ivory fans, the combination of marabout and carved tortoise shell, or the delicate pink made from the wings of the Southern pink curlew—all bringing $5 easily, to see how quickly these perishable trifles find a market.

Elegant imported tables sell readily for from two to five hundred dollars, so it is not alone the hotel coffers that are enriched by the summer citizens. Cottage life, within the Pier limits, is often that of luxury, quiet and unpretending, perhaps, but involving an outlay of many thousand dollars for mere summer adorning. Take, for an example, the pretty "Star Cottage" of Mrs. Butterfield of Washington. It is simple enough in exterior and not over-imposing within, but admirably adapted to summer entertaining. Her dances and five o'clock teas have long been vastly enjoyed by society young folk, and her music room is pretty enough for special description. It is a separate addition to the house, having outer Dutch doors of its own, with fanlights above, beside the connecting door with the main house. It is a most charming room, about twenty-five feet square, with its corners running obtusely across, instead of at sharp right angles. A most dainty, radiant room it is, all white and gold, with its white fluted walls, simulating hangings of silk. The great lamp on the antique Dutch inlaid table in the centre of the room has a small table, for these Friday evening dances are to alternate with old-fashioned teas, between the same sensible hours of eight and eleven. On an iron frame, a huge figure five, hangs the shining brass kettle, and the tea tray cover has ripe strawberries and leaves embroidered around its edges. Overhead, on the white ceiling, are genuine golden constellations, Ursa Major glistening triumphant with the pointers indicating the north star, just within the northern entrance. The whole effect of this charming music room is indescribably dainty and brilliant. The

CANONCHET.

shade of golden silk, with a frilled fall of white lace. The candles are in white waxen clusters in the golden candelabra, and bits of tiny stands alternate with easy chairs of white and gold. The polished floor is oak, with an inlaid Grecian border of oak alternating with mahogany. The broad, high windows are draped oddly and gracefully with snowy muslin, with huge polka dots. Couches of old rose, crushed raspberry, old gold and electric blue plush, piled high with cushions of corresponding hue, stand about the room, and an upright piano is at one end. In a cozy corner is a little tea service on a cottage is crowded with curious and interesting bric-a-brac, exquisite Dutch inlaid furniture lingering about it, Burgundy wine carriages of twisted wire from Berlin, and dining room panels of rare French maple, like polished onyx, exhumed from a half-century's storage in a Washington warehouse.

Nothing, however, in the way of elaborate furnishings could compare with Canonchet in its palmy days, lordly Canonchet, scarce a stone's throw from the beach, and stately and resplendent even now, with its sixty-two rooms, comprising bath rooms with every suite. In the days of Mrs. Kate Chase Sprague there was nothing in simple Rhode Island to compare with it, when in the paved dining room, the old style of Roman luxury was daily enacted, the fountain plashed in the centre of the tiled court, and guests dined to soft orchestral music. The grounds about the fine old place are beautiful as a dream, with the wooded vistas looking out on the flowing Pettaquamscutt, the distant Tower Hill heights and the spreading ocean, with Newport and Conanicut dreaming in the distant sunshine, and white surges always leaping about red Whale Rock light, and the ocean's murmur sounding always faintly in the tranquil air. Canonchet has had a romantic history from first to last, too long and too well known of old Providence citizens to repeat here.

Bathing hour is, of course, the chief daily event; at the magnificent, long, pebbleless beach, with its booming surf, one may see at high noon all Narragansett, either bathing or beholding, with the exception always of the hundred little folk, to whom Narragansett is a true baby's paradise, and who, sheltered in white tent or gay marquee down on the sand, in the care of black or French bonne, dig and delve and make forts and mountains and, above all, pies, of the tempting sand that the roaring sea creeps up nightly to demolish and devour. The babies of the Pier are worth a chapter of their own, such lovable and picturesque and highbred little mites are they.

With the increasing August heat, the number of beach frequenters increases, and there daily gather on the sands a changing multitude of spectators to the great fancy dress carnival that takes place at high noon daily among the tumbling breakers. At first sight, coming suddenly upon hundreds of bobbing red caps among the seething foam, one imagines he has hit upon an assemblage of Turks, in fez and toga; but as arms toss wildly upward in a heaving wave, the picture grows to one of the weird scenes in the "Orlando Furioso," or—yes, like a rabble of French canaille, shouting "Vive la guerre!" and "Down with the Bastile!" anything at all but kinsmen of that gay throng assembled high and dry under awnings and balconies.

The bathing beach is the great leveler of distinctions. Bring the genial autocrat Holmes, that great stickler for aristocracy of birth and breeding, down here by the Pier bath, seat him in one of our particularly hard chairs there for an hour or so, and let him muse on the strange transformations that a simple flannel costume and a douche of sea water combine to produce, and bid him retract.

"If two stranger queens," quoth Holmes, "shipwrecked and destitute, were cast ashore upon a desert rock, each would instinctively address the other as 'Your Majesty.'" Oh, no, Mr. Holmes, they wouldn't, not if they were clad in baggy flannel bathing suits, and little, black tails of tresses trickling down over their eyes. They would have sand in their feet and points in their elbows, and their graceful movements would be hampered by soggy garments, and they would say: "Here, you!" or, What ho, menial!" according to the several fashions of their countries. In the water is felt most strongly that fellow-feeling which makes us wondrous kind, and blue-blooded patricians hobnob with unknown plebeians in a common struggle for egress from an encroaching wave.

The general color effect in this ducking and bobbing multitude, is of navy blue, garnished with scarlet, these colors being largely predominant, but here and there is a variation, especially among the men, who affect the convict garb, and stride manfully seaward with no feminine shilly-shallyings among the seductive lesser waves, or recline in groups along the sand, suggestive of limitless " Dying Gladiators," or, in their plethora of bared legs and arms " Laocoons." Few of the very little folk venture in at all, the roar of the waves and the might of their motion being altogether too much for baby nerves. A few little pantalooned ducklings paddle in the shallow water near shore, or jump Liliputian breakers six inches high, created especially for their small selves, but most of them, setting timorously forth into the vasty deep with an attendant on either hand, speedily emerge with loud lamentation, and scuttle up the beach like so many baby crabs.

It is gala time with the dogs, too, little and big, and the water-loving are kept busy retrieving among the breakers. Far out at sea, placidly bobbing up and down in lonely contentment, is to be seen the season through a fat old man in a scarlet jersey. He looks like nothing in the world so much as a can buoy.

Dripping skeletons and masquerading Falstaffs, Venuses and washerwomen, the hour at last up, go hastening up the beach, and running the gauntlet of spectators with more haste than in their downward progress, disappear among the bathing boxes.

EARLSCOURT TOWER.

The furious surf of a sou'wester often washes in from far away sea groves long ribbons of kelp, green, bronze and maroon, and it is a fantastic sight when the hundreds of bathers duck themselves in these slippery garlands, and sport like so many mermen and maidens in the flying surf. All sorts of aquatic exercises are indulged in at bathing hours; even base ball is sometimes extemporized in the billows; and often there is a mad race of several lightly clad flying male figures through the crowd and far down the hard shining sand toward Pettaquamscutt. The Neptune bathing suit, beginning to be used extensively, does much toward the enjoyment of a bath, for it has a neat little hidden bladder that is filled, and gives one double buoyancy. A pretty girl looks doubly pretty in her dark blue, modest bathing gown; but now and then a portly old lady or hurrying Falstaff ventures down the sands with disastrous effect. The bath is practically over at 1 o'clock, and the great procession moves on to the Casino, to while away the time before dinner, when drives and "rocking" shall be in order. This phrase, a familiar one in the Pier vernacular, has no connection with chair, hammock or rowboat, but is derived directly from its nearest source, the rocks. How often does the solitary wanderer, springing from crag to crag of the broken bowlders, heaped along the eastern shore, spy a brilliant bit of color perched on the edge of the stony plateau he is approaching, and wonders if it be some strange tropical bird or blossom, or unknown sea-growth stranded high above tide mark. Cautiously approaching, he sees this brilliant exotic slowly resolve itself into the top of a parasol, the apex of a coquettish little chapeau, or a flattering rampant bow of ribbon, beneath which, on a conveniently jutting ledge, is seated a rare and radiant maiden, and one of the much-prized, rarer and more radiant young men beside her. Shamefacedly does the solitary traveller beat a retreat, whose noise the booming breakers obligingly cover as they thunder in, and leave the discovered to blissful ignorance. He scales to dizzy heights, or descends to caverns perilously near the leaping billows' onslaught, and thinks himself the first intruder. But ten to one if he do not find ere he turn, caught in some rock crevice, the fragment of a letter torn to bits in feminine fashion, a burnt match or two, a cigarette stub, a shriveled cluster of what were once royally pink pond lilies, first favorite of Pier flowers, and these mementoes tell their own tale. The rocks are indeed the best of Narragansett; heaped in tumbled profusion for a mile or more south of the steamboat landing, they lie exposed to the full onslaught of the swinging Atlantic billows, and there is, after a day of wind and gale, a wild excitement in watching the lifting heads of the wild sea-horses, with white mane flying, dashing themselves to nothingness on the sharp ledges, or springing high and solid against the massive sea-wall. Here is the much-painted and photographed Indian rock, with the customary legend of the Indian, who leaped from its jutting point into the raging sea, rather than be captured. Sunset Rock looms highest, and from its eminence one can watch the reeling and staggering little "Caswell," swinging in or out from the one staunch pier that has been able to stand on Narragansett shores, as she comes and goes from Newport. Day excursionists would doubtless repair here oftener if there were a quicker and more direct water route, but even as it is, the trip by steamer is a charming one, with pause of an hour or two at Newport, and then a rolling passage around Beaver Tail, and across the surging seas at the bay's entrance, in the dancing and rocking little Caswell, as she parts the rushing waves with her glistening bow. The pier frontage is then most picturesque and imposing, as one comes upon it after the flying plumes of spray that assault the red Whale Rock lighthouse are passed, and the steamer swings quietly in to the modest little pier. Half a mile of hotels present an almost solid rampart from the rocks that begin at Greene's Inn to the huge, gray arch of the Casino, whence come faint strains of music across

FIRE PLACE IN GREENE'S INN.

the water. On one hand is the long, yellow line of the beach sand, and the white line of the leaping breakers, and on the other the gray of the tumbled rocks and bowlders, battered by the booming Atlantic, and crowned by picturesque cottages and velvety lawns. It is a rough passage, to be sure, from Newport over in the reeling little vessel, but a most enjoyable one to ocean lovers.

Most exciting is it to cross in one of the famous Newport fogs, when fog-horns are booming dismally everywhere, as the fog comes down and hides the sunlight. High and white against the distant Whale

Rock Light the invading surges spring and shatter, and far beyond it, spectral ships sail out of a low-lying fog bank that stealthily pursues and swallows them up again. There is no Conanicut, no Newport, though the day is fair and sunny—nothing but a wildly rocking little steamer, a veritable maid of the mist, that comes swinging sturdily out of the gray mystery, and bears passengers away to an unknown borne. People who know say that the passage from Narragansett to Newport is worse than the famous English Channel as a provoker of mal de mer.

But ocean fogs are charming—"sea turns," the good old Pine-tree State natives call them. One cannot catch cold from them, try he never so hard; they add a charming variety to the landscape, when they are considerate enough not to obliterate it entirely; and they smell good enough to eat.

Other pictures are many in the changing atmosphere. Go down to the bathing beach, or even along the Ocean road before the hotel front in the dark, and watch the wonderful electric flash of white that shows transiently where the surf is breaking. That is all one sees—those glancing lines of white that fly far to right and left in the black night faster than the eye can follow; now by twos, now by threes, now singly. It is a spectacle that often holds the homeward-going stroller a long, long time. I recall how one summer August came in at the Pier with a wild and rattling hailstorm, and how July went out with a wild and weird picture over the moonlit sea. Red as blood the round moon rose, and went slipping and climbing through sinister black bars and blotches. Over where Newport lay dreaming, a gray line over the dark waters, pink flashes winked momently in the sky, and showed, piled ominously against their transient gleam, great mountains of cloud bank, climbing silently higher. Back to the winking lightning winked the white electric lights of the Pier, the distant lightship, the flash of Point Judith. Only red Whale Rock light and white Beaver Tail gazed steadfastly up to the steadfast evening star above the barred moon, the pink lightning and the heaving black billows, tipped with gray in the strange light of the red-haloed moon. A black silhouette against the pink sky, far Conanicut rose transiently in the lightning's flash, and then sank to dim grayness. To complete the weird picture a brass band on the Berwick's great lawn sat amid flaring torches, and the wild strains of music gathered an audience of slowly passing vehicles along the ocean highway that loomed black and huge against the gray water like a procession of camels along the moonlit desert. Perched all along the massive graystone walls sat groups of si-

WRECK OF THE MAGGIE SMITH.

lent listeners, for all the world like companies of penguins on the rocks, while the surf broke dismally down on the boulders. It was one of Narragansett's strangest pictures, to be long remembered.

The social life of the Pier clusters of course around the Casino, its most picturesque and most attractive feature. All its comforts and conveniences are open to the summer subscriber for a trifling sum for the season, but a single admission is fifty cents. The Casino comprises the offices, the ladies' reading room, the gentlemen's reading room, three suites of furnished apartments, two private dining rooms in the tower, the billiard room, the rotunda, the ball room, the large cafe and kitchens, while the many balconies look down on the velvet green of the tennis courts, where the August tournaments are held, and the paved veranda on the ocean front is packed at the midday concerts by Lander's Orchestra with a gossiping, idle, half-listening audience, robed all in their best, who leisurely listen, and lunch the while away time till dinner. Over the Ocean road is the Casino's most romantic quarter —the breezy upper promenade, stone-pillared, over the springing eastern arch, swept always by ocean's breezes, and illuminated at night by the red glow of incandescent lights by which the voyager knows the Pier for many miles away at sea. This charming shadowy spot is known as "Cupid's Arch," and many memories of our gay summer girls go back to its sheltered nooks, where countless ices and lemonades and other liquid refreshments are consumed tete-a-tete, while the dance music sounds faintly from afar, and old ocean's orchestra thunders weirdly down below where the unseen rocks rise from the black water. Wednesday and Saturday are the dress occasions—the Casino hop nights, besides the countless dances held in hotel parlors: to some onlookers, however, Thursday night, devoted to the little folk, is a far more interesting occasion. Clad in their best bibs and tuckers, little Miss Goldilocks and all her ilk—for small boys are sadly in the minority—hie to the Casino, where a bit of the orchestra, all their very own, awaits them, and plays "York" and all the other pet dances that the mites love, while the grown folk look down applaudingly from above. What matter is it that some of the wee tots don't "know the steps?" I defy a quaint little fairy, all in gauzy white, with flowing love locks, bits of shoulder knots, and silken half hose on her plump little legs, showing her rounded little limbs nearly to her dimpled knees—I defy her to look awkward if she try. And as the wee little feet twinkle so merrily from left to right, and tiptoe round and round with the abandon that only childhood knows, pink, white and blue bits of frocks mingling so mazingly in the merry measures, it looks a veritable dance of the pixies, and the wild dance almost beckons one to

"Rise and go where they flit and fleet,
The little red shoon on the twinkling feet."

And the August carnival, usually under Herr Marwig's direction, calls out the especial bloom and grace of the summer fraternity.

Popular as Narragansett has been for long years, its best day should lie yet before it. Yearly more lands and nations are represented at its twenty great hotels, and yearly the list of celebrities tarrying on its shores grows longer, while the cottage "season" lasts practically half the year.

WATCH HILL.

[Stonington Railroad to Westerly or Stonington, then by small steamer down Pawcatuck river or across Bay. Two hours from Providence. Watch Hill House, the best, $4.00 per day. Seven others, Plimpton House, the best low priced.]

SEEN from the sea, from the deck of a distant vessel, Watch Hill does not look its best. The round bulk of that ancient lookout of the Niantic Indians which gives the place its name rises up and intercepts the view of the rolling hills, hotel-crowned, the western shore, bazaar-lined, and little Narragansett bay, craft-crowded, that help to make the promontory lively. And excursionists come home and report, as we often hear them, that Watch Hill is a bleak, lonely place, all sand and no trees, and it is strange what any one can want to go there for.

boulder-sprinkled bluff. Here is the great white square of the lighthouse, and the huge, gray granite tower, all surrounded by a high and massive sea wall that mocks the Atlantic rollers springing impotently on the tumbled stone below. On the seaward point are also the life-saving station, where keeper Nash has done so long and so brave service, a fisherman's shanty or two, and fish nets and lobster pots galore. Eastward from this wild promontory the yellow shore slants away six miles till it runs out to a southern point again at Noyes Beach, there on to Quonocontaug with its Asha-

WATCH HILL FROM PAWCATUCK BAY.

Watch Hill is, indeed, unique as a shore resort, both in its natural features and in the unity of its social element, which has grown to be a power in the last eight years. To describe the first briefly to those unfamiliar with our extreme southwest possession, while it is to roughly shear the place of all its detailed beauty, may yet give a crude idea of its general character.

A high, rolling and rocky promontory runs straight southwest into the ocean, terminating, unlike most peninsulas, in a point which runs up yet higher into a

way inhabitants, and still on to more familiar but wilder waters at Point Judith, where our own bay begins. The whole eastern shore as far as the eye can reach from Watch Hill lies open to the onslaught of the swinging southern billows, straight from leagues of open ocean. Westward, the sea lies placidly enclosed in the long sickle of slender sand bar that curves out from the very hotel wharves, and, ceasing on one side at Napatree Point, runs on still on its upper length a mile or two more till it terminates at length in Sandy Point, sinking beneath the water and making a submarine foundation for myriads of waving eel-grasses. A remarkable ocean sickle is this, one interminable, undulating sand dune, thrown up by combined wind and wave in long years, and bristling with harsh beach grass.

Half way down it stands the old Peninsula House, once a hotel, and two years ago washed from its foundations in a high gale and tide. It has been carelessly set back on spiles, and is untenanted and windowless. Across the quiet stretch of water thus protected lies Stonington, five miles distant, and the common terminus for most travellers Watch Hill bound, whether by way of New York, Providence or Boston. A little steamer plies constantly across, and it is a vastly pleasant half hour's sail, skirting the long sickle, passing the mouth of the Pawcatuck flowing from Westerly and the north, and avoiding the two treacherous reefs that show their ugly heads, yellow with rock weed, above the water at low tide. The two Hummocks, island hillocks, rise distinctly across the sand bar, and the heights of Fisher's Island are gray and blue in the far away sunshine. On its seaward end the summer cottages are dimly outlined, and other vague shadows unrecognized here resolve themselves from the Watch Hill heights into Long Island, Gull and Block.

The terminal wharf lies right at a hotel's foot, and as the whole place is compact, all the hotels and cottages are within very easy walking distance, though by an up and down route. Sunset Hill rises on the west shore, looking straight across Little Narragansett, and still farther north is Money Hill, one of the many alleged hiding spots of Capt. Kidd's profuse wealth, where more than one of the Watch Hill small boys annually excite themselves and vainly dig. All the way between here and the real Watch Hill looming from the southeast shore is wild, rolling land, the hillocks a tawny graygreen like plush with its peculiar wiry grass, sand-nourished.

From any one of these heights, as soon as the sun has sunk in a peculiar blaze of splendor that only Watch Hill knows, with the atmosphere all a golden mist, in which the distant islands swim, from far and near, east, west and south, glimmer the golden lights from lighthouse towers, Fisher's Island, Montauk, Point Judith, Block Island, Watch Hill, Gull Island, The Hummocks, Stonington, New London, Norwich, Mystic, and the rolling lightship, a goodly company indeed. In spite of all these warning beacons, and the melancholy bell buoy ringing lonely out beyond the southern sea wall, many a good ship comes to grief on these shores, and bleaching skeletons and driftwood, little and big, strew all the pebbly sand of East Beach, where the breakers are always roaring.

From about the pyramidal rocks on Lookout Hill, and elsewhere in its region, have been gathered many Indian relics, suggestive of the days when King Ninigret and his dusky tribes waged their frequent combats with the encroaching Block Island red men from twenty miles out at sea. In the old Stonington courts annals are still preserved of the peninsula's old time changes of ownership. Its ancient boundary lines are very quaintly defined in an old document dated 1688, the conveyance deed of Nathaniel Lynde.

"The persell or neck of land Commonly Called or known by the Several name or names of Pawcatuck alies Squamochuck neck, beginning at a stake stuck in the East side of a Creek one Rod west of the mouth thereof; the said Creek being between two small Necks of uppland, and Runs into a piece of salt Marsh, at the head of a Cove being on the East side of pauckatuck River, which said stake is the North Easterly Corner. And from thence in a straight Lyne South fifteen degrees East to Cross the said Neck three hundred and fifty eight Rod by mark trees and heaps of stones into the salt Water pond Called Mossachuge, which is the south East Corner, from thence bounded southerly by said pond and beach and whatch hill pond and beach as said ponds and beaches joynes unto the uppland with whatch hill peyntt being the south west corner,"

and so on.

The surf beach sinks with a sudden slant down out of sight among the breakers, and in itself confirms the universal statement that bathing there is dangerous and the undertow strong. The bathing beach, a long, safe and excellent one, is on the other side of the slender neck, close to the sickle handle that runs west. None of the picturesque salt marshes that abound generally by surf beaches are to be found near Watch Hill; from an artistic point of view this is perhaps to be regretted, but it is amply atoned for by the absence of those customary midsummer pests, mosquitos and flies. There is unusual life and vigor in the fresh breezes that sweep this high point, and in all the "hot snaps" Watch Hill invariably records the lowest temperature, 77 degrees being its most aspiring point when the mercury the same week in Providence was skipping recklessly about among the nineties.

To these last two facts are largely due the place's wonderful growth; it was only ten years ago that the large Cincinnati syndicate began to sell house lots into which the 160-acre purchase was divided. Now the slopes are covered with handsome and picturesque summer homes of wealthy New Yorkers and Westerners—the north end being peopled almost wholly by Cincinnati guests. Among the finest cottages on the hill are the two Anderson places, to one of them belonging a small salt pond connecting with the sea, where private bathing houses have been erected, and a water toboggan gives one a sudden douche bath. Miss Mabel Anderson, his daughter, died in the summer of '91 here; she was but eighteen, and one of the especial favorites among the many charming girls, and her sudden death cast a gloom over the whole place.

Mr. Anderson, Mr. Jacob S. Burnet, Mr. Lyneas Norton and Mr. Walter S. Jones are among the prime movers in the summer colony's growth, gentlemen known as among the most influential of Cincinnati's citizens. With these powerful leaders, a congenial element soon followed, prominent New Yorkers who were that happy combination of moneyed and modest people also erected cottages, and to-day it would be difficult to find anywhere a summer colony representing the wealth and social prestige of Watch Hill, with equal unpretentiousness. The young girls dress with perfect simplicity in dainty gingham and outing flannels, rather than the over-elaborate raiment at Newport and the Pier. It is true that in our recent stay there more diamonds and other precious stones decked the hands of the fair dames than have blazed forth on us elsewhere in the season's tarrying, but they were worn where they should be—at high tea and the evening germans.

Gov. Howard and his nephew, William C. Hastings, of New York, were the first to build here; the first cottage a modest brown one, stands beside the bowling alley. Mr. Hastings's own cottage is one of the most perfect seaside homes imaginable, a real cottage, not over imposing, with its every room finished throughout —floors, walls and ceilings—in carefully selected hard pine, without a knot, in various tints in the different rooms, paneled and decorated ceilings, the hall walls finished in beveled squares, the dining room in diagonal panels, and the arch between the parlors elaborately carved. With the floors profusely strewn with rugs, the gleam of bright china, ancient and modern, from sideboards and cabinets, the glow of nasturtiums, pansies and lilies from vases and fireplaces, and the whole effect softened and made fairy-like by tall lamps with huge tinted shades and soft chairs and couches inviting repose, it is a most restful summer home. Mr. Hastings is chief organizer of the Improvement Society formed three years ago, to which all the cottagers belong, and which is doing good work in a quiet way.

Some elaborate entertainment for raising additional funds is agitated in the near future. Mr. Hastings is what might be called the "business manager" of the very remarkable Watch Hill Chapel. Remarkable it is in this way, that it is a union chapel, thoroughly non-sectarian, and yet crowded to the utmost capacity of its 400 seats each Sunday; also that not only do Protestants worship here, but there is an 8 o'clock morning mass for the Catholic element among the servants, and an evening service in the vestry for the colored people. Moreover, the pretty little building, built in 1877 at a cost of $10,000, was paid for entirely before the shavings had been swept away, and the organ, worth nearly $1000, was subscribed for and its purchase guaranteed within three days. So, as one sits of a Sunday within its quiet precincts he realizes the sincerity of the golden mottoes gleaming on its walls: "The church is many as the waves, but one as the sea," and "In essentials unity, in non-essentials liberty, in all things charity." Clergymen are engaged for the summer services early in spring and come on from New York to fill the pulpit, and it is a source of pride to the summer fraternity that the shining lights of the pulpit invariably offer tribute to the superior intelligence of Watch Hill congregations. The weekly collection quite defrays these rather heavy expenses.

It will be seen from this alone that the Watch Hill cottagers are harmonious. Cottage life is quiet here, the special diversions being relegated wholly to the hotels. Some brilliant germans have been given, and there is the usual full dress Saturday hop at the two leading hotels, the Watch Hill and the Ocean House. Remarkable fact No. 2, at many of the Saturday germans the men far outnumber the ladies. Think of that, dwellers in the "catch" resorts where seven women lay hold of the skirts of one man!

Concerts, juggling feats, small diversions of all kinds, spring up here and there at a minute's notice, and last the season through. The noon bath is apt to be long drawn out, so tempting are the waters, and so large the numbers, and as fishing is fine, and little steamers put in here daily from Westerly, Stonington, New London, Norwich, and frequently Block Island, a life on the ocean wave becomes almost a literal fact. Some especially pretty little catboats are to let in the harbor. Along the road that skirts the still water edge, dozens of little mush room bazaars, with Westerly proprietors, have sprung up, from tintype rooms to ice cream parlors where, though we can personally testify to the cream's virtues, it is frozen in layers like milk in winter and served with a pewter spoon! There are merrygorounds, flying horses propelled by a real calico horse, and one shore dinner restaurant. No new large hotels have been added, but Columbia Hall, a pale yellow building of pleasing design, stands by the west shore. Mr. Hill now has oversight of the Plimpton, Narragansett and Bay View; the others are the Atlantic, the great white Larkin, and the rivals Watch Hill and Ocean. Beautifully decorated as is the Ocean House's interior, the Watch Hill is and has been first favorite among the eight great houses; it is admirably arranged, and its table d'hote unexceptionable.

The leading hotels are crowded this month, and not only hotel proprietors, but more unprejudiced cottagers aver this to be a rapidly growing and increasingly successful resort. The summer population of the point is from 1500 to 2000. What must this contrast seem to the thirty-six winter residents, fisherman only on the bleak and deserted coast?

Always the wind blows freely over the airy heights, always there are the bathing beach, the row boats, sail boats and steamers to patronize, there are fishing and crabbing parties, and walks and drives innumerable. Noyes Beach and Brightman's Pond, not far east, are worth a longer drive than they require to view. Then there is the Life Saving Station to visit, whose keeper gets more calls in one day of summer than in all his winter service. Mr. Nash, the present keeper, has been at this station eleven years; and in the six years that he has been in direct charge, he has assisted at forty-five wrecks—seven in one season. It was but four years ago that the melancholy wreck bleaching on the eastern sands was a staunch vessel, that, bewildered in night and storm, struck the rocks with a crash that sent her canting sidewise over. The crew—it is a volunteer crew for the four months from April to September, picked from native fishermen and sailors —trundled out their great car of over a ton's weight, which, down on the beach abreast the vessel, bears the gun that fires the projectiles carrying the life-line. A row of these long shot hangs on the station walls. They weigh eighteen pounds each, and it seems hardly possible that they are thrown 300 yards. But they were fired, one by one, at this vessel, and owing to the darkness and the gale, caught or went through the rigging, and it was only by accident that one of the crew, groping along aft, felt the life-line. By the apparatus which this car has, an endless line is formed between wreck and shore, and the passengers, enclosed in a framework of rope to prevent their being washed away by the might of a strangling breaker, are slid ashore. This particular vessel was canted so that the line to shore had a 20-foot descent, and Mr. Nash said "when a man got started he went right along." It is a rather odd thing that in all these 45 wrecks, where life-lines, life-boats and life-cars have all been in use, not a man of the eight who make out the winter complement has ever been injured. It is a lonely life they lead here: the point is deserted, the bay frozen over, and they cross on the ice to Westerly for supplies. They hire a cook, and—should not the Government be ashamed of itself for its stinginess?—these brave fellows have to pay for their food and cooking out of a $50 pay monthly! There is a patrol who must nightly traverse the beach through storm and gale, on the lookout; and whether there are actual wrecks or no, the entire force has to go through the whole beach and launching drill fifty times in its eight months service. Mr. Nash says that though he has called the life-car (the queer-looking, air-tight construction that dangles now from the ceiling) several times into service, he has never chanced to bring in women or children in it. The men rescued have been the working crews of vessels. Marryatt's code is the signal service in use here, but a lengthy description of it involves too much space for the present article.

We noticed the life-preservers—much more simple and pliable and less cumbersome they appeared than those ordinarily furnished on pleasure steamers; they are for the use of the life-saving crew. Over at the Montauk station on the Long Island shore, they have passed all these years without a single wreck, where Mr. Nash has witnessed forty-five—fortune de la guerre.

Mr. Nash said the ladies who visit there sometimes ask him very queer questions; I am convinced he was only prevented by gallantry from saying foolish, for queer does not begin with an f. The favorite inquiry seems to be concerning the number of wrecks he expects to have this year. Let us hope, for their sake and that of the gallant fellows who go to their rescue, that there will be none; and also that Government will wax munificent and compensate them better for their perilous calling.

Personally, the feature of Watch Hill most pleasing to us was the number of delightful old ladies we met, real, genuine old ladies, who had grown sweetly and placidly old without a fight with destiny, snowy of hair and cap, sweet of face and charming of mien.

Some of the well-known sojourners at cottage and hotel are Mr. Page of the Massachusetts Insane Asylum, who has a stately summer house here, far up to the north; Mr. Collins of New York in the red, vine-draped cottage by the chapel; Judge Finckle of Canada; George T. Blackstock and family of the Pacific Railroad; D. M. Wells, Speaker of Parliament; Lieut. Gov. Hale of Springfield; Maj. S. Bradford and J. H. Wesson's family; James L. Morgan, Sr., and Jr., Morris J. Black and family, Mrs. Asa W. Tenney, William Clark of Newark; Mrs. Dr. Seelye and the Easthampton Dr. Seelye, J. C. McMullen of Chicago; Hon. William Brigham, Dr. Vanderpoel, J. M. Belden, Mrs. Frank Hitchcock, Mr. and Mrs. Herbert N. Fenner of Providence; Silas F. Miller, President of the Pendennis Club; William P. Anderson, the Secretary of the American Legation in London; G. Richmond Parsons, Henry Tilden and family, H. F. Richards and S. M. Knowles of Providence.

A full list of names well known would be an over long one. Many of the cottagers dine at the hotels. Supplies come mainly from Westerly and Stonington, and the growth of this summer resort, so little known among Providence people, promises to be greater in the next eight years than in the past—though it has had a Watch Hill House since 1840.

BLOCK ISLAND.

[By excursion steamer Mount Hope in summer, or Danielson in other seasons, direct from Providence, or by steamer to Newport, and Danielson thence to Block Island, four hours sail. Ocean View Hotel largest and best. Block Island House one of the best of the smaller.]

A WIDE line of sparkling green—the ocean; a narrow line of foaming white—the breakers; a level line of yellow-white—the sandy shore, and an undulating line of dark green, flecked with the rectangular shining grey of house tops —the hills; above all the hazy blue of sky. All told, that is Block Island from the ocean, as it lifts its head above the waters to greet the voyagers sailing southward. But what Block Island is to its familiars and friends—that is not so speedily told. A place of many hotels, a charming seaside resting place, it strikes the casual traveller glancing along shore as the steamer swings into the dock; but the real life of the island, the essence of the quaint old place, and the heart of its many histories, is to be gotten at only by long and repeated wanderings among its rolling inland hills.

All among and between the hotels are wild fields and pasture lands, and the convenient cross-cuts that intersect each other at every turn lead through back yards and farm yards, whose gates and turnstiles are ready to swing open at a touch. Ask a direction to any objective point visible in the distance and your answer will be: "Oh, go any way, across lots," and setting confidingly forth the tourist is never balked by a "No thoroughfare." This accommodating state of things is due largely to the islanders' close relationship; literally sisters, cousins and aunts are the women folk. Even the hotel proprietors are evolved mostly from quondam fishermen, so, as a hotel clerk expressed it, they "fight for custom all summer, and shake hands over it in the fall."

Among the early settlers who crossed here from Long Island and Massachusetts two centuries ago, when Block Island was "Manisses" and its only inhabitants Indians, there must have been a few fishermen drifted south with a favoring wind from Nova Scotia; for every now and then one encounters on this island just such a group of the genuine " bronzed and bearded" as artists love to paint and poets to picture. Broad faces, honest blue eyes, high cheek bones, a fringe of beard from ear to ear, and a general weather-beaten air, characterize them as they tramp sturdily over the hills, and a group of them among the lobster pots or the boats or the seines makes assurance doubly sure.

But where do the women of the island keep themselves? A lady assured us the other day in somewhat Cooperish phrase that in all her stay there she had not yet seen a "female native," and on reflection we found that we had not, either.

It is the men who come to the doors of their lonely, scattered houses among the hills to answer questions of strangers; the men who do the marketing. But the island is a religious spot, and the time to catch them is a Sunday at "meetin'." There are three Baptist churches between their Dan and Beersheba, the North and South Lights, a persuasion unanimously adopted by the islanders, and a peculiarly appropriate one.

They baptize not indolently in ponds, though every hill has its hollow and every hollow has its lakelet of greater or less size—usually the latter. No, they take converts down to the rolling Atlantic, where there is "much water;" and amid the plaintive melody of ancient hymns and the roar of ocean confer their rites.

Not long ago an Episcopal Church, newly built on the eastern bluffs by the efforts of the summer guests, mysteriously took fire and burned to the ground, leaving but the one sect dominant. Somewhat intolerant in their virtue are these Block Islanders, advocating the fiery as well as the watery baptism! but a new "High Church" stands now intact upon the shore, and vengeance seems to have been relegated to the higher powers.

When Italy was ringing with the tales and marvels of the new world, three centuries ago, the venturesome Verrazzano, sighting and christening our ocean island, went home and told the folks it was a "triangular island well covered with trees." Alas for the ravages of time! scarcely a dozen trees can one count at a time, look where he may. They have gone the way of all firewood long ago, and when they were finally consumed the people fell to digging peat, of which there was abundance in the hundred swampy warm hollows.

But now, through the many vessels which put in at this very poor apology for a harbor, coal and wood are supplied at prices which assume their proper dimensions only when averaged in with the house rents.

Even the island itself, buffeted by wind and ocean at north, south, east and west, is no longer what it was. Yearly the high boundary line of bluffs retreats inward, and yearly the malicious frost spirits pierce the overhanging banks with seam and crack, and send great masses, tons in weight, crushing down the clayey sides to be swept remorselessly into sea. The great salt pond that monopolizes half the northern territory of the island, and leaves only a small strip of shore between it and the sea on west and east, was once a land-locked anchorage for small vessels approaching it by a natural western breach, and also a profitable breeding place for fish and oysters.

But that fickle builder, the sea, broke in with barriers of rock and sand and filled the opening—how thoroughly and successfully people did not know till they went to dig it out again and found it was a work of two years.

It is now completed, to everybody's joy, and the tides again rise and fall there with their wholesome cleansing rush.

The bathing beach, too, wonderfully smooth and pebble-free, is the work of the sea in the great 1815 gales. Before that it was merely land protected by sheltering sand hills, which the sea leaped and leveled.

The North Light, too, has been thrice rebuilt, for its predecessors were built unwisely upon shifting sand. But far back from wear and tear of ocean the green hills lie far inland in billowy waves. Beacon Hill, the highest landmark, conspicuous far out at sea, and abandoned from its original use, when the lurid glare of a burning tar barrel warned the settlers of incursions by sea, it appears now only an old shell of a building devoted to refreshments and a field glass, through which one may view, if he will, four States. But local characteristics are not visible by its medium, and the four States are as many blue blobs along the horizon.

The North Light, out on the sandy peninsula, where quicksands abound, is an ultima Thule to which brief sojourners seldom penetrate. It is a long drive from almost any starting point, and not especially interesting when one gets there. Mr. Ball, the twenty years keeper there, has now been superseded by the former Whale Rock keeper.

Voyagers to Block Island for one day's excursion only do not get much more from it than the sail, the dinner, and an impression of the general contour of the east shore and the wild, undulating background. Nevertheless, 3000 a week is a low average for such excursionists. Block Island is the one place accessible to those who have but a day to spare where one gets so far out into old ocean as to lose sight wholly of land save the shadowy blue island line for which he is steering. One feels that for the time he has shaken off the world, its dust, noise and cares, and it would not surprise him if he landed on a new planet. Herein, despite one's liability to mal de mer, lies the constant charm of the ocean sail. It is a pity, however, not to spend at least one night on the island. One can return via Newport the next morning and be in town in time for dinner, and meanwhile see something of the real island beside the ordinary watering place that clusters round the east harbor. But if one has but a day here, it behooves him to speed through his meal and engage a carriage, for the thousand rolling hillocks of which the island is composed are trying to the muscles of an "offener," as strangers from the main are called by the old folk.

Let the charioteer have his own way and he and his horse will set off by instinct for the South Light, a structure that gets more visits than even Point Judith, the terminus of the favorite Pier drive.

It is a pleasant ride down to the South Light, up and down over the hills and across the fields, where a small boy, rising out of the ground, appears to open a big gate and look for baksheesh. Thence the road winds along the top of Mohegan Bluffs, an average height of 150 feet straight above the foaming sea. Stones and water and high-flying spray have wrought fantastic pinnacles and headlands all down the bluffs, that one would surely say were solid rock; but the whole great bluff is one vast clay bank. Half way down the sheer side a spring house stands, which would be the right thing at the right time were it attainable otherwise than by a swift slide and a slow scramble. The lighthouse is an imposing edifice, joined to a pretty cottage, both cottage and octagonal tower of dark red brick. And if it chances to be visiting hour— which it will be if one is not over-early or late—some one of the three families whom the cottage harbors leads the way up the three flights of winding stairs and up to the "crystal palace"—the glistening, wonderful thing that a first order light always is, handled so lovingly by keepers and not to be touched by other fingers. It is a very marvellous thing to stand inside it, with the prismatic rainbow lines all about one, and a dazzling shimmer and shine, but alas, it is something exceedingly hot, too. This light proper, of five wicks in concentric circles, burns a

half gallon of oil hourly. The light itself, with its paraphernalia, cost $10,000. Outside on the platform one may get as fine a view of land and ocean as heart can wish. Far to the southeast are the smacks of the Gloucester fishing fleet, and everywhere is ocean, except for one little blue line off in the northwest; that is the Rhode Island shore. In the white-washed building near the water's edge are the two engines that supply breath for the fog horns; a middle-sized voice for middle-sized fogs, and a deep, deep voice for deep, deep fogs. It seemed at first like a case of big hole for the cat and a little hole for the kitten, a la Sir Isaac; but the attendant said it would not do to keep the heavy one sounding all the time, and when we recalled its dismal, booming tone we thought so too.

Of course, being a first-order light, this is indeed one of the wonders of our coast,

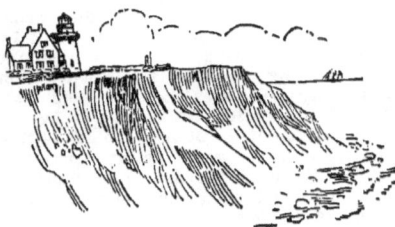

BLUFF AND SOUTH LIGHT.

and its dazzling barrel of prisms is worth getting inside of. But if visitors could see the air of weary resignation with which the keepers plod up stairs after their expectant and enthusiastic guests, and hear their mechanical replies to the same old questions, they would either be more considerate in their calls, or make their douceurs larger. At this day it would probably be impossible to hazard within the lighthouse walls a remark on the subject which would strike the keeper's ear with an air of originality. Unless one cares very much to enter, let him stroll instead to the verge of the Mohegan cliffs that make the southern bulwark more wonderful than any work of man, and see the distant white lines of breakers crawling down on the scant beach 175 feet below. With jutting, serrated edges overlapping each other, as one gets this grand series of bluffs in profile, it seems almost impossible that they are made only of crumbling clay, constantly changing in outline; they look as enduring as old ocean itself. Away down below the passing sails look like flitting white moths out at play, and even the billows of the Atlantic lose their contour, and the sea lies like one great silver plain, crossed by strange wavering lines and letters that wind and tide fantastically trace, meaningless to mortals. Strewn all along this southern shore are smooth round stones, great and small, and not long ago vessels pausing here took away thousands of paving stones or similar design, but the islanders at length protested, fearing for the permanence of the shore itself in the absence of its best protection, and the stones stay. Inch by inch the whole island, "beaten by billows and swept by breeze," is wearing away, and perhaps when shining Vega in the constellation of the lyre becomes the new pole star, Block Island will have ceased to be.

On the top of the Mohegan bluffs is this summer a bit of a red cottage, occupied by Mr. Hyde of Norwich, and supported on either hand by a supplementary tent, inhabited by friends of the Vaill cottage folk. From the south bluffs it is a short drive westward to the Vaill cottages, of which even the islanders know little, and the little they know turns out to be entirely untrue. Various papers have described these cottages as being the sanitarium of Miss Abbie E. Vaill, a well-known New York physician, and details even of her treatment and care of the invalids have been published. In fact, there is not an invalid among the number who make up the isolated southern colony, although the manner of its inception was peculiar. It was eight years ago that Miss Vaill, herself then an invalid, came to Block Island in search of health and quiet. The first she found, the latter, as she summered at hotels, she naturally did not. Impressed with the wildness, the grandeur and quiet of the cliff land, where the cottages now stand, she purchased a tract of some twenty-five acres, had erected a small red cottage for her own occupancy, and induced a few congenial friends to build also on her land. When the time for flitting came, the friends lost heart, declared they never should be able to keep an establishment on this wild island, and begged Miss Vaill herself to establish the chief cuisine. This she did, brought on a force of efficient servants, and from that time on the Vaill cottages were a pronounced success. From New York, Connecticut and from Florida, the patrons and friends crowded the little cottages, and this year a large new building has been found necessary, fitted cosily with sleeping rooms and a great central dance hall, where festivities of all kinds come off. The one dining hall is annexed to Miss Vaill's own cottage, and she and her sister are chief managers. A class of society gathers here wholly unlike that even of the best hotels; musicales, charades, amateur theatricals come off constantly with much eclat. Supplies come down from Providence, and the ocean and a thriving garden help out, largely with fresh fish and vegetables. Carriages cross often from the harbor, though excursionists never find their way here, and but two Providence families are among the guests—those of Edwin Barrows and Gov. Taft. Others are Rev. M. K. Schermerhorn, Dr. S. C. Logan, Mrs. McAllister, Mrs. William Thomson and Miss Elinora Bird, Prof. Johnson of Ann Arbor, Mr. Lee Cushing, Mrs. Wilbur of Washington, Prof. Beebe of Yale, Rev. Chauncey Brewster, and a long list of others, several Norwich people among them, and most of these lawyers, it would appear. It is a very unique and unexpected phase of life at Block Island, vastly independent and thoroughly comfortable. So far from practicing in her capacity of M. D., Miss Vaill sends even the ailing ones of her own family over to Dr. Brewer, as she is pleasantly and fully occupied with other duties. Vale the sanitarium!

The afternoon is long enough, after passing the bluffs, for a further ride to

Beacon Hill, the island's highest eminence, and a view of four States through the glass in the little structure that caps it. The road lies past the ancient harbor windmill with its queer round cap and gigantic arms, over to the West Side Life Saving Station and the desolate flat shore, up to the great salt pond that spreads over half the island's northern land, and makes picturesque sand-dune bordered marshes. Within reach, too, is the old island cemetery, with epitaphs so solemn that they become funny. Off in the southwest, too, is the neglected corner where are the seven graves of passengers on the ill-fated Palatine, wrecked here in 1750, and giving rise not only to the fire ship legend, but to the sale of enough relics to credulous summer guests to compare favorably with the somewhat overcrowded cargo of heirlooms from the Mayflower. Ever since the burning of the old stranded Palatine has the ghost of a fire ship lent interest to these waters, appearing fitfully and spasmodically about the island and in the Sound. Only last summer the phantasm was witnessed by a large and interested audience on the Rhode Island coast, flickering and vanishing. These many appearances cannot be wholly visionary, and now and then scientists interest themselves in the phenomenon and explain it by the inflammable gas theory; but there is many an old island native who still puts credence in the fire ship. The graves, at least, are genuine facts.

Nowhere on our coast is there a spot where so many hotels cluster in so small a space as around Block Island's bit of harbor, the metropolis of the island. Behold the list from greatest to least: Ocean View, Spring, Manisses, Hygeia, Highland, New Adrian, Pequot, Surf Cottage, Woonsocket, Connecticut, National, Eureka, Narragansett, Sea Side, Windsor, South Cliff, Block Island, Central, Union, Mitchell, Rose, Norwich, Bellevue, Springfield, Fern, Fair View and Ocean. When these houses are full, as in a prosperous season, the summer population amounts to some 3000, while the day excursionists swell the number at the dinner table.

Queer contrasts are in these summer hotels, from the great brown leader of them all, the Ocean View, with its beautiful arched dining hall radiant with electric lights, gay with hanging baskets of foliage, and its three or four hundred guests served by college boys combining business with pleasure in their summer vacation—from this to the bits of houses on the hillside, presided over by island natives, with waiters from their own household band, and a sort of nautical flavor in the air. The small and cheap hotels down by the landing are as a rule frequented by rather third-rate people, but one often finds very pleasant sojourners in the quiet, breezy houses upon the hill. Capt. Conley, the well-known skipper of the Danielson, is at the helm of the cosey little Block Island House, farthest up of all, and one expects to hear "four bells" struck for supper and find plum-duff for dessert. It is the pleasantest of all the small houses. Often the Ocean View as well as smaller and less popular houses, is obliged to resort to cot beds in extemporized sleeping rooms. By crowding, the hotel will lodge 487—their highest number. The gay season's close comes comparatively early here, but there are always many to finger for further study of the queer island life after the crowds have gone, and marvel at the glory of the close cropped hills and hollows in their countless hues of autumn's painting, and watch the raving surf as it batters down atom by atom the foundations of the isolated ocean island.

The Spring House has a neat little pavilion over its two springs of iron and sulphur, dipped up by an attendant with accessories highly suggestive of Saratoga. These are the only waters used at the house, but even the most strenuous dislikers of mineral waters could have nothing but enjoyment of the very mild sulphur spring. At the Ocean View a pavilion now stands at the head of the bluff above the dock for the use of the hotel guests, and no more satisfactory improvement could have been made. Otherwise, things are not greatly altered, though the conservative islanders are slowly rousing to their guests' demands for repaired docks, better roads, sidewalks at the harbor, a Sunday boat, an electric light system, a Casino, and an ordinance regulating carriage fares. None of these demands is unreasonable, and all are obvious. Mid Ocean, the paper created by the presence of the ephemeral summer population, is the medium of much agitation on the question, and probably another summer will see an Improvement Society an accomplished fact. There is certainly wealth enough to support it.

Few summer cottages appear on the island; it is a hotel colony wholly. The homes of the natives are mainly plain little whitewashed cottages, though now and then one sees a more imposing one, like Noah Dodge's, or the pleasant old Sands farm, located in a rare group of trees down by the goodly-sized Sands pond. A dozen or so pretty cottages nestle down by the harbor, but they are boarding houses in the summer and not fair representatives.

Weeks of research would not wear out the island's resources. There is the North Light to visit, and there seems something of the supernatural in that, too; for a livery man told us that there wasn't a driver on the island but would rather go anywhere than to the North Light. And why? because you keep going and going, and never get there. For his part, he wanted $20 to go to the North Light and back, he did. Even the island itself is highly elastic in character; sometimes it is six miles long, sometimes seven and a half, and sometimes nine, as one may see for himself by inquiring of different natives. It may be the state of the tide is answerable for this phenomenon; these ocean mysteries are beyond us.

Block Island's mineral springs are well patronized every summer; the spring of iron and the spring of sulphur that never mingle because the sulphur overtops the iron. A small boy politely handed us glasses as we passed, and we said jocularly, "What is that little engine for close by? to pump gas into your mineral spring?"

"Naw!" said the small boy, in much disdain. "It's to take the water up to the Spring House."

The small boy moreover gave us much useful information, and presently, struck by a brilliant thought, said: "Want to see the rams? We've got two rams down here." Always interested in live stock, and bearing the distant bleat of sheep on the hills, we said we should. The small boy and a smaller sister, skipping joyously before, led the way down a very muddy hollow, and paused before two small wooden structures. With the pugnacious character of rams well in mind, we peered cautiously in, but there was only a big iron knob and two pipes through which the water was gurgling and thumping. Politely the small boy explained, and attentively we listened, not understanding in the least; but whether it was ours or the small boy's fault, we know not.

In the hollow between the rams and the sea the way was green with peppery watercress, nourished by medicinal waters. We drank copious draughts of the iron spring, and it was not till we were turning away that we espied a sign whereby visitors were requested not to carry away water with them. But it was too late then.

Visitors are not out in great numbers in July, any more than in other places, but for all that the hotel keepers anticipate a rush in August. The lovers of fishing are early on the field, however, and the morning breeze bears away many a vessel in search of the luckless swordfish, or cod, mackerel and blue fish. Fun is plenty about Block Island, and in the frenzy of the decorative mania which has so long prevailed ladies buy the sword of the fish, tie it with ribbons and hang it on their walls—whether gilded or not tradition saith not; but it seems to me a decorated fish sword would look sweet in gilt.

The summer boarders do not have it all their own way on this fair island. At a majority of the hotels the table hours read: "Breakfast at 7, dinner at 12, supper at 6."

They want to get their work done up, they say, and the boarders may come to their meals or go without, just as they please. They are mild, but firm, and 7 o'clock sees the guests seated at the breakfast table; but vast is the grumbling. And when the languid Pier people are just sitting down to their rolls and coffee the Block Islanders are jubilantly forth at sea. Early hours and ocean breezes work wonders with invalids, and many a long list of testimonials have hotel keepers proudly to exhibit. Autographs of many of our great men adorn the hotel registers, and all, from the smallest to the greatest of the thirty that are known as hotels, are filled to overflowing before the season's close.

Over the whole island a breeze is always blowing, and it is a pity some of the big hotels were not set further up the hills to catch the cool air on their summits. There are the usual diversions of summer hotel life through the season, base ball, tennis, dances and musical entertainments; but a life on the ocean wave is the one preferred of all, and the stay-at-homes take their daily bath and roam the hills and hear the breakers thunder at the foot of the bluffs and see the midday commotion of excursionists landing and exploring. But the "day laborers" seldom wander from shore, and the old sojourners feel that they have the real Block Island all to themselves. Perhaps the very prettiest thing of all Block Island views is the sight of the fishing smacks coming in at dusk for a night's anchorage. One by one, like a troop of silvery butterflies, tired with flitting, the cloud of soft, silver-gray things come stealing in across the darkening waters and gently nestle in the shelter of the long breakwater, while still another and another follow quietly from far out at sea, the masts tipped with the lingering gold of sunset. So gently the eye hardly knows when their motion ceases, they come to rest, and one by one a cluster of shining stars dawns in the dusk to mark their sleeping place.

Perhaps some one gets up in time to see them spread their wings and sail away in the morning breeze, but we have not been so blest.

The little steamer Ocean View, beside her every morning trip sword fishing, which is in the established order of a day, goes daily during August on an afternoon sail around the island, which is well worth one's while and consumes two hours. Then the queer island geography is made plain, with the narrow northern peninsulas, the long surf beach by the western breach opening into the salt pond, the fantasies of the huge southern bluffs, whose only seaward view is by this means, and the clay bluffs to the northeast in a series of pointed ridges, like great solid triangles laid sloping to the sea, with their pointed edges upward. Here the little boat runs nearer the great Searles mansion, sitting white and solitary on the northeast shore.

It stands two miles and a half from the nearest point of approach, wherever one starts from. When the tide is high and every footstep is deep in the clinging sand, it is twice as far. Worst of all, when one reaches there, it is to confront a forbidding sign that absolutely prohibits trespassing, and a labyrinth of barbed wire fence that convincingly seconds the motion. It is a wise prohibition and a necessary one, for the stately white building is even a more tempting bait than a wreck to visitors, and the house would be fairly overrun. On this occasion pen and sword had the customary conflict, pen as usual prevailing and entering triumphant. The great white walls glisten like marble in the sun, and though one sees it is wood on nearer view, the foundation still seems of stone, so skillfully is the wood sanded in simulation. The main house is square, with wide promenades running about it, enclosed in arched colonnades, and protected by massive balustrades. Before the house, running out seaward, is a huge gray promenade, with ornamental arches; the house entrances, front and side, open by long shuttered doors, directly on the balconies. Within the finish of the main house is all pure white, the floors are of polished oak, light and dark, the stairway in the great hall being especially handsome, and a mahogany handrail capping the white balustrade. The ell containing the kitchen, pantries and servants' dining-room is finished in hard pine, and the half-dozen servants' rooms overhead are in Norway pine, walls, ceilings and floors. On the first floor of the main house is the great hall, the promenade before it, and the dining-room and parlor on either side, both shaped and finished alike.

The hall is the main glory of the house; around one end the solid stairways in their red and white glistening wind thrice up to the guest room and the two suites of rooms that open from it on either hand, and up again to the picture gallery still above, under the great white sky-lit dome. The whole, as one stands below and looks up to the glimpses of blue sky through the arched dome windows, gives an impression of even greater space than it really contains. In the great lower hall are the customary polished tables, the rugs, the huge vases, the glittering fire-place andirons, and on the north and south wall are mounted two great snowy owls flecked with black, and their outspread wings and tails making a fluffy halo about them as they stand perpetually on guard. The boudoirs of the upper story are very handsome and luxurious rooms, fitted with every possible convenience. The walls, with a thin coating of white over the wood grain, are hung with draperies. Gray shades hang at window and door, and every door-knob in the house is of white glass. The views even from the grounds are magnificent, and when one ascends to the roof, fitted up for promenading, they are even finer.

The dome grows handsomer on nearer approach, with its ornate Corinthian columns between the Gothic arches, and the curving bands that bend to its apex of glistening gold, as is the great pineapple that caps the whole. Peculiar as the history of the house has been thus far, its final disposition is now the subject of lively comment. Finished in the summer of '90, it was intended as one of the least pretentious of the mansions of Mr. Searles and his "millionairess" wife. As the widow of Mark Hopkins she became possessed of $60,000,000, and this great white house, with its huge rotunda, its white and gold walls, mahogany stairs, and round picture gallery beneath the high dome, was a mere bagatelle beside the million dollar house in California, the two million residence in Great Barrington, or the suburban home near Boston where Mrs. Searles died. Therefore the great white house now stands lonely on the beach at the island, with but one solitary custodian to prevent intrusion and robbery. The summer home was chosen here in the hope of restoring Mrs. Searles's failing health, and only this season a bath house was fitted up on the shore, which has its counterpart only among the voluptuous Orientals. It is also white, and is a small copy in outline of the house above it, even to the round dome.

Of course the transient guest cannot visit these many points of interest, but hotel proprietors say that the number of guests engaging rooms for the entire season is steadily on the increase. Providence people are not, as a rule, among those long tarrying, though they make the majority of day excursionists. Norwich and Worcester are two leading cities among guests. The island is the most cosmopolitan resort of the State, and the great and mighty of the land and the humble kitchen domestic take their daily bath together on the pebbly beach. There are accommodations to suit all purses, and society to suit all conditions.

MILL POND.

But one must not say he knows Block Island till he has seen it in all seasons, particularly in fall, when the bleak, bare hills are rich in gorgeous colors as forest foliage, and the dark pools have ranks of golden reeds. There is coloring then not to be surpassed. Those who have seen it only at midday have not seen it at all. Wait until sunset, when the round hills send long, overlapping shadows across the land, when the beacon and the north light grow black against a crimson sky and the salt pond is a fiery sea; when the white fleet come gently stealing in across the darkening water and cluster in the harbor, when the black night falls and the billows leap white on the shore, and the wild wind brings down from the dusky hills the plaintive voices of the sheep, calling and crying in the dark; when the orchestral music pulses sweet and faint from a distant hotel, and in its pauses the voice of the surf calls rising and falling all along the lonely shore.

Great was our desire to reach the real heart of Rhode Island, which we could never do while summer guests tarried and the natives retired within their shells like mollusks to await their going. We waited, therefore, till September went out and the last summer folk with it; then we embarked again for a more lengthy sojourn at the lonely island.

It was a very queer thing for the staunch little steamer Danielson, bound from Providence to Block Island, to forget the Newport mail, but forget it she did, or the one responsible mind on board of her. And back from "Pine Jude" to Newport plied the plunging vessel, leaving her few shivering and seasick passengers to exchange condolences in the cabin over the agreeable prospect of rounding Beaver Tail thrice in the one trip.

We two, who stuck resolutely to the upper deck and fresh air, were bound to Block Island for a longer stay now that summer guests were flown and island life had resumed its customary torpidity. It proved to be an all day's trip on this occasion, and the vast dark green swells that went rolling heavily by, now and then shattering in foam on each other's shoulders, were getting just a trifle monotonous, when a wild and lurid sunset glorified the clouds that had mingled showers and sundogs around the horizon the afternoon long.

Block Island loomed large to view at last, sharply black against this wild splendor, the north light a death's finger tipped with flame, and the long, undulating line of billowy hills stretching bleak and inhospitable against the cold sky. We had meant to stroll leisurely about, seeking an abiding place among some genuine old settlers, but it was Saturday, and night descending swiftly.

"We'll go to a hotel, any one we can find," we decided weakly. "Some of the little ones may remain occupied through the winter."

We scanned the dusky shore eagerly as our boat glided in. A long line of vehicles, and drivers standing by, stretched along the head of the dock.

"Oh, what nonsense about the hotels being all closed," cried I, superior I, who knew all about Block Island; "there are the teams from half a dozen this very minute." Blithely and triumphantly we gathered up our belongings and pressed shoreward in the rear of two very disgusted oxen who had been swaying back and forth giddily all the afternoon on their thrice-prolonged trip from Newport. And were these hotel teams, after all? Well, if they were, the proprietors had relapsed into their old-time simplicity now that summer was no more. Ox-teams and tip carts pure and simple, and nothing else were they, waiting, alas, for consignments from over the seas and not for us. We paused dismayed, but who was this tanned and weather-beaten stripling, his ingenuous countenance overshadowed by a perplexed smile of half-recognition and a familiar Tam o'Shanter?

"Cornelius!" we cried rapturously. "How nice to find you here. And is the little Norwich House still open, and can we go there, do you suppose?" To all these queries Cornelius gravely assented, and marshaling us to a waiting carriage near at hand, promptly ejected an astonished dog which had evidently been counting on a ride, and bade the extremely youthful charioteer drive us to the Norwich House. Over the winding roads and up the hills madly tore our bony steed, goaded by the shouts and lashings of our frowning infant jehu, in the headlong manner peculiar to Block Island drives; and when we drew up at our goal, there, flushed and breathless, but promptly on hand to do the honors, was Cornelius himself, having sped madly up from the wharf by a series of short cuts through barnyards and over meadows, much to his mother's alarm. For, as that good lady afterwards related to us, "There I'd laid abed the whole afternoon, not able to stir hand or foot, wondering what could have come to the Danielson, and when I looked out and saw that boy, I said to my sister, 'Sarah, here comes 'Nelus, running like mad acrosslots. Something has happened!'"

But nothing had happened more alarming than our advent, matter slight in itself; but when we afterwards learned that Cornelius's mamma had been ill in bed for a week, that her "girl" had just left, and that the household aid consisted of one small daughter and an aged retainer known as "old man William," then, even so trifling a thing must have taken on a tragic significance in our hostess's eyes. Indeed, it was the pathetic pleadings of Cornelius and not our winning presence, that won her consent to our tarrying. That misguided youth pledged himself to be cook, porter, nurse and chambermaid, in the absence of those functionaries, all of which departments, we cheerfully testify, he filled with grace and ease. It was not till the second day of our stay that we gathered from the sepulchral silence reigning in the kitchen as we sat at our solitary meals in the dining-room, attended by Cornelius, still Tam o' Shanter clad, that the youth held sole sway there. But that this was the case, the youth, when pressed, somewhat shamefacedly admitted, "'Nelus is loth to let an old visitor go," declared his mother. "If you had been strangers, he would have said it wasn't convenient, but now he can't do too much for you."

With this passing tribute to the miraculous powers of our mascot, we resume the thread of our narrative.

Bed time followed close upon tea. There was absolutely nothing to do but go to bed. The wind had increased to a cold and piercing blast from the northwest, straight from the sea, as is every wind that blows.

The stars glittered with a frosty brilliancy like December, and dotted all about the feeble anchorage were other wavering stars of vessels waiting for dawn. At our airy upper windows we could see away up north beyond the Great Salt pond that greedily monopolizes half of the island's northern territory, the steadfast gleam of the lighthouse far at the end of the treacherous peninsula of quicksands; and still farther north, leagues beyond the dark waters, a twinkling gleam that flashed and faded and flashed again, showed us where the unseen breakers roared and seethed about the reefs of the sailor's terror, Point Judith.

In the little Norwich House stoves were not yet, and we slid speedily and thankfully beneath our many coverlets, and slept till the lowing of cows in the surrounding pastures woke us to a crisp, clear and quiet Sunday morning with the keen wind still in the air. How silently the whole long island lay under the morning sun rays. About the little scattered white houses among the hills there was no sign of life, but the smoke curling upward from the chimney, and away down around the wharf, where the many hotels cluster; it seemed a desolate town, wrapt in enchanted sleep.

Our walk led this morning, naturally, down along the shore running southward, where sun would warm and breeze cease to penetrate below the banks growing momentarily higher. How still it was! it was Sunday on the sea, even, and the waves broke gently along the rocky shores and the white wings of sailing vessels were few and far. There was the ravine lined with water-cress, moistened with the flow of the mineral springs above, and which looked too icily suggestive to tempt. But the water-cress—how hot, peppery and altogether comforting it was; we consumed immoderate quantities, and, suggestive of that erring monarch of the Orient turned out to grass, strolled on, still browsing. The strip of shore grew too narrow to traverse, and the ascending sand bluffs more formidable, so, moving somewhat inland, we pursued our course over the hills southward, the sea still to our left, though dropping farther and farther below, till suddenly as we toiled up a higher hill, the south light seemed to lie directly before us, across only an undulating pasture or two.

"Oh, let us go to the light," I proposed eagerly. "We can't get in to-day, of course, but you must see those stupendous bluffs it stands on, and we'll get a view of the Atlantic southward." So on we trudged. But let no man be beguiled by an ignis fatuus that flits before at Block Island. Before we had traversed that seemingly brief space, our line of march might have been represented by the wavering and undulating record of a pulse-writer. Up one hill and down another, and a detour round a peat-bog at the bottom of each. There are said to be 200 of these peat-ponds, little and big, on Block Island, and we could easily credit it. Peat is no longer dug from them in quantities, for stoves have supplanted the hospitable old firesides, and schooners bring coal almost daily. Only about a few of the conservative "west side" abodes does the fragrance of peat-smoke still hover, and more rare still is it to find

"Old wives spinning their webs of tow,
And rocking weirdly to and fro,
In and out of the peat's dull glow."

But peat is not peat to a genuine islander, anyway. It is tug: and tug is a much more expressive word, they who wrest it, damp, black and reeking, from its mucky bed can testily. Spinning wheels still abound in Manisses, but they are mostly to be found idle in garrets and cellars. There are plenty of first-class spinners still on the island, but they will tell you it isn't "worth while."

Long on Mohegan Bluffs we tarried, gazing upon the massive jutting gray pinnacles shifting and changing from year to year, but looking now, against their background of blue sea, firm as enduring granite itself. Golden-rod edged the bluffs, rank, rich and fat; there is no other word for the seaside golden-rod, with none of the airy and graceful plume-like beauty of its upland cousin. Our homeward way was by the road lying close to the dizzy verge of the bluffs, and destined some day to be in the air beyond them. Listening, even now, there is a constant tinkling fall of pebbles and bits of sand down their rough sides. Sheep grazed in the velvety pastures, and over the dark and reedy pools flitted sand-pipers, and, could it be? English sparrows. How did the plucky little rascals find their way here? Boarding some sailing vessel down the bay, did some adventurous pair perch on the mast like Jean Ingelow's remarkable dove, and "mourn and mourn and mourn" till they reached Manisses? Here they are, at any rate, quite acclimated, and as fat, saucy and quarrelsome as they are ashore. In the dark pond waters late white lilies were lingering even now. It is something to have these dainty flowers on the island, though arbutus, wild rose, clematis and wind flower, and the hundred and one of our winsome woodland darlings be missing. Imagine children who have never seen woods—and hardly a dozen of the Block Island children have seen them or can imagine what they are like. Indeed, it is by no means a majority of their elders who have ever been off the island, and it is recorded that there are dwellers on the west side who have never even crossed the island and beheld the giddy scenes in the summer boarders' quarters about the landing. There, with nothing but the western ocean and the eastern hills to contemplate, they vegetate till their time for departure, and one wonders if it has been worth their while to live.

Our walk has made us late for church. We hear a bell faintly tolling up among the hills before we are half way home. We have missed our opportunity to see the Baptist patriarchs in council. Perhaps, at this time, too, the native females, of whose exclusiveness the summer boarders complain so bitterly, rally their forces and appear in public. But we see nothing of them about their homes, now or ever, as we roam the island. One day, as I sat alone in a carriage on a lonely road, awaiting the return of my comrade and the omnipresent Cornelius from a photographing tour, there emerged from a neighboring house on the hillside a fresh-faced and graceful young woman, who proceeded to hang out a wash on the line with some difficulty, owing to the boisterous breezes. Her lithe young figure, outlined against the sky, among the snowy garments, in its action and spirit, was like a picture. A little child toddled out of the house presently, and the young woman—she looked too young to be its mother—caught it by the hands and began a spirited dance along the hilltop. Suddenly she espied the waiting vehicle and my observant face, and like a flash she was gone, and I saw her no more. So fled within doors the entire female population, at our approach. They should wear the yashmak, or whatever the Oriental veil is called. My mind misgives me as to the above word.

On Monday we went to see the wreck. It was a coal schooner, and she lay hard aground up on the northwest shore, near the breach that connects the great salt pond with the sea. She had grounded there in the night and storm of a week before, and her masts could be seen, faint and skeleton-like, across the water and peeping over the high sand dunes, from our piazza. Cornelius volunteered as driver, however he found time from his manifold duties; but as we descended the steps for departure, we caught a brief and fleeting glimpse of "old man William" hard at it dish washing. Old man William somehow made us think of pictures of gnomes and kobolds, and those merry little folks of many kinds that dwell in German fairy forests. He had a little home all by himself upon the shores of the salt lake, and he was a bachelor. How he chanced to be wintering in the Rose household did not transpire, but it added much to the charm of our Bohemian banquets, whereat a young and tender fowl was daily offered up, to think that this agile little old man with his long gray beard and twinkling eyes, his cap and his apron, was hovering about the kitchen fire and directing the movements of the youthful Cornelius.

We drove merrily away toward the salt pond; the air was still crisp and cool, and Cornelius had thoughtfully furnished each seat with a bed comfortable, gallantly taking the most frayed and ancient one himself, and speeding through the harbor roads in sublime disregard of the tatters fluttering merrily outside. Here and there a "native female" at door or window, made bold by a compatriot among us, hailed us with "'Nelus, how's your ma?" for Mrs. Rose still kept her bed.

We passed the school house at the Centre, meeting a group of children joyously homeward bound, having just encountered a notice on the door of the teacher's illness. Our mascot cheerfully hailed them. "Turn back, children," he called out, "your teacher's sick, and you're going to have a new one to-day," and gravely proceeded to turn up before the school house door and draw rein amid a dismayed silence. A shout of derisive laughter presently arose, as, having declined to further his deception, we moved on, and shrill little voices called out, "Aha, we knew you was foolin' us!" Fancy the relief.

There are five schools on the Island—the Centre, Harbor, Gully, West Side and one other, whose name we either did not learn or have forgotten. We visited the largest one day. The big boys who will attend the winter school were far at sea, fishing, but there were a half-hundred Balls, Dodges, Mitchells, Roses and Littlefields painfully acquiring knowledge within its walls, and they looked very like the small patrons of a district school elsewhere, except that they were a trifle more bronzed and tanned by the sun and the sea breezes. Quite contented are the large majority with the rudimentary instruction furnished here. The few of overweening ambition, who seek superior instruction on shore, are apt to wash their hands of their native soil, and abide among the "offeners," for such is the name the Islanders bestow on dwellers on the mainland. And when we asked them why, they said, "Oh, because they come from way off!"

We passed also the most picturesque old gray wind mill it has ever been our lot to see, a huge and quaint designed old structure, once an ornament and a service to the harbor, but long since abandoned and moved up inland, to moulder slowly among the low hills about it. Block Island has no trees to take on gorgeous autumn colors, but the hills turn every delicate shade of olive, russet and brown, and look at a distance like great soft cushions of plush, tumbled carelessly about by giant hands.

We passed the old graveyard, more populous than the island, and where scores of the dead and gone members of the island's dozen families or so lie in clannish comradeship. Dates in the 1600's are to be found on the mossy stones, and quaint old epitaphs innumerable. One in particular was remarkably unique, reading something like this:

"She was a woman of rare domestic virtues, of great and exemplary piety— but!"

The young doctor of the island, Dr. Perry—for there are three in all, says that

OLD WINDMILL.

rheumatism and dyspepsia are the chief foes of the islanders, and that their endurance of pain is not made with remarkable fortitude. Rheumatic pains are engendered by their lives of hardship and exposure, and dyspepsia by their poor and indigestible food; and, indeed, when one comes to think of it, he would scarcely covet the Block Islander's winter menu. Constant and increasing intermarriage must also inevitably have its effect on the physical as well as mental well-being of the natives. The only thing that we envied this capable and cultured young physician in his voluntary winter exile from cultivated humanity is his opportunity to study the queer old-time ways and environment of the island folk into whose homes he will have access. Through the efforts of Mrs. Rose, who is herself a descendant of the old Dodges, we visited more than one century-old house, saw the spinning wheels and the "line-gear" and the obsolete devices now laid aside in most homesteads, heard old tales and legends and secured a valuable old relic vastly prized; but after all, we feel that the real heart of Block Island was revealed but feebly for our searching.

Wending their way homeward from the wreck we met here and there an ox-team freighted with dripping coal plundered quite openly and brazenly from the defenceless schooner, borne to shore in rowboats and thence transferred. These shameless wreckers wore one and all an air of jolly bravado, and invariably hailed us with "Goin' wrackin'?"

The wrecked schooner when we reached her lay far out in the water almost on her usual level, the waves breaking dismally over her deck. The captain and one or two of her crew paced drearily up and down the sands waiting the tug's arrival. Dories black with coal dust lay about the shore. Cornelius skipped into one and with never an invitation to follow, paddled blithely out to the deserted wreck, and eventually took up a picturesque position in the rigging, awaiting a transfer to a negative of our camera, and it may not comfort that graceless youth to know that he figures there as a remote object pinhead-size. It was in a furious midnight storm that the schooner grounded, the watch neither hearing nor seeing the breakers till the instant before she struck, and the captain having taken the north light for Montauk! From four miles below, the saving station men hauled their car and other apparatus in the teeth of the storm, got all the crew safely landed and were snugly back in the bed within four hours. Disgusted sailors at the harbor told us that the islanders might have made more money by keeping about their regular work and buying their coal at cargo prices than by their wrecking expeditions, but it seems an instinct born in the hearts of the native islanders, and it is easy to believe in the wild tales of the Palatine.

The island chronicler has been Mrs. Caroline Willis, but she died in the summer of '91, in her 98th year, and her mantle must fall on another. There was no limit to the tales and traditions this gifted and garrulous old lady could narrate, and the island genealogy was at her tongue's end. Another famous character is an old man residing on the west side, who is deaf, dumb and blind, but who is remarkably intelligent considering his limitations, and delighted to receive visitors and small oblations, tobacco exchanged, though he usually jocularly gives visitors to understand that he intends purchasing new garments with them.

We drove everywhere, sometimes mascot attended, and sometimes alone. But ever and anon, in the most isolated quarter of the island, we would start to hear a loud and stertorous breathing in our very ears, and there would be Cornelius close behind, mounted on his old spotted white horse, and ubiquitous as his Tam O'Shanter, leaving dinner apparently to get itself, for it was always gotten somehow. We went to the west side saving station, and all through the bright and cosy building, inspecting the apparatus with a thoroughness which would be commendable in a Government official, and waxing wroth, as we always do, in the consideration of the meagre pay received by these brave fellows. Excitement ran high on the day of our visit. Two hen hawks appeared hovering high in air, and it was astonishing to see what an armed population sprang up and ran to cover, and fired futile shots into the air. We got a fish eagle, a magnificent osprey—perhaps we shot him—and we brought him home and had him stuffed. And we would have brought home another that we picked up, had we not been deterred by an evil and irreverent reference to St. John xi., 39, for the taxidermist's remark on unwrapping the fowl, made by a party who shall properly be nameless.

We drove to the bathing beach, and the sand drives, and the gully school. We drove everywhere but to that elusive north light. Here we were stayed by direful reports of how the big storm had driven sand over the peninsula and blotted out the road, and how we were sure to get into quicksand and sink from sight. For my part, I begin to think there is no north light—that it is a corposant or a spectre like the fire-ship. I would believe almost anything weird and uncanny about Block Island, whose very atmosphere is as unlike the main land as a foreign country. And, indeed, it is said that horses and dogs brought here seldom become acclimated. We do not doubt it, for some of the native horses look as if they were not acclimated, either. Strange sea fowl hover over the island, but there are few birds or animals on shore.

Rustling corn-stacks and golden pumpkins lighten the sloping fields with splendor, just now, but late fall and early spring must see them desolate. Yet, ah, what a glorious place to slide down hill! Think of it, poor little city youngsters, whose feeble descent down a faintly sloping street is liable to end with a rap on the shoulder from a big, big policeman!

But we did not shiver during all our stay. With a sudden caprice, the air grew spring-like, mild and balmy, and there was a fragrance as of delicate flowers in all the air. They were golden days in which we roamed, unmolested, wherever we pleased, and every day seemed like Sunday, with the fishing fleet far out at sea, and only sailing safely home at dusk. It was only fun for the time, to go "shopping," to never find what we wanted, and then pay twice as much as we expected for what we didn't want. But in time this would have lost its charm. The mind shrinks in dismay from such an undertaking as building and furnishing a house here, yet they are built, and when one is rarely empty, it can be rented for two or three dollars a month!

A salt flavor is over the whole island, even to the row boats in the door-yards, flower filled, the full-rigged miniature ships on the parlor tables, the shells on the mantel, and the fish sizzing in the frying pan. And if the solemn asseveraion of the natives is to be believed, the gateway arch of the Spring House is composed of whale's "tushes," from the whale washed ashore years ago. And if whales have tushes ten feet long, the statement is not to be doubted.

The longer our tarrying, the vaster our discoveries, and we would have departed more reluctantly, but for our reflecting that for all times to come, awaiting our return—

"Circled by waters that never freeze,
Beaten by billows and swept by breeze,
Lieth the island of Manisses."

QUONOCONTAUG BEACH.

[Sixty miles from Providence. Stonington Railroad to Niantic, thence by carriage south to Beach 7 miles.]

THERE was no kind soul to inform the ignorant stranger that Niantic was the nearest point to Quonocontaug, so the ignorant stranger journeyed blithely to Westerly, there to take the boat for Watch Hill, and from Watch Hill to proceed east to Quonocontaug by whatever vehicle one could find for love or money.

But the traveller had not counted on finding a liar in Westerly. There was one, and he said a boat went to Watch Hill three hours earlier than it really did. Realizing the mistake, there was no better way of saving those precious three hours than by being driven directly to Quonocontaug. The beach was two inches from Westerly, we remember, which ought not to take more than a half-hour to travel, an inch standing for a matter of two miles. But who would dream that a little pond only a third of an inch long, over which our measure had unswervingly passed, deeming it a road puddle through which our horse could plash, meant a detour of a half-hour? The drive, therefore, was long; but it led through a new and delightful region. It was along the old post-road, where once the gallant stage-coach gayly dashed with its four staunch horses all the way from Stonington to Narragansett Pier. There is a mail-wagon now, to be sure, for there are straggling hamlets of post offices all along the way that lie far from the path of railways; but it is a modest little affair that recognizes a superior and only goes as far as Kingston.

In the wild, barren and unfruitful country, where rocky pastures alternate with sea-invaded marshes, there is little to tempt a man to fix his home, and miles of wild waste land lie between even next door neighbors, whose houses are nearly every one, old, quaint, and gray as the wood of fence-rails or wasps' nest.

What do the people do all alone here? I asked the genial driver.

"Farm it," he replied; "In summer. And in the spring and fall of the year fish it."

Now why that first occupation should seem perfectly decorous, and the second something exceedingly funny, I cannot say; but it is impossible to think of all those desolate 'long shore country folk "fishing it" without rising mirth.

"That is the Quaker burying ground," he said presently, pointing to a rising meadow rich with waving grasses.

"You mean it was once," I appended.

"No, 'tis now."

"But where are the graves—the headstones?"

"Oh, they don't believe in them," said the driver. "Get up, Dick!—here's the Seventh Day meeting house. Lots of those folks in Westerly; it comes handy."

It did, indeed. If one wished to do something of an uncommonly secular nature on Sunday, he had then only to make his plans a day beforehand, attend church on Saturday and then proceed to business.

Off to the right, among green hills and lonely woods, we saw a high white hill of sand—barren and shifting as the sea shore; regular beach sand, the driver said it was, and added that there was much speculation as to what brought it there. There was a great bowlder, too, away in the woods to the left, a gigantic stone of some four or five tons weight on which one might stand, and, bending his weight from side to side, cause it to totter on its base. So old mother earth has been at her antics away down in this little corner, too.

Before another old gray house—a somewhat pretentious structure which was in its day the old Town Hall—there stands a gaunt and spectral buttonwood tree, gray with age and moss, a landmark for a long distance. An old, old man in Westerly—let us hope that this one was a truthful person—remembers to have stood among a curious crowd once long ago to see the last punishment for theft by whipping. A mutton-loving man had stolen a sheep, and he was strapped to the old buttonwood while the Sheriff laid on the prescribed number of lashes.

Are they rather severe on live stock down this way? We came presently upon a cluster of little, cowering yellow ducklings in a side yard, and a sun-bonneted woman standing over them with a long switch. She was not using it as we passed, but I'm afraid she did after we got by. Whatever their misdoing, switching little yellow ducks seems rather a cruel business. Aside from this resolute female, we met all along this ancient road only a young man with cabbage plants, an aged man with patches and a young woman with white gloves.

There was a pretty little boarding place on this road called the Ocean View House, the significance of which title will dawn upon one if he find facilities for mounting the ridge pole. Wild roses bloomed confidingly before it, as they did all along the way, and every marshy pond among the reeds was white with lilies. We learned that Mr. Hoxsie, a native hard by, smoked buckies in the spring, caught when they came up into the ponds to spawn. After musing a while, we ventured to inquire what buckies were. "Why, I guess you call them bony fish down in Providence," said the driver. But we did not, and it was not till he further called them menhaden that we were enlightened.

And now the rain, which had been a baptism and a deluge from early morning till our arrival in Westerly, began again in a gentle drizzle. It drifted north with the ocean-breeze and wrapped us in a particularly damp mantle. The landscape retired, and the only object visible in its entirety was our jogging horse. We went and we went. Was there never a southward turning? Never would we be deceived again by two inches on a map. Why had we not left the train at Niantic, a six short miles from shore? Perhaps the driver had a grudge against newspaper folk and meant to drive and drive at an awful price an hour. We stole a furtive look at him, but his kind face was reassuring. In the language of the present hour, he was all right.

The tall, harsh marsh grass by the wayside rustled like hay in the rainy wind. It was high as a man's waist and leaned straight northward. And as we still went on through the splashing puddles, the horse's hoofs kept beating time to a snatch of Scripture that mockingly persisted in returning to mind: "But what went ye out into the wilderness for to see? A reed shaken with the wind?" Verily, it was the limit of our vision.

QUONOCONTAUG BEACH.

But with a sudden sharp turn we were headed southward, and the beach lay not far away. We could hear its muffled roar. The road was a narrow, stony one, over pasture land, fine massive posts marking the places where as many gates were formerly hung to prevent cattle straying. The driving rain held up a little, and we could see before us a cluster of gay cottages fronting seaward, and a number of older settlers farther to the west. All the way between was one fragrant wilderness of marsh grass and wild roses. The shore line was hidden by the sharp, undulating line of a range of sand hills, mingled green and gray. No one was to be seen on this wild morning, and it was the part of prudence to get under shelter till the shower abated. The driver set us down before a cottage and departed with his horse. A kindly cottager directed us to a place where we could get dinner. All along the front of the cottages on the seaward side a plank walk runs, and terminates at a new building put up recently for the accommodation of guests— the Cafe St. George.

We had not meant to enter so abruptly, but a wild gust from the Atlantic started in at the same time, and we flew in together, accompanied by a burst of rain. The landlord, manifestly not expecting callers from the Atlantic, rose hastily from an unoccupied dinner table where he had been taking a siesta, and advanced in some confusion. We could have dinner, and did, a worsted motto satirically bidding us meanwhile to eat, drink and be merry. But before we had finished the heavens had brightened. By the kindness of residents, and our own observations, we felt quite familiar with Quonocontaug before we left. It was a great surprise—a wild and surf-beaten shore like this, in a corner of our own tiny State, so given to crowded watering places. Far along the shore the breakers were thundering, and it seemed odd that a half-dozen or so of stately hotels were not confronting them. At the west end of the beach, near the pond—for here a large salt pond makes up into the meadows—are the oldest cottages, a cluster of fourteen; they have been built from twelve to fifteen years. Right before them is the bathing beach, the spot marked by a peculiarly fantastic rise of an isolated sand hill at the pond's mouth, a sort of a "tri-mountain" with an undulating triple summit and reedy grass waving all up its landward side. Here one could have no excuse for not learning to swim, for the salt pond affords the quietest possible bathing rink, while braver or sturdier bathers have the wild surf of the south

THE NEW STATION.

shore to battle with. We found, as usual, that the ever-elusive undertow had retreated when we got here; there was no undertow here, the natives said, they had it at Noyes's Beach. The Noyes's Beach people said the undertow was at Watch Hill, and Watch Hill people say they have far less undertow than the bathing beach at Narragansett Pier; and we all know the Pier people pride themselves on the absence of it along their bathing beach. It is something as difficult to find as "down East" or "out West."

"Had much rain down in Providence?" said Mr. Rice of the Cafe St. George.

"A good deal," said we. "But why do you all say 'down in Providence?' It is up on the map, and it's up country."

"Well, I don't know," said Mr. Rice. "It don't make much difference about up or down here—the tide goes both ways."

The fourteen cottages represent dwellers from all about the southern part of the State, and the seven newer ones were built by a party of friends and neighbors, all from Ashaway. There are house lots still for sale along the shore, and they would probably be taken up a good deal faster if there were some public conveyance to the beach. A railroad has been surveyed through here, and a name has been given it—the Sea View—but here it has paused, and the natives do not speak hopefully of its further progress. But a life saving station, long needed, went up in the season of '91, and has already done efficient service among the vessels that have come to grief on the outlying reefs. The only wonder is that it was not long before erected.

Until seven years ago a small hotel stood here at the pond's edge; but it mysteriously took fire and burned down, and has never been rebuilt. There is a building, however, where shore dinners are served, and where a few boarders can be accommodated. Mr. Rice, also, has room for boarders this year, for the trig little building he now has replaces a tent where he formerly dispensed food and drink to guests, but was given up because it was "mighty inconvenient."

Large partes from Westerly, Ashaway and other places often come down for the day, and it is a spot for unrestrained freedom and frolic. What would the fine folk of Newport think, for instance, of the shocking spectacle of a party of young folk in bathing costume—at the wrong hour, too—pursuing each other up and down the bordering sand hills, dancing on their summits and hilariously immuring each other in graves of sand?

Then there are more staid companies of picknickers who come down for a bake of their own on the shore. A fisherman's hut hard by, where two jolly fellows keep bachelor's hall, furnish them with lobsters, black fish or tautog, as they say "down in Providence," and blue fish, and the day goes fleetly by in strolling, shell gathering and bathing, watching the distant track of the passing steamers and the changing shores of Block Island and the blue outline of Long Island far across the Sound.

4

CHARLESTOWN AND MATUNUCK.

[Narragansett Pier Railroad to Wakefield, by hotel carriage to Matunuck Beach. Matunuck Beach Hotel and Cashman House.]

THERE is hardly any section of our small State so difficult of access, so uninviting as to byway drives and yet so thoroughly strange and interesting as the desolate, wild tract known as Charlestown, its southern shores battered by the wild Atlantic, and unsettled wilderness and unbroken forest to the north and west. With two days to spare, one can penetrate quite deeply into its lonely reaches, and by way of Matunuck enjoy a much more varied drive. Whether one start from Providence or elsewhere, the village of Wakefield is the nearest point by rail, and it was from Wakefield that we set forth.

Wakefield itself holds its own with most Rhode Island villages; its principal street, tree shaded and flower bordered, is lined with beautiful old homes, ideal nooks in which to dream away a summer, and beyond is the beautiful Robinson place on the seaward side, all gray stone and mantling ivy. Leading southwest from the village, the road lies never far from the sea, with a distant line of blue always to the left, dotted with the white specks of distant sails, except when woods yet primeval border the hard highway and glossy shrubs show where, weeks before, the magnificent waxen blooms of the rhododendron reigned, favoring only the South County with their wild beauty.

Pleasant as our drive was, it was yet not specially characteristic till Wakefield and civilization were left far behind; then it began to grow peculiar. To the left of the macadamized highway were the usual lush green meadows, stretching distantly to the sea, but on the right rose presently rolling hills, bare and frowning, their harshness only aggravated by gray strewn bowlders that literally peppered the hillsides. Mile after mile they towered beside us, a most remarkable freak of nature, and as desolate as ever a barren Sahara could be. It was surely from here that Block Island was separated in some huge convulsion of nature and washed far out to sea, for here only is its counterpart. The clustering gray stones that follow the undulating lines of towering hillock and sinking valley give a singular look of bleakness and sterility to the whole wild region, though the lesser foot hills are clothed in the

KING TOM'S HOUSE.

short green of bayberry and huckleberry bushes, whose blue-black globes peered mockingly in our faces from over all the numberless stone walls, while blackberries lay dead-ripe in perfect mats all along the dusty, lonely roadside. No fences did we see on either side this highway. It was surely easier work to pick up the countless stones that lay ready at hand and erect these solid ramparts of stone wall which, stretched far into the hazy distance, helped out the weird look of grayness. Flocks of sheep,

CHIEFTAIN OF THE NINIGRETS.

too, ambled in mild fright over the rolling uplands before our approach, and they, too, were gray, and not at all the snowy white that unpractical poets make them.

Now and then a pond nestled in the level green of the more lowly landscape to the left, and if it boasted a tiny islet or a jutting peninsula, that, too, would be covered to the very water's edge with the velvety green bayberry. Its sweet, spicy air made the sea-salt air more bracing, and the birds sang lustily as they wheeled and dipped in the blue waters.

The remnant of the once powerful Narragansett tribes are scattered all along these shores, degenerate and intermixed. Whether more Indian or negro it is sometimes difficult to read in the dusky figures one meets, but it is probably true that half the native negroes about the country have an admixture of Indian blood. In lonely state at the foot of one wild rise we passed, stood a bit of a gray shanty, and out of its open door rolled and tumbled one by one eight little pickaninnies, dusk and shiny as the huckleberries that grew profusely about, and on which it seemed they must have been brought up. With the African love of color, the little dooryard was all ablaze with gold and scarlet poppies. Few and scattering were the homes we passed, and the local architecture in these was striking. One house had its front painted gracefully in the form of a festooned curtain, with tassels depending from the eaves and tucked neatly away behind the windows. Unless memory serves falsely this house was blue and yellow. Another harmony in pink and brown was decorated as to the front door with a perfect sash, bows and notched ends carefully painted. Crude and barbaric as some of these designs were, one grew to understand the craving for brilliant color in this green and gray land, and it was a pretty bit we came upon suddenly, as we went on and on, and Matunuck's shore came in sight. Another little time-worn gray cottage, a huge sheltered wall where bee hives clustered, a rank of crimson hollyhocks, and in among them a morsel of a shiny little black girl standing with hands clasped and head drooping. In the foreground, among a helter-skelter array of sand mats, color boxes and so on, a young lady was hard at work putting this effective grouping on canvas. It flashed up at us as we sped by too fleetly—the dusky little figure, with its crimpy pig-tails, crimson hollyhocks and all.

Just beyond was the turn in the road that led to Matunuck beach and the sea, and opposite this branch stood perched on a commanding eminence the dark red

CRYING ROCKS.

cottage that has been for twenty years the summer home of Edward Everett Hale. Here we halted, curiosity and interest being too much for us, mingled with an all-consuming anxiety to know how Mr. Hale felt to be the originator of the largest social-religious society in the country, and also what he meant by his queer story of the far-famed Block Island fire-ship. Mr. Hale was at home and hard at work at his typewriter in his cosy study, and until he should be at liberty Miss Hale, the sister, entertained us in the breezy reception room looking seaward, a cosy, homelike apartment, with sketches of familiar bits adorning the walls, and on the panels of the sliding doors that shut out the study companion sketches of the regal scarlet swamp lily and pale purple milk weed. Mr. Hale's daughter was the artist here, and she it was who was at work among the bees and the hollyhocks down below. Miss Hale had recently written a syndicate letter describing the summer home in full, and says with whimsical frankness that she much prefers doing it herself to allowing some one else. There are but four who make up the family here; no new neighbors have come to occupy the land, and the whole Hale family congratulate themselves on the perfect seclusion rarely interrupted by invading strangers.

Mr. Hale presently appeared, and was kindness itself to us apologetic strangers. He even confided to us that he did not believe writing autographs was the bore some public men would have one believe —that, for his part, when a modest little girl out in Iowa or somewhere else took the trouble to write him a nice little letter inclosing a stamp for his autograph, he felt it very churlish to refuse. This was indeed amiable. He took us to the beautiful little lake back of the house, where there is a bit of a boat house, and showed us the spreading view from a lofty hillock. He told us how Point Judith took its name from Judith Hull, daughter of the old mint master of pine tree shilling fame in Hawthorne's story; he told us that Matunuck meant "the back way," and said that the road down which we were travelling was the "queen's road," and dated from the time of Queen Anne. In the midst of his kindly talk he plucked for us each a huckleberry bush, but I am sorry to admit that in the midst of eager listening to the explanation of the fire ship story I absently nibbled off the berries from my own and cast it far from me, to suffer vast regret afterward.

The fire ship, then, when Mr. Ingham

NINIGRET LODGE.

and his friends all hastened down to the Matunuck shores in Mr. Hale's Narragansett book, was made to vanish with Felix Carter and all the rest, because, as Mr. Hale said, he felt that the public were wearying of the admirable Felix and

CHARLESTOWN AND MATUNUCK.

Fausta, and it seemed a pleasant ending to speed them off into the mist and mystery that envelop the Palatine's vanishing; a kindly ending, too, for the old Palatine is apt to reappear, and why not they? The "Brick Moon," of which we spoke, was, of course, Mr. Hale said, a parable, meaning to show how possible it was for 37 congenial persons to exist happily with absolutely no diversion outside each other's society; and when we spoke of the good we had gained in earlier years by the series of helpful essays called "How to Do It," Mr. Hale told us the book had been locally adopted as a text book, and he hoped to see it generally accepted some time, as it seemed to him most fitted for that. There could scarcely be a more practically helpful one for young people.

Mr. Hale bears his years lightly and genially, though the silver is predominant in the long locks that fall to his shoulders; he wished us good speed with a cordiality that sent us buoyantly on down the Matunuck road.

Matunuck Beach is a popular spot with Providence people—more so, perhaps, than any other surf beach on our coast, albeit there is nothing, absolutely nothing, there but one hotel, a half-dozen bathing houses and—the ocean. But it is easy of access; carriages meet the trains at Wakefield, and it has certainly a most magnificent reach of shore and surf. There are no rocks, no sand dunes, no salt marshes; nothing but meadows and a level, far-stretching shore. The beach has not the wildness of Quonocontaug farther west; it is too level, too barren; but the safe bathing in the heavy surges makes it a great attraction, sufficiently so to warrant the erection of a first-class hotel. The Cashman House, somewhat back from the sea, though accommodating but a limited number, is an excellent house, and often preferred by guests to the regular hotel on the shore.

We did not tarry long, for we wished to see the heart of Charlestown, so we retraced our way to the queen's road and plodded westward. We would have done better to take the new road through the southern fields, for the queen's road was not of a degree of excellence commonly associated with regal requirements. It was sandy, inexpressibly sandy, and the dust enveloped us as in a mantle, as we ground through it, or trudged up hill in mercy to our perspiring horse, consoling ourselves by plucking frequent blackberries. Far down the desolate road, after we had passed through a whole plain of aromatic scrub pines, making a scant balsamic shade, we passed an old, old house, with a rear roof that

INDIAN MEETING HOUSE.

FORT NINIGRET.

sloped down from a two-and-a-half-story-height to a mild little jump from the ground. It is the home of Charles Church, brother of the lightkeeper at Point Judith and the Pier. Inside are the massive rafters, the cavernous fireplaces, cranes and andirons of long ago.

The house is two centuries old, and has been inhabited by generation after generation of the same family. Down in the fields, on the new road, is the oldest house in the region, and the date 1633 is set in curious figures above the door. The chimney alone would make a good-sized room.

On, and on still, we come to Cross's Mills, which is the real centre of Charlestown. Years ago, before the little stone church in the woods was built, the neighbors say this little settlement was perpetually graced by a dozen or so of Ind'ans, lying about in various degrees of intoxication. While they have deteriorated in blood, they have certainly improved in morals, and the few survivors of an ancient tribe are scattered to various peaceful vocations—farming, fishing and mason work —for the Narragansetts are born masons, perhaps as there is such abundance of stone in the neighborhood. The foundations of many of the finest Pier cottages are laid by the hands of the Indians.

JOE DENT'S RESIDENCE.

the brush back of the church are a few grave stones, their legends cut by the Indians also. The royal burying ground lies further south toward the sea, and beneath its rapidly leveling mounds the bones of Queen Mary and King George Ninigret are said to lie. In the graves of those honored by interment here were placed also bows and arrows, as was the usual custom. Ante-mortem choice was also given of a sitting or reclining posture in burial. A marble tablet erected by the State designates the enclosure and bears the date of 1879. Fort Ninigret, on an arm of the salt pond, bears still some faint trace of its ancient purpose, but the most definite knowledge one gets of anything remarkable in this desolate, thinly-settled region is from some of the few genuine old settlers. They will tell you all about the Baby Rocks, the queer heap of giant bowlders on the western hillside, distinct even from the land of stones, round and overlapping, or grotesquely balancing against each other. Here, in the first and last quarters of the moon, were brought the hapless deformed infants of the tribe to be slain with savage butchery, that there might be found in the tribe no target for a foe's taunt. Even at this late and unsuperstitious day, South County folks avoid the rocks in the waning moon, for they say the wails and cries

UNCLE GID.

The little church stands among the recurrent stones and huckleberry bushes, approached by only a bumpy cart road. It is a severely plain stone building, with a single window either side the door. In

are heard there still. Crowning Rock, or Coronation Rock, is the seat of the ancient coronation ceremony, and has also a State tablet inserted to that effect. By Chockampaug pond stands also the Indian school house, with the original room kept sacredly with all its disused paraphernalia. One of the old historic houses has been made over by a Newport club; it is a plain house with low and sloping roof and broad piazzas, and has witnessed much good cheer within, when the silent woods resound with the crack of the gun, and the abandoned "shore right" is resumed with rod and line. Until within 40 years, an old rule existed granting this so-called shore right to the remaining Indians—the privilege of a certain number of rods along shore with the right to camp and fish; then for weeks at a time tents and shanties would dot the beach and there would be a season of industry. But now all that is changed; there are few distinctive features maintained anywhere in Charlestown, and no special camp, and scarcely a typical Indian to be found on the coast. Uncle Gideon Ammons, whose career was given at length some time ago in the Journal, is probably the most interesting figure in modern Narragansett history, and Daniel Moody, the most thoroughly Indian looking. Joe Dent is another, and has one of the two remarkable old wagon hospitals that impart a suggestion of departed liveliness to forsaken Charlestown. In the tall weeds of the stone wall enclosure are leisurely decaying all manner of obsolete wheeled vehicles, from stage coach to spring wagon. It strikes one as the "port of missing ships" struck the mariner, and only emphasizes the general forlornness. The noble red men are few and far to find, but in their inmost fastnesses far in the hubbly cart-roads there are said to be a few degenerate in shanties and dug-outs. The little gray time-worn huts were the favorite architecture, however, till we turned back to the delights of the new road, and saw again with joy the cheerful paint and bold mural designs of more aspiring South County civilization, and left the strange gray hills behind.

CONANICUT ISLAND, CONANICUT PARK AND JAMESTOWN.

[Conanicut Park, by Newport steamer from Providence. Fare, 60 cents round trip. Jamestown, by ferry from Newport or Narragansett Ferry.]

AS the one boat which deigns to pause at Conanicut Park sweeps in at the dock, a scent of bayberry from the wild slopes is first to welcome one. Next is the one hotel carriage, as one disembarks and the boat speeds down to Newport. It is well that the hotel is pleasant and well managed, for it is "Hobson's Choice;" but it is perched invitingly among the old trees up the slope, a pretty bit of color with its light gray walls and red turrets, and its pillared veranda green and shady with masses of woodbine.

Conanicut Park is emphatically a place of rest; its diversions, though many, are of the mildest, its dissipations none. Its six mile length and one mile width have all the wayside delights of upland and ocean. Wild rose and iris, bayberry and elder-bloom crowd the northern meadow, and by and by a harvest of berries can be had for the gathering. Conanicut Island light, on the northeast shore, is a spot well worth a visit, aside from the views to be gained from the lighthouse tower. Mr. H. W. Arnold, the keeper, a graduate from the Warwick Neck light, is the hero of the Conimicut Light disaster a few years ago—the victim of the ice-flood. He has been in charge here for five years and achieved the most admirable results. The yard of the pretty gray cottage from which the tower rises was then like the wilderness without a jungle of wild growth; it is now a neatly shaven velvet sward, dotted with flowers, and with the finest bed of nasturtiums possible to find in a long day's journey, shading through yellow from white and palest straw color to deepest crimson. Over the entire front of the house runs a great honeysuckle, a fragrant mass of yellow and white, and an uncommonly aspiring jessamine has ceased to become a shrub and run away up to the high eaves and the light tower.

The grounds about the hotel, and even down to the water's edge are also reclaimed from their not unlovely wildness, and form the real "park" which names the place. The station erected by the steamboat company, but sitting serenely above the bustle of the dock, is a pretty feature of the place, and the few quiet cottages are in excellent taste, that of Miss Jennie Lippitt, with grounds sloping to the water, being noticeably inviting, and above it, also near the wild rocky shore, Charles Fletcher's spacious cottage, most imposing of all, with its round tower, clustering verandas and handsome lawns, closed in by a dense hedge of evergreen from the too wild blasts of the east wind. It has been the custom in past years for a party of gay girls, chaperoned by some not over-severe matron, to take possession of a Conanicut cottage for the summer, and have their fill of innocent and healthy fun. It would be hard to say how many charming girls have learnt proficiency in swimming by a Conanicut season, stimulated by criticism and rivalry, and encouraged by calm waters. Their only plaint is, amid the eulogies of beloved Conanicut, that "you can't spend anything there." Papa has neither to forward occasional checks during the daughter's stay, nor to settle sundry later and appalling bills. Conanicut has no store, no bazaar, not even an Indian tent and accompanying basket work. One cannot buy even a stamp there, for addresses read thus: "Miss Blank, Conanicut Hotel, Conanicut Park, Newport, R. I." It is possible to run up a bill only with Mrs. Brown and the stable keeper, Mr. Paine. The stable is the one public luxury, and Mr. Paine furnishes saddle horses and various vehicles and drives the stranger all about the island, furnishing information and prancing steeds at the same time at most modest prices.

with huge, gnarled trunks, where the sun and shade frolic in the breezes that blow up from the salt waves, lapping the rocks almost at its foot. In a hollowed stone by the old well, the birds drink and bathe in a tiny pool, and twitter perpetually. This is Seaside Cottage, and a winding concrete walk leads down to the "children's cottage," under the same jurisdiction, but where the mothers with little folk abide, that the nervous and invalid be not disturbed at the larger house—a thoughtful provision which we would commend to the attention of hotel keepers

CONANICUT PARK HOTEL.

But the most notable and most praiseworthy feature of the place is the institution known as "Seaside Cottage," established now for fourteen years by the Providence Fountain Street Society—the admirable arrangement by which tired, ill or not over-wealthy city women and children may have a week or two of change and absolute rest at the small sum of $3 per week. Mrs. Wright, the matron, has charge for the fourth season, and her domain is a most delightful one. Picture a quaint, low, old-fashioned gray farmhouse, with deep well and flat door stones, enlarged by ell and verandas, and nestled in the heart of a quiet old apple orchard,

generally. Mrs. White is assistant matron here. There are times when the matron has been called upon to entertain ninety in her entire fold.

Mrs. Wright was sans cook on the occasion of our visit, and we found the worthy lady busily engaged in spearing dumplings from a literal boiling sea. Their odor was most appetizing, but we had been taught not to ask for food in a stranger's house, and refrained. Mrs. Wright showed us the mammoth great range recently acquired, with mingled pride and despondency; for though an indispensable, it is not yet paid for. Our errand was hailed with joy, for the matron assured us that the place was seldom "written up" without some kind of response in the form of a much-needed check; and hopes were high that a similar demonstration might follow our coming, and settle the range difficulty, and also the still more vexed water question; for the old well, though mightily picturesque, is not practical, and Mrs. Wright lamented in almost Scriptural phrasing that her five handmaidens had nothing wherewith to draw, and the well was deep. With these two obstacles removed, life would go on smoothly at Seaside Cottage; and surely aid is worthily bestowed on a society whose managers themselves devote days to menial toil of the severest with their own hands when it is needed. Of the good that is done the matron speaks in unstinted measure. "The girl clerks and telegraph operators and hard-worked mothers who come here are dead tired—out and out," she says: "They have no appetite, no strength, no color at first, and it does my heart good to see them improve as they breathe the fresh air, and walk, and bathe, or just do nothing. It is only a little run down to the shore and the bathing beach through the orchard, and by the red gate—and there at one side you can see Mr. Vose's cottage, S. M. Vose of Providence. Good by, and I shall hope so much that something will come of your visit, and I am sure it will." May we hope for response in some reader to whom a check means so little, while the good it may do may mean so much.

Delightful as Conanicut is, it is not wholly pleasant to know that one cannot leave it when one is so disposed. The captain, the ticket agent and the starter all assured us that ferry boats to Wickford and Newport touched at the Park, but they do not. The morning boat from Providence, and her five o'clock return are the only landings, and the natives say the ferry boats have not paused for weeks. The Eolus waxed wroth since her encounter with the Day Star, and has concluded to let the latter vessel have her own way, it would seem. What she might do if one were to stand at the dock's edge in a commanding attitude and beckon in broad capitals, we cannot say, but just now a petition is circulating that the two o'clock city-bound boat may stop there, as it ought.

To leave Conanicut otherwise meant to enter Jamestown, and Mr. Paine's charioteer conducted us away from the quiet north end of the island to the tumult of the south; past Seaside Cottage again, and the bit of an old graveyard where lie the bones of that dead and gone habitant Paine, over whom neighborhood gossip is just now exciting itself to settle whether he was in truth, as a revived tale has put it, a murdering, bloody pirate or a highly respected citizen and an ornament to the community. Past the old, old windmill, 150 years old, with its huge great arms, its revolving cap and its still staunch body, which yet earns its living like younger windmills, up the long slant of Freebody's Hill, the way adorned with youthful turkeylets roosting melancholy on the fence-tops; in sight of stately Newport and the white-winged fleet always hovering in the harbor, past the Champlin House and its opposite neighbor, the Bay Voyage, thus oddly named to commemorate its own trip across seas, and down at length into bustling Jamestown, lively already as in midsummer time, the imposing front of the gray and red Bay View blocking the way, and the docks below, bristling with sailboats and lesser craft, and the towering hulk of the ferryboat Conanicut, swinging in from Newport. General bustle is in the air; and so is the Philadelphia and St. Louis accent, for these two cities populate the most of this growing summer town.

A long-standing mystery is solved. Now we know what becomes of all the boys and girls through the summer—they are at Jamestown. Newport claims the beaux, the Pier the belles and babies, Block Island the men and Watch Hill the nice old ladies—the silver-haired Aunt Serenas; but everywhere has there seemed sad lack of real genuine boys and girls till we landed at the Jamestown wharf, and there they all were, as if the Hamelin piper had piped them all over the ferry from Newport. It is small wonder a new hotel has gone up since last season, and cottages without end, and that the sound of the plane and hammer is still heard in the land. Jamestown is of a growth as rapid as any of the mushroom towns of the West. Six years ago, an old resident says, standing at the dock and looking into what is now the heart of the place, there were but eight houses to be counted—old settlers all, and readily to be distinguished now from their more modern neighbors, from the wee black hovel, with its lone pine tree near the landing, to the fine old Curry place, a bit up the north shore road, with its remarkable apple orchard that should have its home in the "Garden of the Gods," so weird, uncanny and gnarled are its giant, sprawling limbs before feathering into soft foliage.

CHARLES FLETCHER'S.

"Smith's" is another of the old places, transformed now into a quaint, gray English inn by the addition of an ell thrice its own size, and looking like a younger sister of Greene's Inn at the Pier. The houses that are not hotels are boarding houses unless they are cottages, and if they are cottages they take lodgers with few exceptions. It is the liveliest place south of the daily shore resorts. To sit at one's window of an evening, albeit it is pretty well up in a crowded hotel where one is lucky to get a room at all—sitting here and listening to the voices of the night, predominant among them all is the confused babel of many voices like the roar of Broadway, and I do not mean the Broadway of Providence, deafening as that is, but New York.

"What is the chief attraction of Jamestown?" we asked an old settler.

"Well, it's the climate and the quiet," he answered. "Any number of Westerners come here who object to Newport and the Pier because they are not quiet."

Jamestown might, like the proprietor of a certain German spa, copy his advertisement with equal propriety, which reads: "People in search of absolute retirement and quiet are flocking here from every quarter of the globe!"

Of the enthusiastic younger folks we queried, to their raptures over its charms, wherein lies its loveliness? Oh, it is so lively; you can go to Newport or Wickford or Narragansett Ferry, or over to the Fort, or down to the Dumplings, or—oh, there's no use talking, Jamestown is perfectly delightful. It would appear from the varied testimony that Jamestown is desirable chiefly for the ease with which one can get out of it; but I suspect that a prime cause of its popularity is its cheapness. There is the great gray Thorndike, with the varied view across the Bay, and the beautiful Bay View, most admirably appointed, and but $2 50 a day, as contrasted with Narragansett Pier's $4 and $5. For natural advantages it has not one-half Conanicut Park's number, or for the qualities one actually looks for in a place of summer rest. For all that it is constantly growing; its cottages are multiplying and it has had practically three new hotels in a little more than a year. With the half dozen others, the many boarding places and rooms in cottages, the season here is unusually early and busy; the Thorndike is about to begin a series of afternoon concerts by a string band, hops are in progress, attended with fervor and devotion; bathing is chief event of the day, in spite of a pebbly and shelly beach.

It is refreshing to see such activity, though it be somewhat confusing to an alien not yet naturalized. The sojourners are not dozing from 3 to 6 p. m. as a general thing, but are walking, driving, rowing, sailing and attending tennis and ball games with the utmost abandon. The excursions on foot are by the shore road, north and south, as far as one may list; far northward he may go and go and know no ending, along the pebble beach, whose pebbles, alas! are all angles instead of curves, or over the sloping hill. Southward, there is a "cliff walk" along the sea, beginning modestly enough and gradually rising till the way terminates at the rolling hills and the gray crags that drop into the southern sea, where are Conanicut's only fine breakers, and where quaint little Fort Dumpling, like an outcropping of the granite itself, crowns the gray crags, unchristened all these years by the fiery baptism of shot and shell.

From north to south the whole length of the island the main road runs straight as a die, swerving not even for the salt sound that penetrates far inland and broadens into a marshy pond. Beyond it the gray road turns steeply upward over a hill on whose summit the ancient wind mill of the island stands with the maltese cross of its gigantic arms sharply outlined against the pale sky. Off to the right is the quaint and interesting old Weeden place, enshrined among trees; then the old Quaker meeting house, where the devotees were wont of yore to solemnly "wait before the Lord" in stately silence, and further north still is the oldest house on the island. On goes the broad highway, bordered by blackberries fiercely thorn-guarded, and the waxen blooms of the clethra, sweetest of all August wild flowers, while down in the marshy brooks behind the wild hedges stands in stately ranks the royal cardinal flower of the Indians. And at last a branch road turns eastward to Conanicut Park, and the traveller is stayed.

At the cross roads near Jamestown, where high road meets ferry way, a southwest avenue leads down to the sandy bar that is the frail connection between east and west Conanicut. Only at supremely high tides is this frail passway flooded, and the walk or drive to western shore is an extremely interesting one, from Beaver Head on the north—though the natives call it Fox Hill—to the lighthouse of Beaver Tail on the wild southern shore, where even yet the lingering spars of the recent wreck grasp imploringly upward out of water. The cross at the roads is marked by a graveyard on one hand, where on one ancient stone is with difficulty deciphered under the veiling moss the name Pauline, and the date 1745; on the other hand, the religion and morals of the island are represented by an Episcopal Church and one of those white-faced, green-eyed Baptist meeting houses, whose belfries are capped with suggestive spikes.

A mile or so across the island, from east ferry to west ferry, runs another highway, from Jamestown down to the dock, where a smaller ferry-boat, the Jamestown, waits to convey excursionists to Narragansett and back again. By Narragansett I do not mean the Pier, often erroneously so called, but a wee, gray and ancient village directly opposite Jamestown on the western mainland. A grayer little place never existed. A gray old building stands on the shore capped with a crumbling belfry, that once, "before the war," was a woolen factory; and the quaint little handful of gray houses that cluster by were once its adjoining tenements; but a few fishermen occupy them now, and three or four long, low buildings at the water's edge, likewise gray and aged, are the fish-curing houses. Never was there so perfect a color symphony; gray are the wharves and the rotting spiles, gray the rail fences and the stone walls, and the hoary trunks of the few poplars; gray the one road stretching giddily aloft to a steep hilltop behind the settlement, and gray is the narrow strip of slaty shore, strewn with shale and shells. Perched on the topmost pinnacle of this breathless ascent behind the hamlet is the white house of worship, its spire still pointing aspiringly upward with a mute "Excelsior." An incentive to toil and progress, and a type of the difficult path of right doing, it is meant to be, no doubt; but half way up the sheer ascent we were content to pause ambitionless and breathless, and shamelessly retrograde to the rocking ferry-boat. It is funny to watch the horses who make these ferry trips between Newport and the islands; one and all, they remonstrate wildly, when a heavy sea first sets the boat a-tilting; some of them very quickly get their "sea legs" on, and others stagger to and fro at each swell with an air of great surprise.

Where does food come from to fill the small boy sojourners? A half-dozen after supper seated themselves on the piazza steps conveniently within earshot, and after discussing all things else in heaven and earth in that particularly knowing, decisive and final way admitting of no appeal, which is common to small boys, they fell to narrating their achievements at the supper tables. After several boasting Iagoos had chanted their exploits, said one particularly hollow and cadaverous youngling, "Well, I just gorged myself. I had baked mackerel, sirloin steak, chicken fricassee, and eggs—all sorts of eggs; I had omelette, poached and hard-boiled." At this juncture the small boy was suddenly reminded of something, and, searching in his pockets, drew forth three hard boiled eggs, which, proceeding to divide among his comrades, they devoured with relish and thankfulness. "I ate a good many eggs," candidly continued this infant anaconda, "and then I had different kinds of bread—say, fellows, rolls and tea biscuit are just the same, I found when I called for 'em—and then I had stewed and fried potatoes, berries and three kinds of cake. Oh, and two glasses of milk—two or three."

A deep silence succeeded the close of this pleasing programme, corroborated by the boy who had dined opposite, and then the six took themselves off enthusiastically to try a new kind of ice cream.

There is no prettier diversion of a summer afternoon than to make a ferry trip east or west among our harbor waters and the many anchored vessels. Westward through Dutch Island harbor and past the peaceful island, where the Sergeant's home stands high among the upland trees and the grassy fortifications, and the southern point is tipped by the lighthouse of the white light. And off the mainland the breakers are distantly seen leaping about Bonnet Head, where the Rhode Island came to wreck, though the harbor waters lift the little ferry boat with only a gentle swell.

Eastward the big Conanicut, plying be-

THE HOME OF PIRATE PAINE.

tween Newport and the island, glides between forts and islands and lighthouses galore, and the small boats of the training ship, with her jolly young uniformed lads, or perhaps the white-clad crew of the big Norseman, their vessel's name blazoned on their navy caps, pull lustily across the ferry's pathway.

Jamestown is not lacking for diversions, and though in her quiet waters there is not the delightful acquaintance of the surf to make, there is an equivalent in an opportunity for fancy swimming and safe rowing, of which the young folk are not slow to avail themselves. The bathing beach, though small in extent, is a safe and pleasant one, and even a despondent on suicide bent would have difficulty in making way with himself by drowning, so many are the skiffs and catboats hovering always about.

A grizzly bear visited the island during our stay, led by a man in Alpine guise, with horn and alpenstock, and called out the juvenile population in astonishing numbers. He was a bald-headed man, and he reversed the Scriptural legend, for the bear and the bald head wrestled together on the sward, while the mocking children stood about and scoffed unscathed. A touch of dramatic interest attended this scene, when the bald head emerged from the combat with an ugly blood-stain, mark of the grizzly's too-warm embrace. The bear, a great tawny, good-natured looking fellow, also performed various other exploits, turned a few "zomazates," as his owner announced, and shuffled clumsily about in a so-called dance to a mellow barytone song of

"Er-room, poom, poom, poom!
Hey-de-diddle-day room pa!"

or words to that effect. And as the owner presently passed around the hat we asked as we dropped our modest mite, for we knew the man would have to buy a good-sized piece of court plaster: "What is his name?" and received the somewhat staggering reply of "Zhinny!"

A wandering Jew pervades the island— the chair-and-ladder man of Providence. Did any one ever go anywhere in the limits of our State in the summer and not see him, we wonder?

All things considered, it is little wonder that Jamestown is a favorite among the young folks, though it is not Providence people, but Southerners and Westerners, notably from St. Louis, who hie here, and the place is already full to overflowing.

Everybody looks busy and happy, and nobody looks bored, and say what one may, Jamestown is the liveliest, the noisiest and the most hilarious summer city on the Rhode Island coast.

PRUDENCE PARK.

[On Prudence Island, 15 miles from Providence, by Continental steamer. Fare, 60 cents round trip.]

FOUR daughters had the old Indian chief, so the legend runs, Prudence, Patience, Hope and Despair; names a trifle Quakerish, perhaps, but we must not question the genuineness of an Indian tradition here on their most favored soil. To the favorite and fairest—Prudence—he gave the fair and prolific island that bears her name, and so on down to poor little Despair, who must have been an ugly little "nubbin" indeed, if she was at all like her niggardly heritage—one low black rock cropping up above the salt waves north of Hope—the latter not at all a bad place for a summer house, as the flourishing farm of Mr. Hiram Aylesworth can testify, lord of his isle among the tall, shivering poplars that scantily clothe rocky little Hope in greenery.

Prudence, in outline and substructure, is a characteristic little island; most islands are likened, in real or fancied resemblance, to some foreign object or animal, and if Prudence looks like anything at all, in its southern oval and long neck reaching north to Potter's Cove, it is a crooked-necked squash or an attenuated Block Island.

Sailors coming in from the west cannot fail to mark the huge rock ledges of black slate, lying flat and high and ceasing only with the sea, as if all the bad boys of long ago giant days had piled their primitive slates together, and vowed to go to school no more. Straight eastward across the island the ledge runs, tilted far higher toward the mainland, so that the ascending eastward road brings one out suddenly on the opposite shore on the top of a lofty eminence with a dizzy sweep down to the water, where Sand Point light rises white before the long sharp sand-dagger that thrusts into the bay and invites easy shipwreck. Here in lonely calm is the little white cottage flying the union colors, the snug harbor home of another of Bristol's retired seafarers—Capt. Gladding.

On Prudence rises a height second only to Mount Hope, capped by the gray buildings of the old homestead of the Potter farm. The Potters and Chases are the oldest inhabitants; Daniel Chase is one of the best known, now an old man of 76 years, and with a father Daniel before him, and a grandfather Daniel also. When the grandfather, Daniel Chase, was a young man, with plenty of ambition and money also, he built down on the southeast shore a mansion which is standing yet, and which, immediately on its completion, received the title by scoffing and less pretentious farming folk of "Daniel Chase's Folly." The Folly was deserted only in 1891, and looks staunch enough yet, with its huge square brick walls, its broad, deep windows, and its granite foundations. But the floors are said to be settling. Its great kitchen is twenty-five feet square, its stately front hall, finished in cherry, with a handsome stairway of solid carved wood, and all the floors of hard pine. Overhead in all the spacious rooms the huge, dark rafters show, as was then the fashion, and the Folly's building cost $25,000, a neat little sum in the thrifty last century days.

Fewer very old houses are found on the island than one might expect, but it was, in the Revolution, a literal stamping ground for the British, and thirty prosperous and peaceful homesteads went up in flame and smoke, with all the huge old windmills that liberally besprinkled Prudence from end to end.

One Islander, returning for his gun, is said to have been shot; the rest escaped to mainland, and left the island desolate. Had there been an adequate historian the tale would have been sad as the "Exile of the Acadians." Never again has Prudence been so thriftily repopulated by farming folk as she gave promise in pre-Revolution days, though her soil is the richest of all Narragansett's islands. The island's stone walls are peculiar, high and massive and dark, of the flat, black slate that crops out all over the soil. One house only, or its ruins, survives the ravages of ancient war—the old mill house, northeast, by the brook that once turned the mouldered water wheel.

A QUAINT NORMANDY MILL.

Crossing the little wooden bridge over the stream one comes upon its ruins now among the willows where the old blind miller, spared by his infirmity, ground his grist and ended his days in peace. Not far from here is the old neglected grave yard, bearing dates legible beneath the encroaching gray gravestone moss as far back as 1723. Cattle stumble about over half-hidden mounds, and pumpkins and even an aggressive haystack declare defiance of death and decay. Near the cornfield that rustles down by the old brick house is another little graveyard near the quiet east shore, in what is known as the pier meadow, where a score or so of islanders peacefully rest. To a cluster of old mounds tradition has long assigned Indian occupancy, and a zealous antiquarian recently excavated there for possible relics; a skull was indeed found, but it bore, not the glossy raven black tresses of true Indian ownership, but unmistakable African wool, and the explorer ceased his researches.

The southern end of the island is peopled wholly by Albros, a family of them having been the last occupants of the desolate Folly. Mr. Albro, the eldest, has spent nearly 50 years on the island.

But for the invading forces a century ago, Prudence could hardly have been excelled in interesting relics; in fire and smoke went up, too, the old pin factory, the first in America, where pins were made laboriously by hand, and which were far more massive and skewer-like than the modern affair. The family of Mr. Farnum, a resident who has done much toward improving Prudence farms, has some of these pins still.

Inland from the sloping rocky shores are swamps and marshes densely overgrown with wild grape tangles, making the whole island odorous in June as a great mignonette garden. It is one procession of flowers here the season long, growing richly in the fertile earth and the humid sea air. Orioles, yellow birds and song sparrows people the island, and down in the wild jungle of woods in the lonely south swamps great colonies of crows have their uncouth nests, flying in a vast calling and cawing crowd northward in the early morning to feast on carrion washed to the shores by Potter's Cove; and when the sun is on the verge of disappearance below the western land line, they flap heavily home again in a black discordant cloud to their secret haunts.

The fields everywhere are literally black with blackberries, for in the season half of them will decay unplucked; it seems a pity, when one thinks of the waiting hungry mouths of hundreds of our little folk at home prevented by poverty from ever seeing a growing berry.

So much for ancient Prudence, as it is, and ever has been. The summer colony is by far its most striking feature, with its two score of handsome cottages nestled midway of its length by the western shore. W. E. Barrett and G. W. Williams were the pioneers of the movement that led to the present Park Association. It was eighteen years ago that they built their imposing cottages, not far apart, and the only white ones on the island, Mr. Barrett's with red roofs and pointed spire, Mr. Williams's with a round tower and pale green roof with the tint of new shingles, and the enclosed pavilion in cherry finish that looks every way at once with its breezy windows. A sloping lawn is gay with swings, summer house and tennis court, and on the rougher slopes by the water's edge browses the children's pet, Jack the donkey, quite the reverse of him of the supposititious ballad, and with any amount of "go." Mr. Barrett's grounds are gay with flower beds—petunias of unusual beauty.

It was about four years after the extensive land purchases of these two gentlemen that cottages began to go up, but the residents are enthusiastic in praises of Prudence, and every precaution is taken to insure only harmonious newcomers. There is neither existing nor desired inducement to excursionists, except those who come to visit friends or enjoy pure nature.

A social nucleus is found in the recently erected Casino, the gift of Charles H. Perkins, who, with his large family and numerous cottages and farm, occupies about 400 acres of the Park land. The Casino is a double structure, one side being devoted to a bowling alley, pool and billiard tables, and the other, which can be made entirely separate, to the dance hall, gayly decorated with Mikado designs, and used at the weekly Wednesday hops, quite a dress occasion, and with a permanent orchestra of three pieces. Service is held here Sundays, and Sunday school as well, for there are lots of little folks among the cottagers, the door opening to secular amusements being religiously closed.

R. B. Little has a handsome red house with dark green trimmings, and a unique roof balcony, a huge square port hole through which passing mariners may view the blue heavens beyond. This is called the "Crow's Nest," and is accessible by an inner stair. Other cottagers are Ornando Vose, Mrs. P. H. Hollister of Greenfield, R. B. Clark of Washington, whose pretty home north of the bathing beach is furnished wholly with antiques, Mrs. Goodall of Washington, Mr. Fred Perkins, Dr. G. T. Swarts, W. C. Wood of Washington.

On the west shore lie only the neat bathing houses, and the stone-pillared pavilion where sweet babies and their bonnes assemble daily. Shady lake, full of springs, furnishes ice; the nightly boat brings the mail, the supplies and the masculine element; fishing is fine from the rocks; a new road by the town has just been laid east and west, and another is hoped for in place of the old north and south driveway. Insomnia is unknown, and illness and death have never been known among the cottagers until the summer when Mr. Barrett's death cast the first gloom over the island.

BRISTOL FERRY.

[Twenty miles from Providence, on Rhode Island. Hotel and Locust Cottage, Mrs. Kate Burnop, $7 to $10 a week.]

THERE are three ways of reaching Bristol Ferry from Providence: One by rail on the Old Colony, via Fall River and Tiverton; one by the 5 p. m. Fall River boat, touching here, and one by boat to Newport and a quick run up in the train—the price about the same. Our way was a fourth one—by steamer to Newport from Narragansett Pier, then up the island. It was a novel experience to cross so heavy a sea in so dense fog. The little Caswell seemed to float in a little halo of her own, surrounded by a fog bank thick enough to slice, which we were forever approaching and never quite touching. Two men were lookouts down in the bows, where they got more than a mild spatter of spray with each lurch, and signalized the approach of each vessel by an extended rigid forefinger, till the captain, further back in the fog, likewise beheld and shifted his course. These men must have had eyes created to see in a fog, as bats have for darkness, for we strained our eyes to see, and it was always many seconds before even the palest gray ghost of a sail came slipping out of the mist, not to materialize, but to remain a ghost still, only a shade darker than the cloud into which it slipped again. Fog horns boomed and bell buoys rang wildly, Whale Rock's warning pealing after us for miles, and our own boat shrieked back continually. It was startling to hear a deep frenzied bellow shattering the mist close off to our left, like an angry cow bereft of her offspring, and still to see nothing and know it was Beaver Tail's call, where the surges were roaring. The waves were not mountain high, but they would have petrified into very respectable hills, and what space of water was visible looked like an upland country, undergoing a transformation scene. Within a stone's throw a bell buoy writhed and struggled, and raised its huge bulk out of water, looking anything but the flat raft it seemed in a calm. The sudden lull that at last came upon us, and the sight of a lone and bewildered bumble bee, told us, as the twigs and berries did Columbus, that we were nearing land, and, at last, damp and dizzy, we slid in at the dock, and hastened down old Newport's worn pavings to the Old Colony station.

The railroad trip along Rhode Island (and by this is meant the island. Alas for our queer naming!) looks just as it does on the map; the railroad runs as delightfully near the west shore as it is pictured, and soon we left the fog behind us. Bits of island peeped up at the left, the Sisters, and Bishop Rock and Dyer's Island, and by and by the distant shores of Prudence. On the right was always a long stretch of green, bare country, yellowing in the summer sun-heat; long lines of stone wall and distant haystacks representing the only eminences. Now and then a flock of sheep or pasturing horses fled from our rattling progress; once two small boys suddenly rose up out of the water and waved their arms with startling effect, and at last we halted at Middletown, announced in energetic tones. This sounded enterprising, but where was the town, the station even? Off to the right stretched the same barren walled pastures, off to the left the sea. A solitary passenger left us, still hopeful of Middletown's existence, and we sped on. Portsmouth Grove next; ah, this is more hopeful. Giant oaks in abundance to give the place name, a half dozen houses, and white tents gleaming through shrubbery, down on the rocks near shore. The inland country changed now as we sped north, and the bare stone walls were draped with shrubs and vines, and trees grew thickly and distant farms appeared, corn fields and potato fields—and Coal Mines was the next place, wearing an air of depression, but sitting amid pleasant scenery in spite of the hill of slate and coal dust that lay beyond the black buildings. Now the main land loomed ahead; Bristol Ferry light beckoned across the channel, and we stepped out at Bristol Ferry, while the train whisked around a curve to cross Stone Bridge and arrive at Tiverton, on the mainland.

Bristol Ferry is admirably arranged for stormy weather, we thought, as we stood and looked about. There were the hotel, the wharf, the store, the neighbors' cottages, the station, the telegraph office and the post office, all within a stone's throw of each other—and plenty of stones with which to test the fact. It was in the telegraph office that we first distinguished ourselves, on spying the operator's seat, an ordinary chair, but set in four of the green glass insulators used on telegraph posts. Scenting an interesting item on "Electric Freaks at Bristol Ferry," we asked in tones of lively interest, "Oh, do you have to use those insulators on your chair?" Smiling a quiet smile the agent replied, "No, only to make the legs longer."

The one hotel here is a big, white, airy structure, tempered with green blinds and surrounded by broad piazzas, even up to the third story. In its cool setting of great poplar trees, with neatly whitewashed trunks, it looked somehow like pictures of old-fashioned "young ladies' seminaries."

"BOOTHDEN."

The house looks large enough to accommodate twice its stated limit—fifty. However, the ground floor is taken up mainly with large parlors, and a long dining hall; about thirty is the usual number, all the proprietor cares to entertain.

Row boats are let by the hotel, and it is but three-fourths of a mile to the main land at Bristol Ferry light, where is the cosy old farm-house of Capt. West, one of Bristol's retired seamen, and at which, when passing on the Sakonnet boat, I have always felt a wild desire to get out and stay all summer. It is but two miles to Tiverton, and ten to Newport, the broad highway leading straight as a die down the island. Therefore the quiet little place is far from isolated, and its scenery and air are delightful. There are plenty of trees, shrubs and wild berries; there are ample, flourishing farms, and a most enormous number of pear trees, heavily laden. The few cottages in the place are everyone picturesque and in good taste, and are occupied variously by Edward Hicks, Oliver Hicks, E. I. Stoddard, Cross, Devol, Sisson and Alanson Peckham. The home of the latter stands in the midst of a farm and fruit orchard, with large and shaded grounds, and its long piazza is one mass of woodbine.

The prettiest place of all is Locust cottage, with, as is not usual, an easily obvious reason for the name. It is a picturesque gray gabled cottage, up which sweet honeysuckle and purple clematis twine, peeping in at its odd-shaped windows, and it is an ideal boarding place. It accommodates fifteen guests. It is managed by a trig little New York woman, Mrs. Burnop, with four bright children, one of whom did the honors of the house with as hospitable urbanity as if she had been twice her age. Its furnishings are dainty and cosy in the extreme, its rooms large and handsomely furnished, and its guests, Boston people, are enthusiastic in its praise and of Bristol Ferry generally, and assert that it is incredible, when one can live in this beautiful homelike nook at prices between $7 and $10 a week, how Jamestown or Narragansett Pier can still be preferred. There are three summer cottages south of the station, occupied by Taunton people, and all the sojourners wear a triumphant air and consider that they have an immense advantage over boarders elsewhere. In our walk inland we met but one stroller—a pretty young girl with easel and paint box.

A few hilarious small boys went bathing at noon, and we heard their shrill voices joyously making plans for the afternoon. There is a small bit of smooth bathing beach, elsewhere it is stony and rough; and stranded all along are great gray stubs of trees, drifted from some far shore with a high tide and gale.

The one store sits down on the wharf in a big gray building, originally intended for a store-house, though used as a store for half a century. E. I. Stoddard has been for seven years proprietor, and among its miscellaneous supplies we can testify to the excellence of home-made hop beer. In the window is a startling appearance, looking like a big red face with mouth wide open, but on nearer view it resolves itself into a portrait of a can of Cleveland's baking powder.

Altogether, Bristol Ferry is a quiet, restful, dreamy old place, added to our growing list of ideal summer homes. There is little doubt that the palmy days of the whole island, outside Newport, are yet to come, and there are many charming spots along its lonely length that a few years will see converted into typical seaside homes.

BRISTOL NECK.

[Bristol, 12 miles from Providence, by Providence, Warren and Bristol Railroad. Forty minutes ride. Fare, 40 cents. Carriage to Bristol Neck, two miles.]

THE train had borne us south to Bristol, but the carriage that was to convey us thence across the Neck took us back northward for a little space over the stately, broad, hard highway leading up to Warren before we branched eastward toward Mount Hope Bay. Fringed heavily with the leafage of huge willows, the fair highway receded into distance like a green tunnel, and every bending tree we passed was a picture, soft touches of olive in its feathery yellow green, and its knotted, dark trunks outlined with the rich green moss of age. The huge stone wall to the right bounded the grounds of the hospitable Paul mansion, and was built by an old-time local celebrity, whose home was on the island, and who, having taken the somewhat eccentric oath never to enter a boat or ride in a carriage, came to the scene of his labors by this rather roundabout route: From Bristol Ferry across Stone Bridge, from Tiverton around the bay to Warren, and south to Bristol, arriving at the trip's terminus with his tools in a wheelbarrow, which he was said to have propelled all the way from the island. This resolute old gentleman is said to have later transported his wife here also by the same means and in the same vehicle. At any rate, the old wall behind the line of willows still stands to prove his sometime existence.

Turning presently eastward, the way led between gray old pastures, where cows were leisurely browsing, and goldenrod gladdened the roadside like the sun, sulking just now behind clouds of fog. The most golden of golden rod in the State, it seems, is this that blooms in the pleasant country places about old Bristol; and a veritable garden of wild bloom was the swamp that lay just beyond, and through which the road passed, its generous dividing walls giving a sixty feet roadway, though greenly grown up with maurauding weeds and vines that flauntingly declared that

"Stone walls do not a prison make."

Jewel weed, yellow primrose, wild arnica, clethra, the fantastic button balls, clematis, passe but beautiful, elder bushes

BRISTOL'S OLDEST.

bending with their purple black burden of fruit, everywhere the regal golden rod and here and there in a muddy hollow or bed of a wee brooklet, the flame of the stately royal cardinal, a true child of the forest. The swamp passed, a salt breath borne on the east wind gently bespoke Mount Hope Bay's presence before us, and a declivity led seaward, capped by the pleasant homesteads of the Bowlers, Paines and of Lorin Coggeshall, to whom belonged the two or three scattered white summer cottages almost at the water's edge; one of them has been occupied by the family of William H. Dyer since its building; he has summered at Little's Narrows for 19 years. The few sojourners on this lonely shore have chosen their summer homes well, for it is a spot unique for scenery on our coast. On the east side of the Neck as it is, it of course looks east across Mount Hope Bay, and one has to keep his local geography well in mind to reconcile the two facts that he is on the eastern side of Narragansett Bay, and yet when he faces flaming oblong that meant a Fall River factory sunlit. Guests of the Narrows' sojourners are always taken to the local "Sunset Rock" for the sight.

Looking north, where Mount Hope Bay ceases, between here and Fall River stretch one after another the four long sand points that mark the several mouths of the four rivers that empty in close parallels into the salt bay—Kickemuit, Cole's, Lee and Taunton. The Kickemuit is nearest, and its west shores rise

THE COLT MANSION, BRISTOL.

the water, south is on his right hand and north on his left. It is for a time confusing to see the sun rise over the water till the contour of this bay's area is clear. Fall River lies directly opposite this small colony, and on clear days is mapped out with surprising distinctness; when the sun goes down in red splendor it is a sight to see the huge mills over there crimson in the glow and flash fire from all their myriad windows—beacons of flame for many a mile on land and sea. Standing on one of the Lime Rock heights far north in Lincoln, I have seen more than once a to a series of rolling, wild bluffs, with nestling ponds in hollows behind them, and the more distant hill dotted with the wee white dwellings of a flourishing colony indeed—the chicken farm of Mr. William Thayer. Down beyond, in a picturesque cluster of trees and brown roofs, is the establishment of Mr. Bourne, the oysterman, and between it and Providence daily plies the little gray and green Kickemuit, sending a cheery salute as she speeds by, to the saluting cottagers, who make much of the one passing craft. Far out on the water, midway from shore to shore, is the long, low line of Spar Island, indicated impartially on maps as Spar and Sparrow. A deceptive little island, sometimes a seeming stone's throw from shore, but really mocking any but a strong pair of arms at the oars, and again retreating wholly behind the low-lying fog banks, on days when there is no Fall River, but only a wide, gray ocean retreating to a dim, gray horizon. The southern walk along these shores, down toward Mount Hope itself, is most interesting. Among mounds of scallop shells, great and small, lie at the water's edge huge pudding-stone bowlders, pale green and gray above, dark brown below where the waves have smitten, and by and by the tumble of rocks grows denser, and those who know lead the way in triumph to a broad, flat rock of dark graywacke, washed even in the mildest calm with the lapping eastern waters, and point out the famous Norseman's Rock. Still legible to the practised eye are the row of strange characters, ten, perhaps, in all, and above them the outlines of a canoe. ' They have often been copied and photographed, and controversy is still rife concerning their genuineness, as it is of those on Dighton rock, far up the Taunton river above. If they are genuine Scandinavian characters, there seems no real reason why we may not trustfully picture the ancient craft voyaging wonderingly along our strange new land, and pausing here and farther north to carve a memento on these scattered rocks so tempting that even the schoolboys of our own generation have also left specimens of rude art on this and other stones along the region.

Quite near Norseman's Rock is the hermit of the Neck, whose home for eighteen years has been in a black, tarpaulin-covered, one-room shanty down by the shore, about eight by twelve feet, and its one door so low that one enters with an involuntary obeisance. "Daddy Booth" is the familiar name by which this eccentric old gentleman is known—for he has grown old in his voluntary exile—and Daddy Booth was at home as we passed by on our return from Norseman's Rock; and, with the interviewing impulse too strong to be resisted, one of us crawled within the dusky wigwam and engaged the hermit in amicable converse, while the rest of the party waited without in ill-concealed mirth. Daddy Booth's real name was Leonard, he informed his guest, as she sat perched upon the woodpile that graced the apartment, while he fed the new-builded fire in the small rusty stove and prepared for his simple evening meal. His old home was in Pawtucket, but he didn't get along with his folks, he explained with a genial smile, so he came down here to live. Oh, he enjoyed it here first rate—dug clams and sold, and read and went fishing. All he needed, he gallantly remarked, in deference to his callers, was a lady to look after the housework.

The little hut was not indeed in so bad trim as one might suppose, though the simple cot that took up half its space looked not over inviting. The old hermit himself was a tall, upright old man, with flowing white locks, smooth face, and an expression of genial, shrewd simplicity. His accent bespoke him an Englishman, and he found a bond of sympathy at once with his uninvited guest in the fact that he was peeling mushrooms preparatory to a stew, while the uninvited one also carried a kerchief full, plucked from the white dotted meadows. Unlike most hermits, this old gentleman does not shun human kind except in his eccentric preference for a solitary and primitive abode. Strangely enough, he had a successor on this very shore, Ike Simmons, now some years dead, who also occupied a lonely hut on the bowlder-strewn beach for many years, till he was one day found lying dead in the woods near by.

A short walk southward, the beautiful home for invalids in Dr. Canfield's care lifted its red walls among the clustering grove that caps its lawns; and almost in the same grounds, but nearer the waters' edge, is the summer residence of his brother, soft gray among the gray walls and rocks. An odd little octagonal bathing house perches on a high rock before it, and leads down to the quiet water. Bathing in Mount Hope bay almost inevitably leads also to swimming, among its devotees, unhampered by the fear of invading breaker or undertow; the constant waves sound only with a gentle lap-lapping, night and day, except in the transitory surf borne by the passing of the great Fall River steamers from their distant port.

In the tangled woods back of the slight bluffs that border the western shores stands a huge tree split from top to bottom straight through its heart by a lightning bolt; one side is bare and dead, and the other forlornly strives to assert itself still. Along the bluffs by the Kickemuit river were once unearthed far below the earth's surface, enormous masses of clam shells along with a skeleton or two of unmistakable Indian origin; and if the most ardent antiquarian of the place, Lorin Coggshall, be interviewed, he will while away an hour or so very agreeably in arguing for the old Narragansett's occupancy of this spot, instead of the generally accepted Mount Hope, stretching its long green length along to the southeast. Certainly, some ancient tribes must have put in a considerable portion of time here to have made way with the contents of that prodigious accumulation of long-buried clam shells. Mount Hope might have been merely the "Sunset Rock" of the appreciative King Philip, and Little's Narrows his domestic department.

Having exhausted all the walks and drives practicable along this shore, there was yet time for a call at the Soldiers' Home, and the approach to this was by yet another road, with the oldest of old houses resting cosily in the shade of the hoary old trees that border all old Bristol's highways. The Soldiers' Home has so often been described and illustrated that it needs nothing further in that line, but it was a novelty to stroll through its scattered buildings, to inspect the laundry, the kitchen and the reading room where a score or so disabled veterans were assimilating the day's news from Providence papers. The new Home gets a good many visitors, and they must be welcome, for it is an idle life that most of the half hundred residents lead—a few being employed on the regular duties of the place, but most of them having but one imperative duty in the whole long day, the making of the red-counterpaned bed in the long dormitory; and the long receding lines show the soldiers' handiwork performed with military exactness. Of course most of the inmates of this

THE SOLDIERS' HOME.

pleasant shelter are incapacitated for active duty, but to some of them some slight familiar labor would be eagerly welcome. Covered walks stretch from building to building, so that these venerable "boys in blue" can take their airing in rain or shine, a welcome diversion.

The hospital is separate from the other buildings, and here, in solitary quiet, sat two old gentlemen, feeble and infirm, with only the attendants' presence for diversion the livelong day. One of them furtively wiped away tears as we entered. Poor old man! our sympathizing thoughts went back to the day when these lonely two went marching away, eager and young, to the beat of the drum and flutter of the flag, to defend our country. Welcome as is the acknowledgment it is making to-day, in these sheltering walls, it is all too slight, it seemed to us, pitying the infirmities contracted in the gallant aid to make our land what it is. Religious services are given by various Bristol denominations, and I am sure nothing could be more welcome than an evening's entertainment now and then from that and other sources, through the week.

We climbed to the top of the high water tower, and saw where the bay ran in from Narragansett, and the distant town of Warren clustered to the north; and far, far to the northeast a high, blue hill rose towering to the low-hanging clouds that capped the faint and distant forests, and Capt. Hull told us it was indeed Blue Hill of observatory fame, hard by Boston. Indeed, with a glass, the observatory itself could be easily made out.

Once more retracing our way we turned toward Bristol to spend an hour or two strolling

"The pleasant streets of that dear old town,"

and those of us who were strangers in the land lost their hearts straightway, and recklessly declared that trains might leave and boats might leave, but Bristol was the town of their dreams, the ideal they had vainly sought, and in Bristol they should stay forever.

Bristol is a town rare to find now in bustling East or West, where everything seems finished, ended, and now enjoying the placid rest of leisurely old age. Of goodly dimensions, as the stately town is, there is no upstart flimsy architecture of modern growth to flaunt its quiet old-time air; along the beautiful streets everywhere elm-shaded the quaint old homesteads peacefully repose, and the age-loving eye revels in fan lights, knockers and Corinthian columns, in queer old statuary in the old-fashioned, box-bordered gardens, in the marine flavor that comes from the sloping streets that lead to the sea, and in the gay parterres where every ancient flower dear to our grandmothers' hearts blooms brightly as in its native atmosphere. Even in the homes of wealth the architecture and adornments are so quietly unobtrusive, so colonial in feeling, that they are in harmony with the whole dreamy town that seems to lie in an enchanted slumber, waiting for the touch of the magic wand that shall draw the old East India merchantmen again from over seas, revive the mouldering whalers and set seafaring life briskly going again in this abandoned port. Flat roofs have most of these charming old homes, surrounded by massive balustrades, and reminiscent of the days when the daughters and mistress of the old household went aloft to watch the ships come in from sea, or linger through the gloaming in this airy outlook in true Oriental style. We saw wooden bay windows, shutters and all, of solid

THE DEWOLF MANSION.

carved wood, and horizontal blinds above doors and windows; we saw green glass tiles and fan lights in enviable profusion, and we saw more beautiful churches than all Providence can boast. And we longed, most ardently for all, to have been so blessed as to have been born and brought up in the delightful atmosphere of that altogether charming old seaport town, and to have had at our tongues' ends all the old legends and sea stories with which we could feel that the air was full and whose faint, intangible essence we could almost grasp, strangers as we were. And so longing and lingering, we at last reluctantly took our train and steamed with undue speed away from the most fascinating town in all Rhode Island.

SAUNDERSTOWN.

[By Stonington Railroad from Providence, or by ferry from Newport to Wickford. Thence by steamer Wyona direct to Saunderstown, 25 miles from Providence. Saunders House, Stillman Saunders proprietor.]

IT is now for five summers that the quiet old colony of Saunderstown has thrown doors open to our ever-growing summer public, and yet the pleasant, dreamy old spot is hardly known even to Providence folk, except by the newspaper advertisement of a little steamer running there, connecting at Wickford with the 8:15 a. m. train from Providence. A trip by this train gives one a long and pleasant day by the shore, or exploring the legendary Kingston homesteads which Saunderstown lies conveniently near.

From the moment one walks down the wharf at Wickford landing in search of the waiting steamer he feels himself in the midst of a queer, quaint and delightful adventure. The big Tockwogh, waiting for Newport passengers, will be lying directly at the dock, and one must look very hard to spy the tiny Wyona, lying quite eclipsed in the shadow of her neighbor, but seeming to say with modest assurance, "If you please, I am a steamboat, too." No gang-plank is required, and one steps nonchalantly over the infantile guards and seeks the after-deck, comfortably filled on the occasion of our own journey by the half-dozen of us who were the passengers. No one manned the deck but a youth who had escorted us and our baggage aboard, who took tickets and seemed to be in command generally, and we found ourselves humming as we glided round Poplar Point Light and boomed along southward between Conanicut and the main,

"Oh, I'm the cook and the captain bold,
And the mate of the Nancy brig,
And a bos'n tight and a midshipmite,
And the crew of the captain's gig."

DUTCH ISLAND FROM UPPER BATTERY.

But in reality our one attendant was one of the clerks of the Saunders House, which was presently to loom up before us, gray and red, sitting at the water's edge on Saunderstown shore, five miles below Wickford. Dutch Island lay directly opposite, the Government buildings and the green lines of earth embankments plainly showing. Farther east Conanicut's long green shores stretched, like the mainland,

but with gray
peeping over the

of Saunderstown
a stone's throw
Many of them
er cottages, for
ine old settlers
t dozen. Saun-
l, for the Saun-
populated, but
illman Saunders
rietor, but owns
; stretching be-
g establishment,
ason has 18 or
within. It was
dsome 100-foot
ilt for John R.
aller one, newly
the door, and
he scent of the
carpet the en-
bowling alley,
s may play at
ther of the hotel
he boat-building
Saunders himself
cares no longer
grandfather of
onor of the in-
d, in which our
also built the

, DUTCH ISLAND.

ner, christened
unched on these
l her honorable
rnished all the
s is constructed.
a of the hotel is
liu, and directly
proper, are the
walk from the
boats and sail

boats are conveniently near, and water parties of one kind or another come off daily among the young folk, with whom the house is rapidly filling. It is such places as these that our own Providence people find out and frequent, while the many Westerners who swell our summer population fill up the old, established resorts. But Saunderstown, in its fifth prosperous season, is now past being an experiment, and its sojourners are loud in its praise.

BEHIND THE LOWER BATTERY, DUTCH ISLAND.

The family of A. T. Cross occupy the pretty little cottage within the hotel grounds, and dine at the hotel, as do those of Mr. H. F. Richards, who has a cosy and picturesque home in the adjoining grounds. Mrs. Hiram Kendall is here, with a pretty dark-eyed niece, quite the belle of the place. Arthur B. Ladd, Jr., has put in a visit here, voyaging comfortably in his own steam launch; and Saunderstown is also one of the places at which Mr. Reuben A. Guild tarried with his family on their leisurely carriage trip— one of the most enviable modes of travel in existence, and suggestive of the delightful old-fashioned days and pleasant leisure.

The Wyona lies at the wharf all day between her two Wickford trips. She is the property of Capt. Saunders, and has been for five years the only seaward medium of approach to that mysterious and little known port; for even now nine persons out of ten to whom you mention the name will look blankly at you and inquire, "And where in the world is Saunderstown?" The infant Wyona, we should have said, would lie all day at the wharf were it not that, being the property of Capt. Saunders, and the captain being one of the most obliging of men, she is more apt to be off on some brief cruise, bearing most of the hotel guests to Newport or the Dumplings or Narragansett Pier, which is but six miles below. Fishing parties are in high favor, too, and the catch often includes a tautog said to be truly immense. The population of the Saunders House is a most friendly and hospitable one, with none of the clannish spirit common to small hotels. The wandering stranger within the gates is made to feel most speedily and happily at home with a welcome which seems scarcely akin to conservative Providence. Everybody knows everybody, and if they do not a brief trip on the Wyona or the sail boat under the guidance of "Jimmy, the Reefer" —so called, it is said, from his prudent

BARRACKS AND SHIPS, DUTCH ISLAND.

navigation—or in the four-seated and buoyant yellow buckboard, likewise hotel property, serves as a sufficient introduction and dispels formality.

It is the briefest of drives to the famous old Rowland Robinson place—scarcely a mile—with its curious carved stairway worn into hollows, its Scripture-tiled fireplaces, the Lafayette bedchamber, the two-century-old painting on the kitchen wall of a most remarkable hunting scene, and the romance of the beautiful long-departed Hannah Robinson pervading all the quaint old place. The beautiful valley, with the nestling lake and the old snuff mill by the cottage where Gilbert Stuart was born, lies also within two miles of the wharf, and there is not a lovelier spot, historic or other, in all

Kingston. A new but melancholy interest now attaches to the old place since the murder by the eccentric Capt. Kenyou. Then a briefer walk still from the hotel there is a famous old house, which in Revolutionary days served as a fort, and its walls are riddled yet with ancient bullet holes. It is known as the old Casey house. At a corner of the road stands the snug little cottage, with drooping eaves and rustic piazza pillars, which is the old homestead of the Saunders family.

Extending south along the shore is a veritable cliff walk, along the narrow beaten foot path that runs to the old "south ferry," so called to distinguish it from a once existing north ferry, a mile or so above Saunderstown, plying over to Conanicut. It is a scant mile along the rocky shore to the surviving ferry, otherwise Narragansett, and makes a delightful walk, with the rippling bay on the one hand, the meadows on the other, fragrant with hay newly mown, and the sweet breath of the wild rose and white azalea, growing here in unusual profusion and purity. Land and sea lay basking in noonday heat when we strolled southward, but the merry song of the south wind was in the air, and there was even a respectable surf slapping at the brown rocks that lay farther and farther below as we journeyed, and the bluffs grew higher. It is the nicest possible little path to lie near a summer hotel—full of little drops here and there, and an occasional stone stile just to give an excuse for the aid of a masculine hand. Once or twice a wee little brook ripples across the way, to slide down the cliff and raise the tide a little; and before we tired, the last stone wall was reached, and gray Narragansett shone before us in the sun. Here a picturesque herd of cows, red and white, was browsing high above the blue sea, and we slid through their midst, now and then addressing conciliatory remarks and assuring them in somewhat shaky tones that we would not harm them.

We descended the stony footpath to the ferry, a veritable symphony in gray. Its grayness grows as one wanders through its desolate roads. It is a little cluster of gray cottages, an abandoned ferry house and an ancient mill dropping to decay. The wharf, the fences, the stone walls, the paths, the poplar trunks, the fish nets and the lobster traps are all gray—silver gray in the sunlight, steel gray in the shade. Down by the water sits the old ferry house, its windows shattered, its rooms tenantless, and in the one low-studded, fire-placed room into which we peeped the only tenant was a rusty sewing machine abandoned to despair and prone on the earth. A big gray house, with stone walls and deep windows, sits somewhat above this scene of desolation, and by a large sign, "Halcyon," over the door, we wrongly judged it to be a public house. In the days of its former tenant, Joseph Eaton, it was, but the present occupants merely stay here, and not enough strangers are misled by the sign to justify its removal. The place is owned by Edmund Davis of Providence, farm and all, but he seldom troubles its solitude with a visit, and it is sinking rapidly into ruin. We saw but one young girl, who talked as one discouraged and looked unhappy. The old mill has not even the vestiges of glass in its staring window sashes. One end of the old building is gone entirely, and a boat or two reposes within, where looms were once wont to clatter. All around the lonely walls are gray cobwebs, shining in the sun, and from under our feet on the gray shingle a gray toad hopped away. Below the mill are the five old cottages that once lodged the operatives, and before the door of one, to complete the harmony, an old gray horse was stumblingly browsing.

However, there is a big and flourishing store here, in the heart of the general stagnation, and a post office as well, for Saunderstown has no store, and much trade comes from that quarter. Then the ferry boats ply here constantly from Jamestown, and many fine vehicles land at the dock, en route for Narragansett Pier from Newport, a most delightful drive all the way, and with easy ferries both east and west of Conanicut. From the dock the road runs steep and high up the hill, and at its breathless top is perched the Narragansett Baptist Church, a white landmark visible for many miles away, and vastly suggestive in its swift toboggan to the sea of new and improved modes of baptism. Then beyond here is that loveliest of drives along the Bonnet and past the four gray rocks of Bonnet Point, where the breakers chase each other into the silver crescent of Wesquage beach, and past the beautiful Chapin place, as lovely a spot as any Narragansett cliff cottage, and so on to the high, wavering line of pale green sand dunes, the bridge across Narrow river and Narragansett Pier, proper.

R. ROBINSON HOUSE.

In a prolonged stay at Saunderstown, one has plenty of opportunity to visit and explore the two most famous old houses in the neighborhood, and one day our party drove to them both. A scant mile distant rose first before us, gray and old, the ancient home of the ancestor of half the Hazards and Robinsons, who form the chief population of the South county. Enshrined among its sombre willows and hoary lilacs grown to the dignity of trees in an undisturbed dotage, still huge and hospitable, though but half the size it boasted a century and a half agone, is the gray old Robinson farmhouse.

Fresh from "Recollections of Olden Times," wherein this historic old house plays so conspicuous a part, we alighted and proceeded eagerly on a tour of inspection. Yes, here was the very horseblock of enduring stone, where beautiful Hannah's dainty foot was pressed—so many years ago. It makes one sad to think—beautiful Hannah who furnished so charming a legend for our local historians by running away with her music master. It is a pity no sort of portrait is preserved of this wonderful belle of olden time. Her loveliness was so rare that it called forth a compliment from a Quaker; and a legend is extant to the effect that one "Dare Devil Harry," a dashing young officer, who had seen the world, and kissed a queen, was so overcome on first beholding her that he sank to the earth before her, and imploring her in faltering accents, to "let the lips that had pressed unrebuked those of the proudest sovereign on earth, now be permitted to touch the hand of an angel," or words to that effect, proceeded to do so.

The heart of fair Mistress Hannah was, however, engaged in another quarter, and the old lilac bush before the door is the identical one into which she was wont to drop billets for the comfort of her lover concealed among its foliage, and the rather cramped quarters of an upper bedroom closet mark another hiding spot for the amorous master of music, whose lurking propensities were developed by the somewhat uncertain and peppery temper of Robinson pere, who evidently had some more eligible suitor in his mind's eye.

Old Rowland Robinson must have been the very ideal of the old-time bluff country squire; all manner of traditions yet abound as to his fierce temper, his recklessness and obstinacy and the kind heart behind it all.

"Bring me a glass of water," so his descendants relate, was once his historic dictate, as unseen footsteps sounded without.

"I'm de coachman, sah," answered that functionary hesitatingly, evidently seeing that he was mistaken for a house servant.

"Oh, you are the coachman, are you?" his liege master replied in the suave tones of well-governed rage. "Very well; go down in the fields, catch the horses and harness them to the carriage."

This Pompey accordingly did—I suppose his name was Pompey—after severe exertions, and when he at length triumphantly drew rein before the door, he was bidden to convey a servant who stood waiting with goblet in hand, down to the well for a glass of water. When this errand was finally performed, no doubt with some shamefacedness on the part of both—"Now, sirrah," thundered old Rowland Robinson in his might, "let this teach you never again to presume to dictate to me as to what your duties are!" And let us hope his goblet of water cooled his wrath.

There came a day when, like Xerxes of old, Rowland Robinson stood on the sea shore and wept, as he beheld a fresh cargo of slaves arriving from across seas—not because of new-born compunctions as to the propriety of slave owning, but because he felt himself too old to be flying into rages with so many of them; and importations ceased. But we are digressing from the fair Hannah, like her original biographer, who heartlessly leaves her on a litter half way home, while he goes cheerfully ambling all over South County for the space of a half-dozen chapters, and then, suddenly bethinking himself, ingeniously proceeds, "as the bearers of Miss Robinson's litter passed on through all this charming country which I have endeavored to describe."

Miss Robinson finally eloped, and after a brief term of stolen happiness found herself deserted by her fickle and unworthy husband. She became seriously ill, through grief and anxiety, for her father had forbidden all communication between her and members of the family. It was only when, from her far away home in Providence, tidings reached them of her unquestionably dangerous condition, that the proud old squire in any wise relented, though Hannah had been his favorite child, and then it was only in so far as to admit of his performing a daily journey on horseback to the city, and inquiring of the servant at the door as to her mistress's health. But full forgiveness came at last, and poor Hannah's piteous entreaty to be allowed to return home was at last acceded to; and as she

accomplish the
four men ser-
ar her home by
She died soon
t is a long and
have been pre-
of detail in the

and interesting,
iture is still pre-
dence, the house
mansion it must
ies, as New Eng-
t. Many of the
y and handsome-
with the oddest
iles—brown and
a what was once
e Scripture tiles
the fire chamber
y agreeable half
eplace, guessing
iich these start-
neant to depict,
y a-field.
 would certainly
, had it been pos-
ront an odd and
mosaic; exqui-
rith that loving,
not possible to
the globe. One
. in it a twin to
y Poore.
l, one does not
stairway in an
oned farmhouse;
up the winding
ie balusters are
lows are worn in
the hollow of a
cond floor, over
yette room," the
afayette occupied
e quartered here,
ary days. This,
id boasts more of
the ancient fire-
i! what a delight-
; wheels, hetchels
saddles, and the
iey crumble at a
, leather and all,
t a hearty shake

and vanish like a dream. Indeed, everything seems dreamlike in this old house,
with the spell on it still of an ancient day;
and, queerest of all, maybe, is the old
hunting scene out in the kitchen, over the
fireplace, and slowly browning and disappearing beneath the smoke and stain of the
cavernous fireplace for a century and a
half. It is boldly painted in oils, directly
upon the inviting great wooden panel, and
commemorates a deer hunt which took
place on the premises while the house was
being built. The deer is madly, though
faintly, scuttling across to the right, and
in a long row behind him four spectral
hounds in Indian file can be seen pursuing
him, if one stands in the right light. To
the left—ah, were ever such gallant horse-
men—a pair of them are standing very
straight and stiff in their stirrups, and
what must have been the gayety of their
trappings and the brilliancy of their but-
tons, that they are shining faintly still.
The horses' tails are describing wild para-
bolas, and in a tree above their heads, on
a delicate twig, sits airily poised an os-
trich or a róc, or some such thing. It is
not as big as their horses, but it would
hold its own with the deer. The name
of the artist whose hand wrought it is unknown, but it is strange to think it has
been dust these long years, while so frail
a memento survives. There is a treasure
in the cellar; a Newport clairvoyant once
graphically described it and its situation,
but no one has ever dug it up yet. It is
a funny thing that clairvoyants do not
themselves dig for treasures and say nothing to anybody, but probably they are philanthropists or haven't got time.

Reluctantly we tore ourselves away from
this interesting abode, where we had painted, photographed and asked questions to
our heart's content, according to our
various bent. The present occupants are
descendants of the old Robinsons, and very
kindly told us the old tales and showed
us the old furnishings, and in their hearts
voted us awful bores, I have no doubt,
though they gave us pears and asked us
to come again, as we rode away grasping
twigs of the historic lilac bush, and with
our faces set to the Gilbert Stuart place.

Two or three miles beyond, the way

leads by a stony descending lane down into the green and beautiful valley, where the famous old-time painter was born.

At the head of a little lake, tree-enshrined and green with lily pads, stands the little box of a house beside the old mill that now grinds grist, and once ground snuff for the noses of our great-grand-parents. There were four in our party; two had come to sketch, and time was precious. The miller met us at the door, for we felt that we must have one look at the very room in which Stuart was born. He was of a massive, majestic and patriarchal demeanor; the fact that he was barefooted and clad in the habili-

GILBERT STUART PLACE.

ments of toil did not detract from the stateliness of his mien. He led us, solemnly and impressively, through the small kitchen and by a doorway where most of us had to stoop, into a bare, little square chamber, where one dominating object met the eye—a bed. "Here," said the miller, "history tells us that the famous painter, Gilbert Stuart, first saw the light of day. Subsequent history also conveys the idea that—" One of the artists glanced at his watch. "It is very interesting," he murmured. "I think I'll go and get a good place to sketch it from the outside," and he slipped away. Slowly and with more impressiveness the miller began again—"It is related that, when strangers occupied this unpretend-

ing house, years after the grand mission of his life was finally accomplished, unknown, unassuming and unwilling to create any ostentation, the aged Stuart returned again to his boyhood's home, and craved permission to enter and muse a while in the very apartment which you now behold. That permission was granted. The—"

"This lady will stay and tell us all about it," murmured the second artist; "we should be so glad to hear, but we have very little time." And with her companion the other two slipped away, and the narrator of this chronicle was left alone with the patriarch and the history of Gilbert Stuart.

We returned to the little kitchen, neat as if a woman's hands had been busy within, but this hoary custodian is miller and housekeeper as well for the wee house of five small rooms. He can relate "historic escipodes," as he says he is fond of doing, with great force and dramatic power; but somehow I think I should have to see him whipping up an omelet or popping corn, for instance, to believe he could do it successfully. He told me of his own family history, gave particulars of the time "when Lincoln was massacreed," and thrilled me with a sentence I had never before heard, said to have been addressed to Dr. Hammond: "Doctor, you air a dressing the wownds of a nation."

It was very, very still in the little room. The sketchers were far away; the clock ticked dismally. The old man's tones were resonant and came from deep down in his chest. He told me of the graveyard hard by. "In that sacred enclosure," he said, while his eyes rested impressively and sadly on me, "in that sacred enclosure the mortal remains of two of my brothers and one of my sisters somewhere reposes; where, I do not know."

Tick, tick, went the clock solemnly. "Have you a cat?" I inquired, irrelevantly, and mayhap flippantly, but I was picturing the old man alone in all this solitude. "Yes; I have a cat," said the tragic miller in stately cadences. "He is—away, mostly. He is black and white; or, perhaps I should say, scory and white. I will see if I can call him." He advanced to the door with majestic tread, and uplifted his sonorous voice: "Here, Ro-ker, doker, ro-ker, ro-ker, doker, ro-ker?" but no scory and white cat appeared in response to this mysterious summons, though the industrious artists without subsequently professed to have been greatly terrified when these words smote the air, and to have been on the point of organizing a searching party for the missing one of their number. "I will read you," said the kindly patriarch, returning, "some portions of the life of this celebrated man." He seated himself in an armchair opposite, opened a pamphlet, and began with his magnificent voice sunk an octave or two lower: "In the old mill house standing at the head of the stream, Stuart, the painter, was born, Dec. 13, 1755; died in Boston, July 28, 1828. On the little sandy beach here, the boy artist outlined his playful fancies. Not many years ago was destroyed a small chest filled with outlines drawn in youthful days. As the traveller halts here, he sees around him that natural landscape which gave the youthful artist his first lessons. Sketching was his play, and in his school days the thought was ever near. Finally he went to Newport; thence to Virginia, and thence to England, where he matured his studies and solicited patronage. Here he labored and here he lived during the great struggle for independence. Here he lived, doomed to hear his people denounced and declared ungrateful and rebellious subjects. He was prudent enough to keep his thoughts to himself; but his soul fairly shouted when his people were victorious. There can be no doubt that Stuart was strongly suspected of American sympathy, and that his patronage was measured by those sentiments. His soul was maturing the grand conception to paint Washington, the great chief, and this took so strong a hold upon his mind that it excluded all other plans. When the Duke of Kent offered unusual inducements, and offered to send a ship to America to bring him back, all was declined respectfully. Not a Duke of England, with all the power and patronage behind him, had a face so dear to his pencil as that of the great Washington, his country's deliverer."

"Thank you ever so much," I interposed, hastily, as he paused for breath; "my friends will be expecting me now, I think; I—"

"Stay, young lady," said the hoary miller, with uplifted hand. "You may intrude upon your friends at their painting. I will relate to you an anecdote of Gineral Washington at the house of my great-grandfather."

The anecdote, in brief, narrates how Washington, incognito, remained over night at the hospitable Col. Rose's; how, through the thin partition, they heard his voice uplifted in evening prayer; how they saw he had a military aspect, but were far from guessing the truth; how, in the morning the stranger guest with sublime disregard of Lindley Murray, inquired, "What has me and my pony cost you for our keeping?" and how the elder Rose replied that to take anything would be a breach of Narragansett hospitality. Then said the unknown: "If you will accept nothing, I will tell you who I am. I am Gineral George Washington, Commander-in-Chief of the Armies of the United States!" The effect of this modest announcement is wisely left to the imagination of the hearer, and the anecdote closes with the ferrying of the unknown guest, by one Gideon Northup, over to Newport from the old Beach ferry, to keep his tryst with Rochambeau.

There wasn't any funeral going on, and we were not in church, but somehow when I finally slid out of that humble cottage, hearing for final delectation an excellent jest the parson had recently made, to the effect that if the Lord had intended people to use snuff, He would have made their noses the other side upward—when sunshine and blue sky were all about, I breathed more freely. And now time was up and so were the easels, and gayly our buckboard buoyantly bore us back to the homelike little hotel in Saunderstown.

TIVERTON HEIGHTS.

(Providence, Warren and Bristol Railroad, 20 miles from Providence, 55 minutes ride.)

IT is a pleasant trip, and not too long a one, from Providence down to Tiverton Heights by the Warren branch of the Old Colony. It is practically a water trip, if one sits on the right of the car skirting the salt water's edge, flitting by the stations that mark the successive shore resorts into which half Providence yearly pours, turning inland at Barrington, drawing up briefly in Warren, flitting on to Fall River, big, crowded and citified on the steep hillside down which runs a broad and conspicuous highway, giving Fall River the appearance of having its hair parted in the middle. Then the way lies seaward again, and Mount Hope lies off to the right across the bay and Rhode Island runs out a barring arm against further passage. Brown & Brightman's oil works loom up close at hand, and across the water Church's big factory on the island gives evidence that we are nearing our journey's end; with Tiverton's heights rising green to the left of us, and Narragansett's waters rippling blue to the right of us, we slow up at our destination and alight, and the train whisks around westward and glides over the long railroad bridge and plunges into the heart of Rhode Island in search of Newport, its goal.

We are stranded on the high platform of Tiverton's station, and a modest chorus of primitive hackmen shows us that visitors are expected. This platform view is the most unfavorable possible to Tiverton, and it is not well to tarry long. Either climb the hill and get a bird's eye view of ocean and inland or take the lower road and view the water front. Tiverton is one vast terrace, its first stage rising from the lower road to the bluff road, on which stand most of the many summer cottages, and from which numerous railed stairways toboggan abruptly down. Its second rises up and up till it leaves the spreading village behind, and stretches in a level plateau or lonely farmland eastward till one trips up against the State line and falls into Massachusetts. The map tells us that the good folk of Tiverton and Little Compton manage to thrive in a very stingy little corner of our not over-big State. It might appear, indeed, by the map, that a stalwart Little Compton six-footer might stand easily with one foot on Sakonnet Point and the other on Massachusetts soil, but this is not really the case, as one may see, if he climb and look eastward on all those lines of stone wall and pasture-land, undulating off toward the rising sun, and is told that all those goodly acres are in Rhode Island. Nothing but scattering farm houses lie off here till one gets well over the border; all the bustle and activity are along the shore between the bridges, where the train halts and the Queen City, too, either to land passengers or to struggle with the draws; and the callous natives have now grown indifferent to the little boat's occasional wrestle with the tide and the insufficient passways.

From bridge to bridge, and village to village—Stone Bridge Village and bridge to the south, Tiverton and railroad bridge to the north—is just one mile, and it is a brisk and springy walk indeed, if one goes on the lower road straight south from the station, for there is a plank walk all the way. With the crisp salt smell in the air, and the wind freshly blowing from leagues away at sea, it is with buoyancy one traverses this elastic sidewalk, and notes with astonishment the number of fishermen's shanties and fish markets that lot the water's edge. Signboards beside them read: "Bluefish, Squiteague, Tautog Live, Scup, Lobsters, Clams, Quahaugs, Clam Diggers and Boats to Let." It is a fish-consuming as well as a fish-catching village, but it has a large summer population. In a massive row, drawn up the beach above the caprices of the tides' assaults, are the great fishing boats that used to journey down to Sakonnet for the big scup catches of the spring, and menhaden that come later, but the old boats are now condemned for rough sea voyages, and will be sold and end their labors in safe still waters, like faithful old steeds turned out to pasture and children's petting. Many of the pretty little summer cottages on the terrace above lead down to bathing houses on the beach below, and the nautical flavor is here strongly manifest, for one of the little retiring rooms of the Narragansett Venuses is an old deck house that seems to have been once at home on some lumber smack, and further south, down before the handsome Robensen place, is a pilot house doing similar duty. It looks very funny, indeed, with its rounded front, its green shuttered windows at the back, and its open casements either side, the invisible wheel, where one expects momentarily to catch the gleam of blue uniform and brass-buttoned cap, hear the harp clang of the pilot's bell, and see his weird little bathing house go suddenly gliding, ghostly commander and all, into the inviting salt waters. The home to which it belongs is one of the finest in Tiverton, large and massive, with broad lawns and a sloping circular driveway. Mrs. Robensen has recently died, and the property descends to an adopted daughter.

The two chief houses of entertainment stand on these first terraces. The Bay View House has been in charge of Mr. .. Tallman, an old resident, for years. It is no longer a regular hotel, but a house of entertainment for transients, and weekly clambake resort. Special parties from Fall River much affect Tiverton and its clambakes, and the Bay View House is a pleasant and breezy spot. Somewhat to the southward stands a pleasant white cottage, and here Mrs. Kate Grinnell serves her famous Thursday clambakes. A stranger is surprised to find how much of a resort Tiverton is for those who know it. Mrs. Grinnell often entertained 300 guests at her airy, out-door dining-room. But it is not from Providence that either the clam-hungry folk or summer residents come. Tiverton is practically an unknown bourne to Providence citizens, and not one among the many new cottages that are popping up like mushrooms on every hand is designed for our people—at least, so far as was known at Tiverton. One and all, they were for Taunton families; twenty have already gone up new, and it is said that there will be thirteen more in readiness for another season. Not only along the shore and on the heights are they stretching along, in the favorite "down-the-river" combinations of brown and yellow, red and white, blue and gray, with a legend "Rose Villa" or something akin over the door, but they have ventured out on the island also, which stretches invitingly near shore here, and is connected by the railroad bridge. Right across from Tiverton village rises a looming crag, decked with evergreens and more lowly vines, and half a dozen gay little cottages nestle on the landward side at its foot. This lofty and picturesque elevation is known locally as "The Hummock," or in the fisherman patois, "harmock."

It is little wonder that this particular spot, Tiverton Heights, has come to such rapid crowning by cottages; the view is one of the fairest on the bay. The island is at its prettiest here, with numerous peninsulas striving out landward and the great, dark hummock emphasizing it all. Stone Bridge Village is a cosy little hamlet below, with its second span across the bay, and the square gray house, that was once the bridge's tollhouse, far across on the island end. Below the bridge lies the fair little jewel of Gould's Island, and away up north, is the euphonious but pleasant Hog Island. Bristol Ferry light looms white before the green shores northward, and away east, across the indenting bay,

Mount Hope rises, blue and dreamy in the distant sunshine. Everywhere is the sparkling water of the blue bay, and scudding white sailboats bending to the breeze. New and old residents are enthusiastic over their pet view, and it must be seen to be appreciated.

One wonders, though, as he continues southward, still buoyantly treading the elastic planks by the shore's edge, where are all the old houses, for the little town thus far has seemed very modern. Few of the old settlers are by the shore; most are away back east on the scattered farms. There is one, though, fairly down into Stone Bridge Village, a little white gambrel-roofed cottage, quaint of design, and with a worn, narrow footpath leading through the grass to its back door. The ell of the house is its oldest part, and its loose clapboards are black with age. Compassionate woodbines have draped its picturesque decay with heavy feathery masses of green, and the old doorstones are worn and ancient. Within, the huge fireplace fulfills the promise of the great outer chimney. It stretches half across the room, and when two families once amicably kept house together in its limited domains, each housewife had her range in her own corner of the fireplace.

Horace Grinnell occupies this veteran abode at present; away down below, in the bit of a shore hamlet known as Bridgeport, there is an older house still—the Barker place, now occupied by Mr. Anthony. Stone Bridge Village and its one pretentious store reached at last, its most conspicuous feature is the closed hotel, "Stone Bridge Cottage." It is a pale gray, piazzaed house, pleasantly situated at the water's edge, and its lack of patronage seems to have been not so much by reason of non-coming guests as its high prices, some of the front rooms expectantly waiting occupants at $25 a week! However, it is expected the hotel may revive and reopen another season under new management. A Newport banking company has possession. Meanwhile signs of life pervade the house, for a thrifty Tiverton family have let their own furnished house for the season and rented this hotel for a modest sum. As it contains forty-one rooms and their own family is of four, they find themselves amply accommodated, and cook in the office and dine in the parlor in delightful ease. The hall of the hotel is especially handsome, supported by cedar posts untrimmed, with the dark red-brown hearts of the knots in rich contrast with the polished yellow wood. The broad-railed stairway had its posts and banisters of the same picturesque material, and its effect is unique and beautiful. The broad front piazzas look directly down upon the water, the new band stand and the funny little beach shanty, which will be remembered as the scene of the exciting "beach contest" of a past season, where the Old Colony Railroad and the Baptist Church represented a war between religion and progress in their struggles for the land on which the unoffending wee homestead stood. During its progress the worthy couple occupying the tiny house, Mr. and Mrs. Manchester, enjoyed a free ride with their household effects all about them a mile down the beach and back again, religion moving the mansion one way and railroading the other. Most of the soil whose title was originally disputed, is said to be now under water, and Mrs. Manchester now peacefully washes dishes at her sink and beholds the same view thrice daily, instead of a slowly moving panorama.

Most of the summer cottages are built on the railroad company's land, on the island as well as a strip along shore. Cottage builders annually lease the land at $5 a year, and build wherever they please on the company's domains. Menhaden is the chief fish sought here now, and between farm and salt water, two stores and the Queen City's supplies life is easily supported. The large white cottage that caps the northern end of Rhode Island's eastern peninsula was formerly owned by Mr. Wilkinson of Providence, but has gone over, like its neighbors, to Taunton occupancy, and is owned by Waldo Reed, a lawyer of that city.

Daily the combined store and Post Office of Stone Bridge village is visited in summer by two young men, who row

TIVERTON HEIGHTS.

us haunt out in
t amid the heavy
land, where there
g. They are two
ling from Provi-
y contented with
summer outing.
and captivating
to be bought for
stow a most in-
modities, in their
shoot away again

HOTEL.

citement clusters
rrow drawbridges
ng wished for one
ices at the draw
, and one spring
from New Bed-
it steamer Harry,
oat was already
falling as we
t, and passed the
uld's Island, its
against a golden
ulate as to our
draws in a tide
e.
p before us, and
ir whistle for an
echoes along the
not, alas, startle
is evening repast,
he is at present
re pause, we even
again and again,
presently comes
ard our ancient
in the dusky dis-
'Handy Gid," as
along with other

titles less complimentary in nature. " Fid-dlin' Gid" is regarded with a certain respect for his rescue of three out of a family of five who went in bathing at a southern point here, and began to drown with a beautiful unanimity, unpremeditated though it was. In its own good time our draw swings around, a roaring wall of water piles up in our pathway, and runs before us into the filling bowl that lies between Stone Bridge and railroad bridge. Captain and pilot are both at the wheel now, and in a wild confusion of ringing bells, revolving spokes and escaping steam, with a rush and a roar we whiz through with the filling tide, swinging so close to port we can jump ashore if we are so disposed, and No. 1 is safely passed. The dusk deepens; Stone Bridge village behind us hangs out twinkling lights one by one, and a red eye winks from the railroad bridge before. Here will be our worst struggle, for the draw is eight feet narrower than the other, 32 only, and the little Harry has a width of 24. Only four feet leeway on either hand, and with the tide rushing down this time it will take a miracle to go through without scraping, to say nothing of crashing. We ponder silently awhile on the cause of the flow tide running down through this draw, where it ran up down below. We have never understood it, we do not now. Listen, then, while our captain enlightens us. "You take a bowl with a hole in each side, and plunge it into water. Long as the water rises it rushes in equally fast each side—see? Here's your bowl and the tide rising. In from above, in from below, too; oh, you're not the first ones that didn't understand it."

. Though we whistled at Stone Bridge to wake the echoes, we may whistle again at railroad bridge before our draw swings. Not hastily from the westward, but leisurely from the eastward this time comes Jerry in the fullness of time—Jerry of fewer titles and less speed. He is not our menial and will not hurry for any craft. We are the only voyagers through to-night; with a wide draw the schooners and the "fishermen" would have been glad to get up to Providence this way, but they have long ago given up beating against the wind, and anchored down below. Hasten, Jerry, for a train is soon due, and that draw must shut again. Now for it, then. Again we rush forward, again the spokes fly, again the pilot gives her "one bell," "two bells," as the case may be; that four feet leeway looks even on either hand, the steamer's nose pokes bravely in, the wild tide catches her, she struggles, she succumbs, and with a bump and a bang we bring up hard to port, hesitate and drift down stream. There seems nothing for an ignorant landsman to do—or but one thing. A bowl of hot tea, for our refreshing, keeps warm on the small radiator. He can rescue the bowl, at all events, if we bang again, for half its contents flew over this time. Again we turn down stream, get up headway and charge at our needle's eye once more. In we go, in the roar of the falling water—on and on, are we doing it? Alas for the power of that swift torrent! Over to starboard we slide, steering all in vain, and bang, crash! with a will on the other hand, while we clutch the bowl. Down we go in the current's grasp, quite ignoring the engine, bumping viciously once more before we slide hopelessly down into the filling bowl again, gray in the growing dusk. "That's a strange tide," muses the captain, "a most tre-men-dous tide; don't understand it. No moon, either. Well, it's about time for that train, John. It's no use, we've got to tie up and wait for slack tide."

"But, captain," quavers our companion, with apprehensive eyes, "isn't it dangerous to charge into the bridge this way?"

"Dangerous—well, yes," cheerfully replies our captain. "Quite a number of vessels have been sunk here, a steamer or two, and two or three sailing vessels." And, quite unconscious of the dismay he has awakened, he descends jovially with his friend for a smoke, as though the delay were the finest thing in the world. The draw closes, a red glare creeps around Pocasset Hill, where other household lights are twinkling merrily in the dark; above the babble of the wild flood through the draw comes a low, faint rumble, and the belated train creeps upon the bridge, the glow of the headlight flashing all the way across the water to our waiting vessel. The long lines of light flash above and flash below in troubled reflections and are gone. The sky is full of stars; the night is perfect. There is plenty to eat on board, and the rescued tea smokes even yet. Why should we grumble? Refreshed from their smoke our commanders return and await slack tide, we talk, we sing, with the babbling waters accompanying, while the night grows older. We fall to discussing our memories, infantile and otherwise. Our substitute pilot says he remembers when he was two years old, and our captain derides it. Pilot waxes earnest; goes on to furnish details. Says he lived down on the Cape at two years of age, and a dog bit his sister, and he remembers it. "Oh, ho," laughs our captain. "Don't believe it—you can't make me believe that."

THE OLD BRIDGE.

Our pilot dives deeply into his pocket, brings up a handful of small change, and proceeds to count it. "There," cries he, holding it forth in anxious entreaty. "There's eighty-five cents—I'll give you that if you'll believe it."

Amid our hilarity at this improvement on proof, a change comes o'er the tide. The lines are cast off, all is again excitement, we slide down stream, and once more rush up toward the black shadow of a bridge, one of us clutching the bowl, one thinking of all those wrecked vessels, and again we go at the big bridge, which is luckily higher than the draw is wide, or we might get stuck on top. The roar of water is fainter, the boat minds her helm a little bit better, we gain on the black shadow—we enter it; it is sliding by on the right, on the left, a cloud of steam flies around us, and with a rush and a roar we are through without a scraping, and the black bridge, surrounded by a climbing cloud of steam, dies away in the night, and the red eye winks knowingly at us as it vanishes. Once more we are on the wing, and have not sprung a leak.

Have we made too much of our small adventures? It is only to show the delightful experiences frequent among voyagers on the Sakonnet river. If the very liberal corporation that controls those draws ever sees fit to widen them, not only local commerce, but State, will rise up and call it blessed, as a gance at the map will show. Meanwhile mariners will continue to bump, scrape, go to the bottom, anchor or pass the other way.

SAKONNET POINT AND LITTLE COMPTON.

[By steamer Queen City, 30 miles from Providence, three and a half hours sail. Fare, $1.00 round trip. Sakonnet House, J. L. Slocum.]

STARTING at the foot of Planet street, the neat little steamer Queen City makes a daily trip now direct to Sakonnet, leaving the wharf at 9:00 a. m. and giving excursionists three hours at the shore, unless they care to longer tarry, which most of them do. It is pleasant company that one finds on board the Queen City, kindly and social, and not bent every one heart and soul to the absorbing business of looking out for number one. The purser and various employes will treat you like long-lost friends, and be gently solicitous for your welfare. Did we not mislay one of our belongings, and speedily find a half-dozen anxious searchers? Was not the steward, or whoever he might be, serving a lunch below to a small party, and did he not promptly accede to our request for some specially delicious watermelon, and reply to our query as to price with utmost cordiality, "Oh, nothing—nothing at all!"

Did ever anybody hear the like?

The Sakonnet trip forms a pleasing variation on the old familiar way between Providence and Newport. It is to the east of the island the boat turns, instead of proceeding southward by the west shore; turning east by Poppasquash, between Hog Island and the mainland, and running close enough to shore to set all the passengers staring at Mayor Lowe's quaint conceit of a house, high on the rise from shore. Picture one tremendously long, broad ground floor, with every conceivable compartment therein, and a roof placed lightly above it. Then imagine the roof pulled up ever so slightly to a central peak, just enough to tuck in a few more rooms on the second story; fill in with wee balconies, ancient windows and bits of port holes, picture the whole thing of a uniform gray, and you have the residence of the Brooklyn Mayor. The gentleman's idea was to allow his whole family to reside on the same floor, and unless they are rivals of the famous old woman in the nursery classic, they may well do so without overcrowding, while the servants' quarters are above stairs.

"Seaconnet," "Saconnet," "Sak"—is there a spelling bee going on among the Queen City's excursionists as we come suddenly out upon the after deck? "Not at all, but merely a lively dispute over Sakonnet's proper orthography. 'Sakonnet' is the proper spelling," said with modest confidence a pretty girl at length. "I am very sure that is the way the old Indians used to spell it." She was an extremely pretty girl, and had a most engaging little lisp, and it would have been the height of rudeness to suggest that the old Indians were not, as a rule, given to spelling, or to show off by remarking that the oldest spelling extant is "Saughkonnet," but so it is. However, Sakonnet is the Government form and ought, therefore, to rule, rather than the anglicized Seaconnet.

Up into Mount Hope Bay the steamer passes, by the Bristol Ferry Light, at the point where Captain West's comfortable old farm house nestles among the trees, with Fall River far to the northeast, and the awe-inspiring pinnacles of Mount Hope on the left hand; then the narrow draw of the bridge rises before us, wind and tide are in our favor and we thread the needle successfully, and the little boat glides deftly through and enters the eastern arm of the bay that is called for unknown reasons the Sakonnet river. At Tiverton Heights we pause to take on ice, and the deck hands indulge in badinage with the grinning, weather-beaten old fellows that line the wharf; then steam on through the Tiverton basin and down toward Stone Bridge Village and the second needle's eye. The pretty hotel known as Stone Bridge Cottage has gone into new hands, the former proprietor not having been vastly encouraged by his first experimental season. It stands airily and picturesquely on the site of the former Lawton House, and looks a pleasant place enough. Various summer cottages have sprung up of late all along the eastern shore here, and it may not be long before a gay little Queen Anne will cap the wooded summit of that green little morsel of an islet lying just below the second draw, through which we now also shot triumphantly.

"Heard you and Captain Ricketson had a bad time getting through here last time you came," observes Captain Pettey, the wheel spokes flying through his hands. "That was the worst tide we've known for years—got stuck here myself the next day."

"And what are the prospects for wider draws?"

"Well, not very bright just now. The Old Colony Railroad has, so to speak, 'sat on it,' and there will have to be another agitation and a few more shipwrecks before anything is done now."

But the Queen City is a small and safe little boat, and passing the draws is, from her decks, but a mild and momentary excitement.

Full of frolic the little steamer waxes now, and tilts merrily up and down the long green swells, to the singing of the wild south wind. Over the crags to the southward and up the sides of the dark red lighthouse, the feathers of foam are whitely flying, and above the sound of the vessel plunging through the seas, comes the pulsing beat of unseen breakers.

Into the quiet dock the vessel swings; a half dozen carriages wait on shore, and from over the inland roads that cross the meadows, a quiet party of equestrians have ridden to meet friends. A dozen farmhouses are in sight to the eastward, half as many summer cottages, that of Dr. Gardiner's of Providence, the most pretentious, away 'on a rise to the eastward, and, praised be Allah, not a bowling alley or a merry-go-round near at hand. Nothing but a house of entertainment a little way down the grassy road, and just beyond it, a stone's throw from the red granite rocks and the tossing ocean, the Mecca of pilgrims, the Sakonnet House. Not a pretentious hotel, but a big red cottage of some 40 rooms, every one filled, broad verandas and pleasant parlors, and a table at which an epicure need not scoff, in the cosy little dining room. The house has been open since '86 under the management of Mr. J. L. Slocum of Providence.

For long years, however, the Point has had its devotees, and the dozen farmhouses have sheltered summer boarders these 30 years. One Providence family, that of Mrs. Thomas Brown, has summered here regularly for a score of years. Yet the Point will never, with its present facilities, be a stamping ground for tourists, lying, as it does, the length of the bay from Providence, a three-and-a-half-hour's sail; 20 miles overland from Fall River, and an arm of the bay interposing between it and its distant Newport neighbors, who are not greatly given to gadding.

A veritable land's end is Sakonnet, tipping the modest heritage of the Tiverton and Little Compton folk, dwelling apart between Massachusetts and the sea.

Standing on one of its ocean-lashed pinnacles—

"On cliffs by clouds invaded,
With wreck of storms upbraided,
With wrath of waves bedinned,"

and looking southward with a telescope of the proper power, there is an excellent view to be had of the South Pole on a sufficiently clear day.

The place is unlike any other on our Rhode Island coast. Right off shore, indeed, the rocks and breakers have the same familiar look that Newport, Conanicut and Narragansett Pier rocks and breakers wear, though the picturesque red granite bowlders add touches of warm color to the landscape that seashore rocks are wont to lack.

Did ever any one sail to Sakonnet and come home disappointed? Breathes there a man with soul so dead, who ever to himself hath said, "I don't like Sakonnet?" Quiet little corner that it is, it has all the grandeur and beauty of the wild Maine coast, the breeziness and freshness of the wind swept meadows, the strength of the hills and the majesty of the sea. Unspoiled by hordes of excursionists with the inevitable peanut bag of the adult and bobbing balloon of the juvenile, unpolluted by any disreputable inhabitants or fourth-rate hotel, it offers sweet, wild freedom and rest to the seeker. Its one hotel, the little Sakonnet House, stands at the very ocean's edge, the salt spray moistening one's face as he paces the ocean piazza in a storm, and with the ceaseless murmur of the waves on the shingle in gale or calm. It is now enlarged to twice its former size and the wide piazzas run entirely about the house. The broad windows of the cozy dining room look directly out upon the Atlantic and the dim far shores of Narragansett Pier with the high vague landmark of the Hazard tower peering across seas. Its rooms are quiet, airy and inviting, its cuisine almost the best on the coast with the "real country vegetables," cream and butter, and its fish, one hour struggling in the net, and the next sizzling in the pan. More Providence people patronize Sakonnet than any other coast resort—Jamestown, Newport or Narragansett.

Its lawns are now improved and beautified by flower beds. Henry B. Franklin has now a handsome cottage close by the red Sakonnet House, and its yellow walls and dark red turret make a pretty bit of color against the green of the meadows and the blue and white of the sea and sky.

Opposite the Sakonnet House an outdoor clam dinner is now served for those who wish, and the old restaurant also flourishes. These are the only distractions of Sakonnet. Elsewhere are the rolling fields, the high sand dunes and the marshy hollows, the spreading shore and cavernous cliffs of West and East Island, lovely in a calm like that in which we so easily recall it. The red-brown rocks reflected in long waving lines in the crystal clear water, the hazy white clouds sailing again in the glassy mirror below, with only a tremulous ripple when the song of the south wind suddenly rose and piped in the rustling reeds. In the salt pools along shore dozens of crabs with butterfly backs sidle and swim; star fish and anemones and paper nautilus have their haunts along the shore, and everyone finds fascination in that marvelous pebble beach on the south shore, whose like is not found on Rhode Island's coast.

Like the admirable youth in that subtle vehicle of morality, the reading book, we regard, morning, noon and evening in turn as the most delightful hour of the day; but when dusk descends upon the water as we stroll along the rocky shore, and the sunset light flushes the faint and distant sails, while the wind lulls and the air grows quiet and hushed but for the breakers' sobbing, when the wee salt lake that nestles among the hillocks turns to a sea of glory fading to grey,—then we are quite sure it is best of all. The best tonic for mental and physical exhaustion is this ozone-laden air—

"Blowing o'er fields of dulse and the gardens and grottoes of ocean;"

absolute quiet and rest are here, and sound sleep that comes for the asking, wherein the breakers' voices come not as a disturbance, but a lullaby.

And when one leaves this enchanted corner, if leave he must, there are three ways to get away. He may be taken to Newport, and set down at Taggart's wharf or the cliff; he can be taken by carriage to Tiverton, there to connect with train for Fall River or northern stations; or he may return by boat to Providence. And in that case, let him bless his lucky stars if he see the steamer pass by Church's factory, for if he pause there to take on "phosphates" he will sail to the very port of Providence wrapped about in not exactly an odor of sanctity, but in a very "ancient and fish-like smell," indeed; but let him not grumble, for what has he

nyway, if not for a change
shore is rich in aquariums
s of the deep. Starfish,
rabs, anemones and Portu-
var are frequent finds, and
ebble beach on the south
the sand hills and the out-
f the Oriental story-teller
l pebbles for—" and the sec-
at the second grain of corn,
life might have been pro-
ore indefinitely. And what
comes out of the deep, all
.thern shore, mingled with
wash of the waves? The
intless stones that strew the
one against another? Oh,
is the mermen and the sea
; their teeth in rage to be
ortal offering.
ere are mermen as well as
who can doubt? And as
lusively puts it, "the wise
e no right to say that no
exist until they have seen
es existing; and that, mind
y different thing from not
babies."
il ribbons of kelp that come
l and fringed in all shades
wns are proof positive of
ies below the waves.
roads are pleasant, too, and
es away the artist Burleigh
e. The road northward over
e curve" is an interesting
iles eastward one may come
ed black lines which divide
Island from pink Massachu-
I fear me the geography
of the impressionist school,
oducing effects pleasing to
somewhat untrue to nature.
get over to West Island or
mpanion, a huge rock split
divided by a roaring flood
id joined again by a wire
dge, 100 feet in length, built
lience of the club fishermen.
on the wild parapets of the
sses to the south, and, buf-
and bewildered by the roar
waves, in deep sounding hol-

lows below, look first to seaward over the heaving billows and see the infinitely distant ocean meet a sky-line unbroken by cloud or island, and then landward over the sloping sunny pastures and the quiet shores, whose population at this vantage ground may be with difficulty estimated to be a dozen; and let him say, if it is like anything else on our bit of Atlantic's borders.

West Island has for years remote been the property of a famous club of 30 members—principally New Yorkers. Bass was the much-sought, highly prized and popular fish, but of late bass have died out or sought other waters, and the sport is not so ardently prosecuted. Fortunately, however, other fish abound and the club still flourishes.

Petticoats were said to be tabooed on the island, or the wearers thereof, but if such be a law it is not rigidly enforced, for we saw some when we were there.

"If you would like to visit the island," said Mr. Slocum to us, "go down to the point where the little landing is, wave a handkerchief, and a boatman will put off from the island."

This seemed a simple process and a harmless experiment which we resolved to try. We betook ourselves to the point among a hopping multitude of tiny toads, that rushed frantically out of snug burrows in the dry sea-weed, and fled to left and right. We waved our handkerchiefs, and—it was quite like a fairy tale—a boat was instantly to be seen, like James's "Solitary Horseman," putting off from the island wharf. Across the deceptive plain of waters, West Island seemed to lie close at hand, but the boatman who ferried us over said it was almost a half-mile distant. The club buildings, with the exception of one rather pretentious cottage, are plain, unadorned structures, mostly of plastered stone. But from the massive causeway of iron-bolted granite that bridged the outer rocks to shore, to the hen yard in the rear of the club houses, everything seemed built "for keeps." A garden, prolific in all sorts of "sass," in the fertile spaces between the rocks, whole families of clucking hens and peeping chickens and a browsing cow, showed that the jovial club men were not dependent on continental domain for the good things of earth. The term of island residence is limited to two weeks, and the number holding possession at once is a half dozen, so that in the season's round the whole club may have its share. But there are cooks and menials also abiding here, and each club man has a "chummer"—a baiter and retainer who must, beside his daily $2, be feed lavishly; the sailboat which carries the clubbers to Newport costs them $1 50 each, as it might an outer barbarian and to say nothing of the assessment levied on members at the season's close it costs a pretty penny to maintain even this free and easy life. Crossing the broad causeway, strengthened by massive breakwaters of granite bowlders, one comes upon the favorite fishing stand—the great fissured cliff that rises sheer out of the boiling sea cauldron. All about its edges are the iron stands that prevent trespassing tidal wave or energetic bass from pulling the angler out to sea. Once, years ago, a Fall River gentleman was washed off this very crag into the leaping breakers—as some say, pulled sheer off by the strength of his catch, and others narrate that in the excitement of playing his bass, he failed to see the mighty encroaching wave that swept him down. Be that as it may, it is a spot where one would not care to linger in the mad revels of a sou'wester. In the outermost crag, one can at one moment peer down into a black hollow fissure where only the hollow gurgle of the retreating ebb sounds and at the next be deluged by the flying plume of spray that is springing up twenty feet above it.

"Oh, do you hear the thunder
  On Darramona's rocky isle,
The wild waves sweeping under
  The ghostly cliffs of dark—West Isle?"

sang one of us. Three winters ago in a wild storm the billows arose and knocked at the doors of the lighthouse north of West Isle. They beat and they battered, and refusing to believe in the social fiction of "Not at home," burst in and flooded the kitchen, thirty feet above high water mark, and left the two keepers barren of fresh water. Fortunately some liquid coffee escaped the salt baptism, and the twain drank sparingly thereof till the waters lulled enough to let them venture landward.

The western cliff of the island is another curiosity, higher even than the others, and with a summit broad and level enough for the site of a small village. Poised here in isolated grandeur, the only one of its kind or, indeed, any other, is a black slate bowlder, 200 feet from ocean, and we one and all said "Glaciers."

Long we lingered on West Island, haunted by memories strange and sweet, and as we disembarked again we said,

"Take, oh boatman, thrice thy fee,
Take, I give it willingly;
For all unperceived by thee,
Spirits twain have crossed with me."

Said it to ourselves, that is; for otherwise the boatman might have interpreted our pensive quotation literally, and he got quite enough as it was.

It is a pleasant seaside stroll among the few pretty cottages that dot the shores and the rising meadows; some day the general public will awake to Sakonnet's loveliness, and then will the cottagers and the boarders in the quiet farm houses lament the good old days of peace and bliss; but meanwhile the Point is an ideal resting place, visited only by refined and appreciative guests. There is no pleasanter sail possible from Providence, for by no other route is a three hours sail available without more or less rough handling by the indiscriminate billows; when one returns by the same boat, there are three hours on shore, but the Sakonnet House has always open doors, and sunset tempts one to linger. Then is the quiet little nook at its fairest; a green hill rises near the rocky shore, where one may climb to see the day die; far across the bay the sun drops golden behind the Kingston hills, the land grows black and the billows foam whiter in the dusk along the rocky shore; the sweet little voices of the friendly sand pipers sound plaintively as they hover fearlessly by; the crisp sweet smell of growing things blows down across the pastures and mingles with the pungent salt odor of rock weed and Irish moss that the Atlantic tosses at one's feet; the gold and crimson die, and the night creeps up out of the vast Atlantic, and in its wake twinkle the beacons from far Beaver Tail, Brenton's Reef, Point Judith, Whale Rock, Hen and Chickens, Cuttyhunk, Vineyard Sound and distant Gay Head. The Atlantic guards are all on duty, and the cheery glow from the black shadow of the lighthouse tower out in the surf answers them back. Reluctantly one seeks at last the shelter of the cosy little hostelry, and the ceaseless waves sing an all-night's lullaby. Surely, the Rhode Islander whose heart is not wholly turned to fashion and gayety must place Sakonnet first on the list of our multitude of summer resting places.

NO livelier industry is plied during May and the early part of June on the New England coast than the scup fisheries about the craggy point of Sakonnet, at the coast corner where ocean ends and Narragansett Bay begins.

The Sakonnet House, perched at the very border of the sea-swept granite rocks and undulating line of roaring surf, is one of the first to open, and though few take advantage of the fact except a party of gunners from Providence, whose yearly rendezvous it has long been, it is worth one's while to be on the spot when the fishing boats spread thickest on the bay, and the gray lines of countless "leaders" of seine stretch well over toward the Newport cliffs and up into the quieter waters that flow by Isaac Wilbur's chicken farm.

Scup migrate northwards like birds, in vast and gregarious companies. Sakonnet's ocean-piercing point seizes them first and most profitably. But the time and manner of their autumnal southward voyaging are secrets that no man has yet fathomed; it is doubtless in deep waters, yet warm with summer heat, that they return to winter haunts.

Clustered about the apology for a breakwater—for even the staunch little Queen City, Sakonnet's one link with the metropolitan world, cannot always make a landing in these tumbling waters—are a half-dozen fishermen's shanties, and down by the south shore, with the air full of the never-ceasing crescendo and diminuendo roar of sliding sea-polished pebbles in the ebb, are two or three others. These are the habitat of the "gangs," Church's and Brightman's, and independent parties, taking the entire precarious net profit instead of the smaller but certain salary offered by the large corporations. Below the low-water mark the salt waters are free to all, and the gang that early in spring sinks its seine first and establishes its bobbing barrel buoys as a token of claim pre-empted, is best fellow. Some lively rows usher in the scup season's advent, but, as a rule, the same gangs establish themselves yearly in the same spots, and always in rough water. Perhaps the disturbed waves hide better the gleam of the entrapping twine, but experiments have proved that traps set in the still reaches of the Sakonnet river yield a return of only about four or five barrels a haul, to the same number of hundreds in the swell. It is estimated that there are about $80,000 worth of seine stretched about the shores of Little Compton alone; 500 men are sometimes hard at it together, and Church, the largest owner, employs about 100. As to catches, it is difficult to make an average, as a haul of a single net will run to such extremes as five barrels on one hand and 1000 on the other. The fishermen say that on one occasion 2300 barrels were captured from a single trap of Church's.

If one has a day at his disposal, he can make the rounds of the fishing grounds and get a fair idea of the modus operandi, though a landlubber gets sadly perplexed by the sea jargon that flavors the explanatory speech of the obliging fishermen, native Yankees for the most part, and the majority hailing from that chief birthplace of fishermen, the State of Maine. It is also perplexing till one has straightened it out by furtive, pencilled notes, to understand that white fish and bony fish and mossbunkers and alewives may all mean menhaden, that flounders are flukes and sculpin are sometimes grunters and sometimes not; herring, too, may be bony fish, blue fish are rock bass and cunners chogsits, and skates are sometimes monkey fish, sometimes old maids, and sometimes, in local vernacular, "Lyddy ——'s," in honor, so they explained, "of an old maid up on the island," and whom they were supposed to resemble.

With this tangle somewhat straightened, the foreman and a stout sailor or two will pull round the Point and take visitors aboard over slippery, barnacled red rocks, and pull out over the undulating green swells to where the long cork line of the leader terminates in the trap and pound. The trap is the ordinary seine funnel, with the large and small openings, through which the unwary school enter and find no escape. To right and left stretch away the arms of the leader, nothing other than a submarine fence, to compel the fish up to the central trap, the weighted net that will by and by discharge its fast filling contents into the square water pen called the pound, or fill at once the "carrying away boats" for the delivery steamers that ply back and forth from Newport with their cargo. Four boats surround the trap, one on each side, with three or four men to the boat, and begin pulling in, closing more and more together as the slack of the net gradually grows into a dark, dripping heap in the bottom of one boat, while in the other stand the fishermen, watchful, alert, ready with their long-handled scoop nets to push back in the weighted net bottom the tangled fish that show more and more thickly struggling in the net meshes. Soon the lively commotion of the one central spot of water shows that the huge bulk of the catch is almost out, there is a gleam of fins and even a desperate leap, high in air, of a bass now and then—for the sea bass jump like sheep, and all the pounds have a double-edged protection of cork-floated seine, "aidgin'" the fishermen call it, or the trap covering of seine known as the veil. Now myriads of fish begin to show, and the scoop-nets grow lively as they plunge into the mass and toss their contents overboard again, where they promptly disappear with one last wriggle of freedom. These are the sculpins, the goats of the flock, and the fishermen seem to be exercising a careless indifference as they scoop them out, only now and then selecting one or two and tossing back into the net; but the foreman will tell you that the surface fish are almost invariably all sculpin, that they are a clannish tribe that fill the scoop nets first of all.

Faster the nets fly as the bulk of the catch comes up, fewer fish take their glistening somersault back into the wide ocean, and a glittering, wriggling heap grows higher in each boat, rising and sinking on the dark green surges till one wonders how the four boats toil in unison. Up comes the fishing steamer alongside, the Hathaway, perhaps, the Seven Brothers, or the Ocean View (known to all Block Island habitués as the scene of sword fishing excitements in August, but chartered now for the scup and menhaden season), and once more the protesting, many-colored throng are transferred, and once more weeded out in the process, and still a good many black sheep adorn the little steamer's decks. There may be caught in the traps beside its legitimate load the skate, the sculpin, cuttlefish or squid, squiteague, flounder, weakfish, sea trout, flatfish, butter fish, tautaug, cod, cunner, dogfish, sturgeon, sharks even, though these engaging monsters generally haunt warmer waters. A whale once got into a trap at the breakwater, and did nearly as much damage as the traditional bull in the china shop before it was rid of him. It is a long list, the fish that haunt Sakonnet's shores, for the hotel proprietor can give you a list of twenty-three edible varieties that grace his table during the season.

Away steams the little steamer to another trap and goes the rounds until her cargo is completed. Packing and icing are next in order, the vessel's hold itself forming the huge ice box, and all hands set to work, with first a layer of ice, then of fish, and so on, till the end is reached, and she steams for Newport, to be repacked at the wharves and shipped to the markets as promptly as possible, New York getting the chief consignments, and Philadelphia, perhaps, following next. Duty is not yet over for the day, by any means, though the most energetic fishermen have been out since the first faint dawn. Pounds may break, and buoys may drift, and leaders may shift, and there is always more or less net mending to do, beside the rents that are promptly repaired when the dripping net comes up.

In the wake of the fishing steamer are often two or three small boats, friends of the fishers, in search of a fat fish or so to grace the dinner table, always freely bestowed as the prerogative of the fisherman.

In a successful run the "pound" is filled constantly from the ever-filling trap. It is sometimes impossible to load and carry away fast enough to keep the trap free, and again the whole catch will not cover the men's daily wages.

One season the net profits of one corporation were $40,000, and the workmen's wages took out but $3000 more. The gangs who fish for themselves lay up tidy little sums also. George Gray, the manager or foreman for Church's gangs, is putting in his 35th season at Sakonnet, and there is very little about the fishing industry that he doesn't know. Maine fishermen, he says, are greatly preferred here to the local workers, for one can be sure of them and their steady adherence to work. They can't go home over Sunday, he explained, and are always promptly on hand Monday morning. Life in a Sakonnet fisherman's shanty is not the bleak and dreary thing one might imagine, though there are no softening feminine touches. A typical one had one huge unplastered room, and an open door leading into another unseen. In the first there was a huge hotel range, whereon a colossal coffee and teapot simmered. All up one side of the room, cool and sweet with ocean's breeze, ran a triple line of bunks, like an old fashioned steamers, without white counterpanes, to be sure, but with some degree of tidiness. Down the centre of the room were long benches, the board table, set with granite ware, and on it still, though fish had been consumed, bread, cheese, gingerbread, doughnuts, sponge cake, pound cake, jelly cake, and three kinds of pie. The cook, a little dark-eyed, bright-faced foreigner, hovered about, and smiled deprecatingly at our exclamations. The fishermen are their own tailors, and do their own washing.

We afterward came upon their wash tub in a stroll seaward. It was in a natural hollow in the summit of a huge rock that rose beside the humble dwelling. There the vari-colored flannel shirts lay soaking in a pool of rain water. Mr. Gray told us afterward that until recently one man who furnished dinners for the gang had considered it necessary to set forth the table with seven kinds of pie at once. The Down Easters must indeed be a luxurious lot.

Though the run of scup dwindles in May, the gangs, some of them, fish for horse mackerel and blue fish all summer. As a rule, fishing runs into November, and one Christmas even it was still vigorous in Brother's Cove.

Some of the men dry fish for their own use, and take home a supply secured while off duty—herring, mackerel, and the best part of the sword fish is also salted for home use. Many of the waste and useless fish are dumped ashore and sold as fertilizers, and Church's factory, up on the east shore of the island, disposes of thousands in this way. Storm, sea and broken pounds make sad loss now and then. In one severe southeast blow over 5000 barrels were lost in the storm. Though there was little wind, there was a tremendously high sea; the fish were bruised and battered in the pounds; the sand filled their gills, and they perished by thousands.

It is impossible to load and pack in weather like this, though the speed at which it goes on in a favorable time is something almost incredible, from 400 to 700 barrels sometimes being taken in in 40 minutes.

There are other diversions beside watching a day's fishing. There is a charming drive northward through Little Compton, first turning westward along the shore. All along Sakonnet coast the house lots are taken, but very few are as yet built on, and only a half dozen stand on the south shore. Other regular cottagers are H. B. Franklin, C. C. Gray, C. A. Franklin of Providence, and Dr. Eddy of Fall River. Mrs. Alden of Troy is always first to arrive at her Warren's Point cottage, and Mrs. Clough of St. Paul is a close follower. Most of the farm houses are filled up, Bundy's having the largest number, and Kempton's next.

The quaint little gray, modern residence of Mr. Sidney Burleigh is noticeably pretty, also that of the Rev. Mr. Slicer, which has an ancient gray windmill incorporated in one end. The loveliest summer home of all is the old colonial homestead which recently fell by heritage to Miss Edith Church, a girl who evidently appreciates and has vastly improved the dreamy old place.

A few miles up the road is the wee village known as "Little Compton Common," containing one of the oldest graveyards in the country. It is a most remarkable sight, the hundreds of crowded leaning black gravestones, gray with moss, and with legends often wholly undecipherable. Many stones bear dates two centuries back, and among the oldest are the Churches, the families of the old Capt. Church, whose name will be always coupled in history with King Philip's.

Treaty rock is near here, where the famed treaty with the Indians was made, as well as the Indian rock, with its timeworn hieroglyphics.

A lover of mortuary lore would be interested, in this old Little Compton burying place, in the evolution of the cherub, as depicted on the head stones. There are twenty-five distinct varieties, from the rudimentary globe with dots for eyes, a long U for nose, and the equality mark of mathematics for mouth, to the full-fledged simpering angel, with towering finely feathered pinions. The old epitaphs were amusing, but the Little Compton mourners did not appear to have "dropped into poetry" to any considerable extent till the beginning of the present century, when the quaint spelling and long-tailed s's were gradually going by.

PAWTUXET, OLD AND NEW.

[Electric cars from Providence, 5 cents, 40 minutes ride.]

"DID you go to the funeral?" asked one woman of the other, as they met on Pawtuxet bridge, under which the wild waters, fresh from their mad plunge over the rock-dam, were tumbling past the dreamy little hamlet and on to meet the sea.

"Yes, I did," responded the other, who bore upon her arm a moist and dripping basket of clams. "And 'twas as pretty a funeral as you could hope to see."

"How was it—pretty well 'tended?"

"Well, yes, 'twas, considerin' 'twas low tide."

The two housewives walked on, their voices lost in the roar of the waters, and we were left reflecting.

That was Pawtuxet—old Pawtuxet, the very essence of it. A slowly mouldering handful of quaint old homesteads, practically unchanged in a century and a half, and dependent now as then for the provisions of this world and reminders of the next, on the turn of the tide.

"I suppose you will be busy to-morrow," remarked a lady to the village barber, on Friday's eve. "I intend bringing my children to have their hair cut."

"All right, bring 'em along," assented the jovial barber; "but come when the tide's out."

And what general exodus does the ebb tide betoken! Clamming, to be sure. Every man Jack of old Pawtuxet's settlers is out to sea, reaping a harvest of rheumatism, neuralgia and clams, and the little fleet float triumphantly in with the rockweed and the flotsam of the next flow.

A fishing and a clamming community, and a brotherhood of "odd jobbers," the male portion of old Pawtuxet get through the year with financial triumphs incredible to outsiders. More than one old clammer clears his straight thousand a year at this amphibious calling. Bloomer's jewelry establishment of recent date gives employment to several natives, to be sure, and some of the rising generation work up in the city and travel back and forth in the electric cars, but the majority are quite content with a stay-at-home existence, and the mild excitement of unearthing the most succulent of bivalves with the clam hoe.

A church and a school house boasts Pawtuxet, and the ultra-ambitious seek further educational and religious privileges up in Providence. The electric cars are the only communication as yet; where the steam cars stop is two miles away, at New Pawtuxet, otherwise Lakewood, which is the new name of our latest settlement, whose families to secure an enduring title engaged in an extremely polite though determined squabble, firmly refusing to endorse that ancient and exploded sentiment that a rose by any other name would smell as sweet.

Two Pawtuxet families, Rhodes's and Gardner's, have been engaged for some years in the lucrative employment of letting row boats for pleasure trips up the fair and winding fresh river, and "up the Pawtuxet" has become a household word. Even when nature is "in the sere and yellow leaf," the river is far from deserted, and is at its loveliest in the eyes of autumn lovers. But go down to the little cove below the fall, where the salt of the incoming tide is felt in the seaward current of the river; down there where sail boats and row boats fairly hustle each other in the "off-hours" of fishing and clamming, one would think it an easy thing to hire a craft for an hour's sail, but it is like trying to hire an outfit for an afternoon drive in the country. Every man owns a boat, and no man cares anything about letting one; it is a vastly independent community. But rage as the disappointed would-be yachtsman may, he can but admire, from the road leading past the cove, and joining ancient to modern Pawtuxet, the fair and peaceful picture of the sheltered little fleet lying at rest in the tranquil waters below with perhaps a pink sunset in the sky to flush the dusky waters and gild gray masts and glorify patched sails. Over across the little cove, opposite the white leaping outline of the falls that shows under the gray arches of the bridge, rises a sound of tinkering and hammering,

GARDINER'S ON THE PAWTUXET.

and there, lying about under the willows and reposing on the green banks, like old salts ashore, are sail and row boats undergoing painting, repairing, and even in the crude process of manufacture. The sloping yard, the shed and the old white gambrel roofed house above on the road, are the premises of Mr. Crandall, Pawtuxet's veteran boat builder and repairer. Under the old willow that shades the invalid crafts, is a circular structure like the ground plan of a summer house, and on it in bold and business-like characters is the legend "Jeanette and Jeannot." It has a seafaring aspect, even with its fringe of weeds and grasses, and on some former day it sailed the seas figuring as the top of a catamaran. Mr. Crandall's old house was once used as a barrack and gunpowder storehouse in Revolutionary days. Across the road opposite, where a grass grown eminence overlooks the bay—for we are on "the Neck" now, and left old Pawtuxet behind when we passed the cove—was once a veritable fort, erected for a time of need, which happily never came, and still giving name to the modern houses now—homes built for summer occupancy—and with the exception of the Chase house, opposite Mr. Crandall's, and the Day place just beyond, the avenue is lined with modern and rapidly growing houses.

The Chase house is the oldest on the Neck, and Mrs. Chase relates that thirty years ago, when the house was one of eight which comprised the Neck's sole population—the Day place being another—she and her husband had an opportunity to buy the entire Neck for $400! That they did not do so, is no doubt a matter for present regret, when they reflect that single house lots now bear prices mounting well up into the thousands. A queer little brick house, partially whitewashed, stands near by with closed and barred doors at the corner of the avenue. It is the property of the Watermans, and rumor says that they have declined an offer of $20,000 for the house and lot. It is an ancestral possession, 150 years old, and retained merely as a family curiosity and heirloom. Occasionally its owners open it and make it the rendezvous for a clambake or fish fry or such like junketings, but for the most part it stands silent and deserted. It is in these same family annals that tradition narrates the death of an old gentleman who in the early years of this century occupied a house standing where the present avenue runs. When the great 1815 gale swept the salt bay waters and the turbulent Pawtuxet together up the roadway, this erring patriarch, who refused to budge from his house when the waters were rising, gave utterance to these historic words, "If my house goes, I go." He did go. His wife was borne to high and dry land through water up to the bearer's waist, but the partner of her joys and sorrows was swept from his moorings with

south wind, and
ng in his flooded
with his life gone

ost the one place
is purely pictur-
filled with intelli-
ple. Its pleasant
high along the
owered in foliage,
eculiarity, one and
older to feel sure
st view anywhere
s to the next one.
fus Greene place,
the most homelike
mer cottages, and
a Horton cottage
are everyone fair,
y trim. Austin's,
its, Dr. Millar's—
ay and are among

little cottages.
uresque salt cove
autiful grounds of
in a small grove
the water's edge,
and well-designed
qual is scarcely to
outlay anywhere
vard lies the old
the newer red one,
turesque and hos-
ded on a rock in
ich every summer
its half-dozen re-
inine element of
ts contend for the
. The club-house,
of the finest dwell-
designed by archi-
Gould & Angell,
ouse here, though
pretentious, is per-
t any at the Point.
gray of cedar, sun
broad piazzas and
with interior fin-
floors, and walls
burlap, walls and
er, tinted a pale
an artistic slap
riously tinted, and

with the seaside proprieties deferred to in rope picture mouldings, and with the most enticing little windows of all shapes and sizes peeping out of alcoves north, south, east and west upon the flowing Pawtuxet and the salt sea. On a panel at the turn of the staircase, burnt on in shaded browns, we read in fanciful letter- ing the name "Cedar Side," and the date of its building. The two huge dolphins disporting themselves on panels on either side the entrance have been gravely pro- nounced by an ancient native fisherman to be "something like a fish he's caught down below, but didn't know the name of."

Far down at the point's extremity, stands the old oyster house, deserted now, and, drawn up on heaps of oyster shells above the daily baptism of flood tide, is the old watch boat, a safe and favorite play ground for the children of summer sojourners. The oyster beds have moved down stream; sewerage affected them, it is said. Eastward, sticking up above the waters like a melancholy wreck, is the crumbling foundation of the old "Spin- dle," the beacon that tottered to its fall years ago, and round which fishing boats are always hovering. A faint, sweet odor fills all the air down here—a scent which is neither from rock-weed or hay fields, but seems a mingling of both. It rises from the sweet clover that grows here in sparse and desultory patch—the elusive plant, which when you pluck it, causes you to say, "Oh, it is not this after all." But gather a handful, with its fragile white bloom, take it home and let it dry, and it will prove a dainty sachet.

Far across to the right—for there are some fine old places over in old Paw- tuxet—one sees the ample grounds, the massive old elms and the white walls of the Butler place and its neighbor, the Alexander house; away beyond it, the Country Club hold their junketings. In one of these old homesteads near Paw- tuxet, lives a man who cherishes in their original state all the little properties and possessions of his wife who died years ago; her dresses, her work-basket, her favorite chair—none of all her little be- longings has he suffered to be touched by a vandal hand. There may be something touching in such constancy, but there is something vastly morbid, too.

Far across the river rise the bluffs of Riverside and Camp White, and far across the river, too, ply the steamboats, which advertise to stop at Pawtuxet during the summer, reserving to themselves, however, the agreeable right to "change without notice," and causing many a wrathful Pawtuxite to put in many a bad quarter of an hour in baleful meditation on the wharf. A ferry ran across to Riverside at one time, an arrangement that met with approval, but that, too, being "subject to change without notice," languished and died. I observe that two long benches have been recently erected on the wharf, from which it is to be inferred that the hearts of the summer sojourners or the Continental Steamboat Company cherish hopes of steamboat connection next year.

But let not Pawtuxet be in haste to fill up—as she is, fair Pawtuxet is simply perfect, even housewives admit, when conveniences city tradesmen are loth to bestow flourish and abound, and where a thing is perfect, a change must mean a change for the worse. So we leave her seated by the sea, and flushed with sunset radiance; and hailing a car, are homeward bound.

FIELD'S POINT.

[From Providence two and a half miles. By steamer, 10 cents; by Pawtuxet electric cars, 5 cents.]

PROVIDENCE is a favored city. Its diverging car tracks, radiating to north, south, east and west, bring one in a few minutes ride not only to pastures green and beside still waters, but also within easy walking distance of the shining blue plain of salt sea that penetrates our modest territory, and well-nigh severs it in twain. We take a Broad street car to-day, for the brisk south breeze brings an alluring sea breath with it. Most westward bound cars have now a new and interesting feature added to their view—the monument on the square, with its polished granite pedestal upbearing the well-known form of Mayor Doyle, whose calm chiseled features seem to gaze with bland and majestic benevolence directly down upon the hill-climbing passengers. Even now at almost any hour of the day little groups may be seen gazing upward with affectionate interest at the massive figure; but our course leads us too far away, though a hard-featured working woman beside us leans eagerly forward hoping to catch a glimpse of it, and announces with prideful pleasure that "her husband used to go to school with him when they was boys;" and we express gratified astonishment.

Trinity square, which we presently pass, has profited by the despoiling of the Cathedral square to make place for the new monument, and the Stars and Stripes will now flutter aloft between churches and burial ground on gala days, and the golden angel that "shows which way the wind blows" will sound his trumpet over the heads of the pious dwellers on Christian Hill. Does everybody know the pet name of the Swedenborgian Church on the square? It is called the "Heavenly Wedge," and its significance may be learned by walking a few paces down Bridgham street and gazing at it from that vantage ground. It would seem a somewhat needless assertion to add that the Swedenborgian Church is not composed wholly or even principally of Swedes, had not experience shown us that the contrary is a popular delusion.

Here is the cosy little brown cottage within the cemetery walls. Does the good housewife alone at nightfall have dread anticipations of spectral visitors; and is her snowy linen cheerily flapping on the line never converted in fearful eyes into an eerie dance of restless ghosts? "Buried from his late residence in Grace Church Cemetery," a funeral notice read a while ago, and perhaps puzzled readers. But it was all right, and meant only this little cottage, for Death would not even spare a familiar dweller on his border lands.

Our attention next turns to the elegant residence on the corner of Dartmouth avenue. Its novel and effective finish of polished cypress wood makes it a charming feature of the landscape. It is the home of Mr. I. B. Mason, and, together with Mr. Potter's handsome new house on Trinity square, form notable additions.

But it is not houses that we came to see, and we journey till they grow literally "small by degrees and beautifully less," for there are yet remaining a number of quaint little old-time houses far out on Broad street beyond the park. Is not Broad our longest street? for we noticed on one of those funny little cottages, just as we strolled past it to take our return car, the number 1570, which was doing pretty well for Providence. We alight just this side of the old trotting park, where a big sign announces, coupled with a guiding hand, "Field's Point." Years ago there was no path across these plains and hills, but now a hard-beaten road winds among the daisied fields. Somewhere along this road we found a small thicket of the plumpest, the most enticing young thimble berries! It does not matter just where, because we intend to go back there and get them ourselves when they are ripe.

The strip of blue, sparkling in the South, broadens as we advance. In the strong breeze tiny white sails flit like errant butterflies along its surface. Midway between the shores lies Starvegoat Island, looking like a long steamboat overgrown with foliage; and the flag pole at its prow carries out the illusion. One would not think, looking at Starvegoat, that it was big enough to boast a pond of its own with a boat on it; but such is the case. The long, white breakwater that bounds it glistens in the sunlight. Its barrier against the invading shock of south-coming waves is ample in ordinary weather, but if in some tremendous tidal disturbance "a mighty egyre rears its crest" and charges upon it, the dwellings of modest little low-lying Starvegoat will go to be playhouses for the mermen's children.

Dark green between us and the shore lie the verdant salt marshes, with treasures of shell and seaweed lurking in their tangled pipes of reed and lakelets lingering as an earnest of the flood tide's return. It is over these moist meadows that the breeze snatches its choicest aroma—the salt and spicy smell that fills one like food—for a time. But before the road drops to their level, we turn to the left and tramp through the fruitless fields of daisy and sorrel to reach the highest hill summit. After a century of wear and tear, it still keeps the form of the old fort, thrown up in so hot haste, though all too needlessly, when our British cousins were expected to come sailing up the bay, their war vessels belching hostile thunders and lightnings. Across the bay on Fort Hill is its twin, and below us, on the point, is a third one. But this elevation is not one to be scorned. From our lofty seat on the old grass-grown ridge we may view the city if we like, though we prefer other views, or we may see the long green point off which Conimicut's light shines by night, away down where Providence river becomes without question Narragansett Bay. Along the Pawtuxet shore the many pretty cottage roofs show among the foliage, and over on the east bank an almost unbroken front of green hides the thickly clustered summer settlements, and with it deprives the observing stranger of the knowledge of good and evil behind. Some of our shore resorts are delightful places, but there are a few on the east shore that attest a growing fondness among certain citizens for dust, heat and garbage-bedecked roadways, and general hubbub. Field's Point, close to Providence as it is, is never anything but clean, green and tranquil, and the pleasant cottages that cluster along its southern banks are every one inviting.

Over opposite is picturesque Kettle Point, where it is said the first American steamboat was built, and we can make out the red roofs of the Squantum Club buildings among the gray craggy rocks and reedy shores. A steamboat passing throws the waves of its slow wake with a resounding slap high against the distant wharf and the rocks that chance to be in bathing. We can see the tossing white plumes of the evanescent surf from here. A sail boat off Sassafras Point—so named because of a singular lack of sassafras—plunges and courtesies in a mad dance, and as suddenly is still again. Overhead a plover flies whistling. There is no other sound but the booming of the bees in the fragrant clover heads that have scaled the fort, and with a valiant troop of buttercups, taken possession and planted their colors. Their weapons are only the numberless green spears and lances that old mother Nature sent to their defence, but the marauder bees defy them, and flounder dustily about on their very points. Far to the north stretch the strange billowy Field's Point hills—hills unlike any other in the State in contour and vegetation, short, close and always green, though barren of tree or shrub; and for every hill there is a corresponding hollow. I am convinced that the whole neighborhood might be made one vast level by simply slicing off the hills, inverting them and clapping them into the nearest hollows, where they would fit to a T.

There is something about this strange billowy region that seems oddly familiar as we stand meditatively on our ramparts; and suddenly it comes to us—it is like the model of Palestine at Chautauqua. That tallest summit to the north, crowned with the snow of dasies, is Hermon, the Providence river speedily becomes Jordan, and for want of something better, the Field's Point settlement will do as Jerusalem. Yonder is the brook Kedron, and Jacob's well; now if the smallpox hospital on its lonely elevation were but tenanted—but let us be thankful it is not, and pause here. By no means a hideous feature of the landscape is it, albeit somewhat barren and shadeless. But we think of that miserable little shanty that travellers on the Worcester road may see near Berkeley—a plague-stricken looking hovel enough lying across the misty marshes to the left and a dreary cluster of gravestones suggestively near by. Surely who enters there leaves hope behind, if it has an interior to match.

As we turn at last to descend the hill a sudden, terrifying sight greets us. Up toward the city a long railroad bridge built out over the water is slowly moving shoreward—slowly, but with an air of resolution. We gaze in speechless amazement at this mystifying spectacle. Do they take the bridge in at night, or is there something the matter with our eyes —possibly with our mental faculties? Still slowly the top of that bridge is gradually abbreviated, and resolves itself into a long line of slowly moving coal cars, drawn by a hidden engine on shore. Much relieved, we resume our journey.

Field's Point is still in curl papers, so to speak, and we have the whole shore practically to ourselves. The current that sets strongly around the Point has changed its shape greatly in past years. Though it is now ebb tide, and quite a respectable tract is ours to traverse, as we journey around it listening to the foamy

FIELD'S POINT DINING HALL.

slap of the waves on the beach and trying to imagine ourselves on some distant "stern and rock-bound coast;" yet the narrow white strip of dry sand in the centre shows how little the advancing tides leave to boast of and make one feel like chanting Aunt Tempy's opening address in her Cape Cod exhortation:

"Lo, on a narrer neck o' land,
'Twixt two onbounded seas I stand!"

and bring vividly to mind her closing peroration to the "benighted critters that stand before me this evenin', a straddlin' this poor old hopeforsaken Pot Hook!"

What has become of the myriads of dainty scallop shells, white, golden, crimson and brown, that strewed the shore in long ago childhood days? Search as we may, not one do we find. The good old times are gone.

The deepest channel is right off the Point. A few summers ago I remember passing in a steamer a fine, large schooner with all sails set, sitting comfortably high and dry on the Point's sandy extremity, having ventured a wee bit too near. Her crew, broadly grinning, were hanging over the rail and bandying jokes with our passengers, waiting for flood tide. It seemed a very ridiculous sight, somehow. The Point looked very frail to support that stately vessel, but doubtless it has firm foundations. Field's Point once also furnished us occasion for more mirth, when an enthusiastic old gentleman of the party, a stranger to the vicinity, descrying the old powder house in the sand bank north of the landing, went eagerly about inquiring of everybody what it was. A wicked young man said it was King Philip's tomb, and he subsequently affirmed that it was worth that blot on his moral tablets to see the air of gratified joy with which that old gentleman was to be descried pointing out to his family the last resting place of the illustrious sachem.

Nestling in the shelter of the earthworks back of the dining hall is the original Field's Point cottage—a low, old-fashioned, little white cottage, looking strangely out of place beside the red and brown piazzad—to coin a word—summer cottages near by, and with day lilies and white roses blooming half way up to its eaves.

Past the bake grounds we strolled, happily recalling nocturnal feasts here, when caught by calm in sailing parties, and turned our way homeward. Had we not been refreshed by rest and a kindly proffered glass of ice water, we might have been disloyal to our horse car, and taken convenient passage on the next homeward bound boat. But our pedestrian vigor was good and we returned over the hills, being rewarded by a charming wayside picture grouped for our admiring—a placid pool in a hollow, reeds and rushes in the foreground, a cow standing knee deep in the unruffled water that showed her placid reflection, and a whole group of them disposed picturesquely about the rising hillside above, while a swampy grove and a group of dark cedars broke the monotony of the background of undulating hills.

A boding blue bank of clouds that lay low between sea and blue sky, drifted north with the wind, and before night wrapped the city in a misty "sea-turn" to make our outing seem the longer, with its faint breath of ocean.

NARRAGANSETT BAY.

ONE wonders where would be the summer exodus of Providence but for the inviting shores and waters of the salt bay, and whether brief suburban railway excursions and "buggy rides" could compensate for the foregone delight of sunlight or moonlight sail down among the islands, and out into the swinging surges of the old ocean. Our bay offers three thoroughfares to passing craft, albeit the voyager must run the risk of paying an extravagantly high toll at the niggardly Tiverton draw in the way of collision or wreck, for the privilege of passing down the East Passage, otherwise absurdly known as the Sakonet river. It is the easy solution of an annual summer problem—our bay with its many waiting steamers—and quickly and happily answers the question, Where shall we take our guests for their entertainment? Even to the ignorant stranger our bay is beautiful, but to one familiar with its many bending shores and their history, it becomes a voyage richly suggestive. Swinging slowly first down through the big draw of the Point street bridge, fitfully termed by taxpayers the "bridge of sighs," and catching perhaps a glimpse of brave Frank Baxter, bridge tender and life saver, the vessel passes the dingy western reach of Fox Point, at whose wharf lie the colossal New York steamers waiting for night and their rolling passage round Point Judith's inhospitable reefs. From here back to the steamer's dock the river's banks are lively with waiting craft of all sizes and descriptions—the little steamers that ply hourly between the city and the nearer shore places, the bigger vessels bound for

CONIMICUT POINT AND SHAWOMET BEACH.

Rocky Point, Conanicut and Newport, the little New Bedford steamer Harry, the Queen City with freight and passengers for far Sakonnet, the big excursion steamer bound for Block Island or perhaps just a day's sail round Brenton's reef and over in sight of Narragansett, and farther down the bay one will come upon the waiting ferryboats that connect dreamy little Saunderstown with Wickford, Narragansett with bustling Jamestown, Jamestown with Wickford again, and Wickford and Narragansett Pier with

Newport, the queen of the bay. There is a vast choice of routes. Upper Narragansett, however, is fair enough to content the eyes even with a modest little sail of an hour's extent. Perilously near the long slender sand peninsula of Field's Point the channel seems to lie, with the queer cropped green hills undulating off to the westward, and all the crowding shore resorts showing faintly off across the water, for the east shore thus far leads in popularity, though in picturesqueness famed salt-water chase of the Gaspee and the little sloop Hannah, and the prompt and dire revenge of the Revolutionary patriots of Providence, who, assembling at the old Sabin House, set forth at nightfall in companies of row boats, and pulling down the Bay to the grounded schooner, seized and fired the hapless Gaspee, leaving her to shoot up red tongues of flame to the midnight sky and crumble into the black water, leaving no trace but her title to rechristen the old Nonquit Point.

THE "CLUMP" AND ROUND ROCK.

it compares poorly with certain opposite shores. The wee, rich hued islets of the Squantum Club, capped with their tasteful club quarters, are the gem of the upper river, though on the heights above Riverside below, the Pomham Club house towers most proudly. Starvegoat Island, like another slender green steamer ploughing upstream, breaks the wide expanse of water and looks as though it were merely biding its time till some huge flood tide should wholly submerge it. Gaspee Point stretches its sandy length westward just below, with its memories of the far- Between Gaspee and Rocky Point, once the prime magnet of excursionists and still leading in the way of natural beauties and wild scenery, summer homes are rapidly growing, and the trains of the Oakland Beach Railroad pause every moment as they bend around eastward to their terminus, the railroad's namesake, known most familiarly as the annual camp ground of the Rhode Island militia, where the boys "rough it" for an August week, and tramp back into town sufficiently tanned and dusty to be greeted as true war-scarred veterans. Eastward

ll into Coweset or Greenwich Bay, the
ain or the vessel may pass, by lovely
ayside and old Warwick Neck light. East
reenwich, the most thriving town on
ese shores, is known far and wide as
e seat of an academy, and the most
ourishing headquarters for the scallop
dustry. It is puzzling in the ears of a
n-resident to hear the drawling an-
ouncement of an old fisherman here, that
proper begins. Whether one turn now
far eastward, rounding Poppasquash,
and pass up into the quiet waters of
Bristol harbor, for a water view of
the quaint and dreamy old seaport town,
round Bristol Ferry Light and the pleasant farmhouse at the water's edge and up
into Mount Hope Bay with its guarding
hill, peopled with Indian history; or
whether he elect to try the East Passage

MOUNTAIN ROCK.

e guesses he'll "go daown t' the shore
id scallop it a spell." But we are stray-
g too far from the Bay proper; the real
ghway lies to the west of Conimicut
ght, and in sight of Nayatt's abandoned
ore lighthouse over eastward, and the
eautiful summer homes on the rising
ounds above. Thus far, Nayatt is easily
ader in point of summer residences
rer all the east side. Once outside this
int, with Conimicut left to the north-
ard, the river ceases and the Bay
and the perilous draws, or to take the
Newport boat's course between Prudence
and Conanicut, and by Coasters' Harbor
Island with its school ship, the Jamestown, and its white-clad bands of cadets
peopling its decks and shores; or whether,
last of all, he will try the wild West
Passage, most perilous, if most picturesque, as the history of wrecks along
its shores will show—all this depends on
the nature of the craft in which one
voyages, and the clemency of its cap-

tain. One certainly cannot exhaust more than one in a day's outing, and a week's diligent cruising is hardly too much to give one who wishes to assert with truth that he knows every shore of Narragansett Bay. Descriptions of the Sakonnet sail, of the four islands dubbed respectively Prudence, Patience, Hope and Despair, of Newport's harbor and of Conanicut's long green stretch, are to be found elsewhere among these pages, as well as the rough passage via the rocking of the Pier with its endless line of breakers, and the old Hazard tower lifting its head curiously across the forest, the shores are strewn with driftwood, and the melancholy fragments of more than one wreck wash in here with the tide. Northward, fortified Dutch Island stands as a coast guard, and the broad beacon of Beaver Tail light vies with the red flash of Whale Rock out in the raging seas, but despite their warning and the bellow of the huge fog

THE "GULLY" AT THE "HORSESHOE."

Caswell from the island eastward to Narragansett Pier—an hour of delight to true rough water lovers; but there are wild rocks and corners about the seldom-seen West Passage that are worthy of picturing, and the several sketches inserted here show better than any words, the lonely, surge beaten coasts that lie about Bonnet Point, the "Round Rocks" and the "Jeffrie." All the way from Narragansett Ferry, on the west shore, opposite Jamestown, down the high and storm-swept coast to Boston Neck, which overlooks the long sweep horn down on Conanicut's southern point, the rocks of the Bonnet have pierced holes through more than one goodly vessel. Here the coast ledges and bluffs run highest, and the outlying rocks, gold and brown and slippery with seaweed, cluster most thickly round the stern coast, and though they are famous fishing grounds at a proper state of the tide, they are wild and weird spots, suggestive of wreck and drowning. Inland, keeping pace with the high coast, the long ridge of Tower Hill runs north and south, and looks calmly down on the wild turmoil of the constant battle of wind, waves and rock; and turning but a mile or so eastward, the rough coast gives place to the calm and pastoral reaches of the Pettaquamscutt river, gliding down to meet the Whale Rock beacon.

In its entire length, our bay presents an almost unlimited variety of marine aspects, whether in calm or storm; and when one thinks he has exhausted even its many resources, he will find that he has still a fruitful fund of entertainment in viewing the interior of the many lighthouses, some of which are easily accessible from terra firma. Those that lie inaccessible out in the salt water, even between Conimicut and Providence, are but little known, and their inspection occupied the writer and the artist one entire day.

Conimicut Light, the most graceful one on the river, was said to be a mile out from shore, lying equi-distant from Nayatt and Conimicut Point, but it was a short mile as our sailboat sped, and we transferred again to the rowboat, for treacherous rocks were ready to stave a hole through the catboat's bottom, and with difficulty effected a landing on the strewn rocks, brown with slimy rockweed, that form the sombre and limited door yard of this unique abode. The tide was low and the piled rocks slippery, and as we scrambled precariously about in search of an iron ladder wherewith to reach the upper regions the keeper himself appeared, rowing from the eastern shore. To our

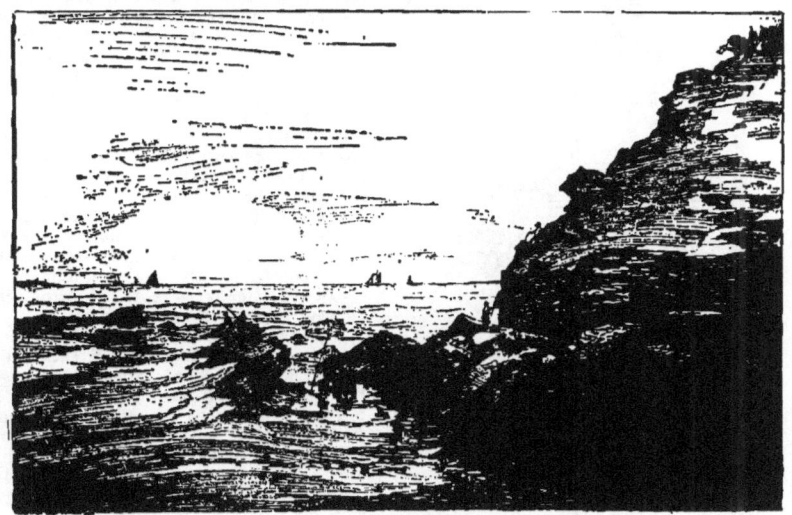

THE "JEFFRIE."

jocular query as to which was the front door, he replied that they were all front, and we were to go up anywhere. So up the slanting ladder we scrambled and through the hatchway up to the solid stone platform that surrounds the tower high above the restless waves. Such a solid structure as this great round tower is! Brick, iron and stone everywhere, fit to battle with wilder Atlantic rollers than are likely to break here. Builders learnt caution from the fate of its predecessor, which some eighteen years ago went over in the ice break-up that made ravages all down the bay. Only the tower was then of stone, the house of wood, and when it went, the keeper and his young boy went too, down into the icy waters of a midwinter's day. The house went over bodily, battered by the huge ice-cakes, flat on its side, and the two managed in some miraculous manner to free themselves, call for help and cling until a tug made its way through to the rescue.

CONIMICUT LIGHT.

Capt. John Weeden, the present keeper of Sabin's Point Light, being on the eastern shore at the time, volunteered to row out at sunset and light the signal in the abandoned tower; while up aloft he looked northward and spied one isolated ice cake speeding down the river and heading straight for the wrecked lighthouse. He ran down with the hope of saving his boat, but it splintered like a toy under the crash, and the great block went on through the submerged and fallen house, slicing through it like a knife through cheese, and leaving Capt. Weeden to the pleasing prospect of an indefinite stay in the isolated stone tower. He spent the night there, made a forlorn breakfast of a meal and tea fondu, baking johnny cakes thereof in the hand basin, stirred with a dipper handle, and brewing tea in a lard pail. A furious snowstorm then set i and delayed his rescue, but he rang tl fog bell assiduously, and at night w: taken off.

The new tower will hold its ov through any moderate attack. The pre ent keeper, Edward L. Hunt, is the thi in charge, Arnold being the first ar Gray the second. A fog bell hangs alo in this tower, too, outside the light roor its ringing regulated by a weight attac ment that runs in a great cylinder dov the entire tower like an old-time cloc It is regulated to strike four to tl minute, and as Mr. Hunt wound up tl machinery and set it agoing for our u derstanding, the fishermen far and wi on the bay must have looked up for a instant from their exciting sport for possible fog bank. It was a fine vie from this topmost, breezy outlook, o the clear morning with the calm wate one great sparkle up to the sun, and tl whole land world stretching to the va level that seems endless, viewed fro this height. South was the blue of t. ocean—but north were the waiting ligh houses, and we must not tarry.

In descending order were, first, t "spare room" and various closets and room; winding down another flight t bed room, taking the whole round of t tower, with about a 20-foot diamet Such a dainty, pretty room as it w: with its soft blue walls, the neat ash s and matting-covered floor. In the dee set, arched windows, bright lambrequi had been deftly fitted, and the dra shades tapped lightly on the casing the brisk breeze. It seemed odd to tu from side to side and see only the glancl bright ripples through the open caseme One bane of housekeepers was surf spared here—dusting.

Mrs. Hunt was at her own home land with a tiny baby, soon to be int duced to lighthouse life, and meanwb the lightkeeper was housekeeper as we Everything was in immaculate order these delightful round rooms, and t pretty sitting room, one story below, w as cosy with its gray-tinted walls and : viting easy chairs as the breezy bl room above. Down still another flight was the kitchen, convenient alcoves in the deep walls acting as cupboards, one or two neatly curtained off. The range stood in the centre, its slender pipe backed by the big funnel case of the bell weight, which, colored like the room it passed through, and frescoed about its top, made quite an ornament in the various apartments.

A window full of pinks and petunias relieved the omnipresent marine view that the window arches framed in on every side; a door led again into still lower depths of cellar, which we did not penetrate. It was a most romantic home, and what a place in which to spend the honeymoon! Had the keeper's wife been there we would have asked her all about it; as it was we roamed about in a most inquisitive manner, looked at the official volume on the desk, which recorded time, wind, weather and expenses, and whose leaves lay open at June 8 and 9, with the brief legend for each day, "Wind N. W., light. Foggy."

The small Government library stood in its neat case inviting examination, but the literature which has fallen to Mr. Hunt's lot this year does not chance to be of the most enticing order. One or two novels, a bulky set of "Queens of England," a Holy Bible and Common Prayer, a dozen or so miscellaneous works, two or three marine works—of the whole collection, Mrs. Brassy's "Yacht Sunbeam" looked most inviting. However, Pawtuxet was hard by, and so was Drownville, the nearest post office, where supplies were also obtained, and life at Conimicut is far from being an isolated one. It is a famous fishing ground, and visitors are frequent, many fishing from the rock foundation itself, and every now and then one getting storm or fog bound, and taken in by these marine Samaritans for the night. It would have been great fun to be captured there ourselves, and it seemed at one time as though we might be; for when adieux were over and we were safely afloat again and about to "spread our white sail to encounter the seas," something parted up aloft and down came the whole sail in a tumbled mass. Our sable captain broke out in no profanity; he was calm, but sad. Aid was finally invoked from the lighthouse, and after a good deal of pulling and hauling, and being hoisted up and down the lofty mast, repairs were finally effected. If the artist did not get a good sketch of Conimicut lighthouse it was not because he was not given time to contemplate it. It was high noon, and the sun's beams fervent, and dinner was hours away; our state was not of bliss, but it had an end.

BULLOCK'S POINT LIGHT.

The old lighthouse tipping Nayatt Point no more echoes to the tread of visitors up its winding stairs; the first built on the river, it has been long unoccupied—ever since the New York steamer grounded on the treacherous rock midway between there and the new light—where the red buoy claws out of water like a floating lobster. Conimicut was deemed a safer place then, as vessels can steer very near it with safety, while the Nayatt Light was to the hidden rock as Scylla to Charybdis. Westward of the present Conimicut Light a long shoal runs across the river, whose visible terminus is Conimicut Point, and this side of the tower shows no light. In the cottage part of the Nayatt house rooms are used by the coachman of the present owner, Charles Merriman, who found the lighthouse property a desirable addition to his own domains; and children play in the empty rooms.

It was washday at Bullock's Point Lighthouse, and white raiment was airily flying about the high railing like a flock of sea birds seeking shelter. What the inmates of these various lofty abodes thought of us as we emerged in the upper world through the hatchway like sunburnt mermaids they did not say, but they were kind and hospitable. Here was a jolly family at the Bullock's Point Light, and plenty of room for them in the square gray cottage, with sharply sloping roof that stood railed in high above its granite foundation, with another tumble of hewn rock around it even scanter than Conimicut's. Here live the family of Joseph B. Eddy, four children pursuing their education under difficulties, it would seem, but managing to accomplish it with as much seeming ease as the shore folk. Each morning they descend that terrible ladder, with its rounds planted at appalling distances for youthful limbs, enter the waiting rowboat and row over to the east shore, where they tie up and tramp off to school at Drownville. Mrs. Eddy remembers but one mishap during their stay here—a tumble off the staging into the salt water by a frisky small boy, who was picked up, however, without much harm being done. The somewhat limited quarters did not seem to trouble the household at all—the lack of door yard and neigh-

INTERIOR OF CONIMICUT LIGHT.

bors' children to quarrel with, and so on. This was all thriftily attended to on shore during the day, and morning and evening gathered them in to the cosy little six-room cottage, where there was never lack of fresh air. Supplies were brought over easily enough in the Government boat, and sailboats came down with coal, which was hoisted up and dumped into the cellar. Cisterns held the rain water, which was pure, sweet and cold; on the whole, Mrs. Eddy considered that her abode was more desirable than a country farm inland; it was easier in a sudden dearth of household supplies to run ashore in the rowboat

nd purchase than to harness a horse
nd drive down to the "centre" in an
solated country spot. As for neighbors
nd visitors—well, in the summer season
here were too many rather than too
ew. Fishing parties paused here frequently, and summer guests made it an
xcursion from the down-river resorts.
torm has never long confined them.
he ice had been the worst the recent
emarkable winter when the Bay froze
ver and the New York boat stuck fast
n the ice above, greatly to the children's
the low whistling rumble sounding here
as it does over every light, caused by
the drawing wind. We peeped into the
oil room and spied, among other paraphernalia, two modest brass lamps with red
glass chimneys. Were they the real
origin of the beautiful red glow that
flashed for miles over the dark waters,
answering the steady white gleam of
Conimicut? They were, indeed, and had
we been composing poems on the subject
would have acted as a sad damper. The
cottage was cool and pretty with hard-

NAYATT'S ABANDONED LIGHT.

oy. There had been some fear of the
lighthouse going when the ice broke up,
nd invitations to go ashore had been
many, but the family had stood by their
ome, and when the time came the jutting point of the rocks on the north
ide had acted as a fender, and the ice
loe, parted by it, had divided into two
streams and left the wee rock islet in a
lear channel. The small fry had been
vastly chagrined at this denouement, and
oud had been their lamentation that they
ad not felt a shock. The light room
nere is in a picturesque little railed dome,
wood finish and tinted walls; is there anywhere a lighthouse with papered walls?
If so we have not chanced to see it. As
we sat in the cosy sitting room, a sleeping baby tucked away on the lounge,
open doors showing bed room on one hand,
kitchen on the other, with a sunny-faced
little maiden busily at work amid the
familiar pots and pans, it was hard to
realize that the heaving waters of the
Bay hemmed us in on every hand. One
could only believe it by stepping to the
open windows. Five years this family
of six have occupied the little six-roomed

cottage, the light having been built about 15. We disappeared at length as we had come, down the iron hatchway and the long straight ladder that led to the slippery green rocks and the lapping water, one of us receiving a compliment as she departed on her tranquil descent. A good many ladies screamed and cried, Mrs. Eddy informed us. But was it for us to shudder and wail where infant footsteps daily trod—with one of the very little heroines herself looking smilingly

SABIN'S POINT LIGHT—INTERIOR.

on? Never; and down we went, and rowed away once more to our patient sailboat, drifted pretty well down with the seaward tide. As Sabin's Point light drew nearer and Bullock's fell astern, the former grew to bear more and more a fantastic resemblance to one of the new sailor hats for ladies' wear—a square crown, a projecting rim, and then another band beneath—this being the stone foundation, the rim the broad platform, and the crown the low, square cottage of gray stone, with brown French roof. No tangle of piled blocks is there here to climb over—the foundation stones are mainly huge flat slabs, some seeming to wave and creep in the tide that covered them. We were getting to be experts now, we proudly felt, and skipped out of our frail bark and up aloft to domestic quarters with great agility. If Bullock's

Point light had seemed li cottage, this was even was the abode of genius, here in the square, airy a musical corner indeed supported, like Horatius, guitar on one side and other; across the room and elaborate bookcase, or altogether in the lighthous Capt. John Weeden, allu the Conimicut episode. of home manufacture and manship, graced the din Sabin was one point ahea keeper was ironing, whil neighbor, so to speak, s airy pennants of the fan whole Marryatt's code at

The square roof gives and pretty sleeping roor tower containing the lig and lofty from one end There is the least bit o top of the tinted walls, shutters kept out the wh shine on the dancing w The song of canaries sou cottage—there had been Point, too—and all sorts dustries abounded. Dov with the familiar smel cellars, compounded of s the general damp, was the eldest of the four customed to make enam hours at home. Here cistern with a capacity running dry but rarely tracted drouth, and Ca arrangẽd a siphon com wash tubs.

Above, fancy work winter days for the w Weeden displaying a k most intricate design, own hands, and an el tiny, brilliant bits, piecec daintiness in the patter " tree of paradise" by had spent the winter h esting relics from wreck too, collected by Capt. many years service.

occupied this house almost ever since its founding in 1872, the first keeper, Mr. Bowles, serving but two years. When the "Ill-fated Metis" went down off Watch Hill—some twenty years ago, was it?—Capt. Weeden, who was in the vicinity, captured from the billows some elaborate pieces of carving, thought to have been purchases of the passengers. Two of these now adorn brackets here—one a bird and nest in foliage, another a group of stags. A wooden box with a set of fine china was another prize, Mrs. Weeden producing some cups and saucers of brilliant hues and dainty design, on which we cast covetous eyes.

We went up to view the light in the tower, of course, also a white fixed light. The lamp proper is a humble and ordinary affair enough, and it is only when it is set in the gleaming crystal barrel that it becomes a beacon afar. It was always a pleasure to step from the hothouse atmosphere of the light-room to the breezy balcony without, and we lingered here long, picking out the familiar features along our "picturesque Narragansett" and hearing the history of the funny old oyster house down on Sabin's Point on the east of us. Capt. Weeden remem-

ROCK FACE AT POMHAM.

bers when it occupied quarters away up on Market square, near the horse car station, and throve as a meat market. This true Peggoty abode was once the schooner Elizabeth, one of a wrecked and abandoned pair, the other being an East India merchantman, and carted off to Drownville, to be also usefully employed, but perversely burning down instead. A newer oyster house now stands beside the battered Elizabeth, and the present use of the nondescript old ark is as a stable and workshop.

Up on the high lighthouse platform is a pleasant resting place on an elsewhere torrid day, and it must be almost equally delightful in the night and storm. Birds do not perish here in any numbers, the keepers told us, though they often hear the blow of their contact in a night of wind and storm. They seem to be stunned more often than killed, and eventually recover. It is only the little English sparrows that oftenest meet their fate here; and their loss ought not, I suppose, to be deeply regretted.

We were off and away once more for Pomham Light, the last family abode on the river, and with the most picturesque founding, Pomham Rock figuring in pastel and oil as well as newspaper sketches. The original Pomham was, of course, a departed Indian chief, and the pretty white cottage with the tower at the water end is built on the larger of the two rocks, so that it has a goodly foundation some quarter acre in extent. The cottage is the most pretentious of any of the river lighthouses, and its keeper, Mr. Salisbury, is the veteran keeper, having occupied it since its erection in 1871. Visitors have been many here always, as the rock lies hardly a stone's throw from shore, and in the days when the keeper's very pretty daughter was unmarried and lived at home, Pomham had an added attraction. No traces of her presence are here now, save the portrait on the piano in the darkened parlor. In the hall at the foot of the stairway that winds up the tower to the light is the desk with the official volumes and the regular visitors book well filled here. The cottage contains seven rooms, and the kitchen is an especially spacious and convenient one. Quite a garden flourishes without, in the crannies of the conglomerate rock that is its under bed, and the radishes at least are flourishing prosperously, as we can personally testify. Pomham Rock boasts two curiosities in the shape of rock profiles, one a small one best seen from the garden looking west down toward the water, the face turned to the left and much resembling the "old man of the mountain." The other is a colossal one on the landward side, visible even from the railroad track on shore, but best seen in a rowboat half way between shore and island, and with its massive brow, its well-modeled features, moustache and fine chin, it seemed to us to bear striking resemblance to a well-known M. D. of Providence.

Mr. and Mrs. Salisbury have the island all to themselves at present with the exception of big shaggy Sailor, the successor to old Major, who used vociferously to greet the passing mariners.

The library here is a better assorted one, as it is at Sabin's Point, where new books of travel, biography and many bound volumes of Harper's abound; the new ones are said to be much better than the old, and as they are changed about yearly, everybody gets fair play in course of time.

We had dismissed our colored captain on landing at Pomham, and he had long ago gone sailing hungrily home to his delayed dinner, so the obliging young painter put us ashore in the Government boat, and boarding a train which steamed in at Silver Spring, we gave up lighthouse inspection for the day.

PART SECOND.

Inland and Upland.

IN AND ABOUT PROVIDENCE.

THE city of Providence, crowded as it is with manufactories so detrimental to beauty, has yet in it much of the picturesque, even in its busy heart, and many of its environs, accessible by horse cars, are both fair to the eyes and historically interesting. Like two distant cities are respectively the "East Side" and "West Side" of Providence, separated by the last widening flow of the many named Blackstone into the salt bay. The East Side, in its tree-grown, stately quiet, in its clustering universities, in its conservative "first-family" abodes, is to the bustling, rapidly growing, more cosmopolitan and democratic West Side what England is to America; and between its several citizens there is always an unacknowledged, but easily discernible, small spirit of antagonism. But the West Side, less beautiful though it is, has distinctly the best of it in the matter of growth and prosperity. All cities, like all nations, grow to the westward; and all endeavors in the opposite way must fall flat, as repeated history will testify. Between the two sections of the city, at the "great bridge," a square of pave, highway and multitudinous traffic, is to the southward a scene that is always fair by day or night; the crowded harbor, gay in summer time with pleasure crafts, large and small, the blue water rippling in the distance far between the ever-retreating shores, Field's Point's bills undulating roundly westward from the point where "the river widens to meet the Bay," and fair Narragansett stretching dim and hazy down to her distant islands. For the best view of the winding river and the Bay, the roof of the Narragansett Hotel is to be commended if practicable; otherwise the spire of the First Baptist Church over on North Main street will do admirably. The favorite East Side lookout is Prospect Terrace, off Prospect street, a lofty eyrie indeed, and showing the city proper in all its entirety, though to our own eyes it shows to more advantage softened by distance from a more remote hill top than one of the seven on which, like Rome of old, the city is founded. Providence is not a city of parks, though the future promises great things for us with the acquisition of the Davis estate and the prospect of Neutaconkanut some day. Hayward Park, off Point street, and near the salt water, is a young and promising scion, but the two fairest, Blackstone and Roger Williams, are outside the city proper. Roger Williams Park not only enjoys the distinction of being a remarkably beautiful one, but the way thereto is the most attractive ride that Providence can boast; turning through Mathewson street, where the slender, graceful spire of Grace Church marks the junction with Westminster, and where perhaps the weird chimes up in the belfry are picking out a tune with clanging, hesitating vibrance; on and around up Broad street, the abode of physicians, and where at the hill brow are always two rival blooming flower beds about two stately homes; past Grace Church Cemetery at Trinity square, and so into Greenwich street, our newest acquisition as a boulevard, and the most beautiful avenue on all the West Side, unlovely nowhere in its entire length, and with charming little side streets, likewise tree-shaded, leading enticingly away on either hand. A detailed description of the park is wholly unnecessary, so familiar is it to all our own citizens, so easy of access to the stranger within our

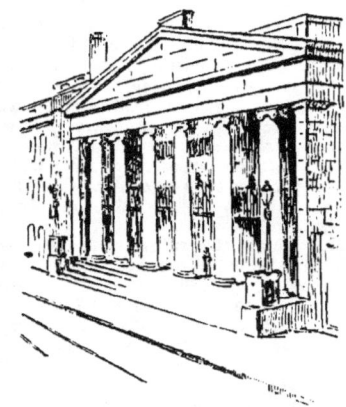

THE ARCADE.

gates. Its eastward approaches, level lawns, with winding walks and borders always gay with flowers, lead past the pretty little pavilion at the terminus to that house of entertainment and refreshment known as What Cheer Cottage, that stands cosily at the wood's edge on the hill top by the beginning of the chain of lakes that make so much of the park's beauty. Here it is always lovely, what with scores of well-filled rowboats, plashing fountains and gliding swans in summer; and still more gay and picturesque on winter evenings, when the red balls hoisted to the flagstaffs down in the city announce "Skating at the Park." Half the young folk of Providence, one would think, were out on the ice in jaunty winter costume, illumined not only by moon and stars, but flaring bonfires around the border. It is a question if the park is not better patronized in winter than in summer, for it is only for a brief season indeed that pleasure-drivers, equestrian parties and bicyclists are missing from its firm and pleasant wood roads. There are many charming wooded nooks, wandering brooklets and primeval swamp hollows that add largely to the park's attractiveness, and are more pleasing to the lover of out-door life than the more artificially beautified portions. For its size it would be hard to find a more attractive park, in natural features, and for the diversion of young folk it has a large and constantly growing menagerie, as well as various equipages to let for drives within its borders and a varied flotilla on the lakes. The old Betsey Williams cottage, the Roger Williams statue and graveyard are prominent and interesting features of attraction. Band concerts on summer evenings give the whole beautiful spot a double charm.

Quite at the other extreme of the city is the smaller and wilder Blackstone Park, close on the borders of the picturesque and romantic grounds of Butler Hospital for the insane. To reach it we take a Governor street car, and proceeding southward turn the first many corners that emphasize the way to Blackstone Park. A not over agreeable impression of the charms of this ride would a stranger receive at the outset, for it lies among those wretched shanties that defile the space between South Main street and the river; hovels over which one wishes he might wave a wizard's transforming wand to our fair city's credit as well as the comfort of their inmates.

But the way grows fairer, and on the heights the south breeze brings salt and spicy whiffs of sea air northward to us. The atmosphere is laden with the refreshing breath of the "green things growing." Narrow door yards give place to ample and velvety lawns, and lawns to daisied fields, where cows are browsing. Near

ROGER WILLIAMS'S MONUMENT.

our journey's end stands a magnificent elm by the wayside—not one of immense girth and marvelous spread of limb. It would no doubt tremble before Holmes's fatal tape-measure—his distinguisher of greatness—but it is graceful, luxurious and stately, and around its trunk, clasping it with dainty feathery greenness from root to branch, a twining woodbine runs riot.

We whisk around a few more corners, pass the charming grounds of the happy dwellers on the park borders, envying now and next winter conpassionating, and reach the terminus. Shall we follow the brook up to its source, where lies a less and lovely park, or down to its union with the Seekonk that flows by the forest, by way of the fern-bordered ravine? Each is equally fair, and many crowding wild flowers, according to their season, mark all the way. This is a favorite spot for picnickers—this deep rustic glen, the brook tinkling merrily at the foot, and great overlacing trees, showing the sky in blue network overhead. In June pink laurel grows thickly here all about the grounds as the plain above. At the car's terminus, an omnibus awaits to conduct passengers to famous Swan Point Cemetery, a spot in its tranquil beauty well worth a special trip. Many beautiful monuments are in its enclosure, flowers of the fairest, and its entrance gate is unique and charming. But we may also from the park limits take the path that leads northwest to the hospital grounds, straying to right or left as daisies or buttercups beckon. We pass the funny little hamlet that lies in the wilderness, distinguished by a barn whose clapboards were shot on, instead of being applied in the usual way. We make this statement on our own authority, but it is self-evident. We pass through the fence opening and take the beaten path that leads up to the hospital. The woods are cool and silent. Do the birds feel the spell of the sad spirit that broods over this tranquil place? For bobolinks and thrushes were jubilant without; and here, listen as we may, not a bird note sounds. And now, if one will take the first beaten path to his left, or, in other words, follow up the first brook he sees toward its source, he will come upon one of the most beautiful nooks in the neighborhood. A silent woodvale, bounded and shut in by lofty, gloomy slopes, dark with pines and musical with the liquid babble of the broad, shallow brook, whose barrier some kind hand has broken by stepping stones. Ferns grow here in riotous numbers, and the sunshine leaps gladly from the unresponding ranks of pine to their fragile, feathery fronds that seem to create a sunshine of their own where they lie. Some venturesome spirits have visited this spot, for midway between it and the main path a sturdy beech is covered thickly with names and dates, 20 to 30 feet upward, and all distorted with the spread and wear of the growing bark.

The red walls of Butler Hospital gleam presently through the trees; the tangled undergrowth gave place to well-kept shrubbery on velvety lawns, and the whole long picturesque building stands before us, quiet and peaceful in the afternoon sunshine, as if it were the abode of saintly spirits rather than the shelter of shattered and clouded minds, a restless multitude for whom unceasing vigilance is needed.

The outer doors stand hospitably open; but the barred and grated windows belie their welcome. Now and then on the quiet air comes the faint sound of a woman's moan, or a man's voice raised in dramatic and meaningless declamation, or, saddest of all, a burst of uncanny laughter. But the walls are thick, and inside the building one would not suspect its character. Every corridor has its heavy door with lock and key, and it is a work of time for an official to make his way from end to end of the mammoth building. The establishment is wisely and judiciously managed, and there is no doubt that its inmates are as comfortable here as it is possible for them to be. The violent patients have their own place, and their vagaries are not left to work harm on the sensitive nerves of the monomaniacs or sufferers from melancholia. The wards are bright and sunny, and tastefully, some of them elegantly, furnished. The central sitting rooms, from which doors open into separate chambers have their books, flowers, and sometimes musical instruments, furnished by patients or their friends. The inmates often retain their love of melody, even when they discard all other diversions, and musical entertainments are quite common. Of course among the many confined here, a large proportion trusted, and serious disturbances are rare. Indeed, some refractory inmate is often put on his best behavior to earn his evening's diversion. And if now and then some vagary not on the programme crops out among the participants, why, the audience, being sympathetic, is indulgent.

The head nurse has been in her present position for twenty-five years; it

ENTRANCE GATE, SWAN POINT.

are persons of culture and refinement, and among them they often contrive an evening's programme that would be a credit to people supposed to be in full possession of their faculties. Tableaux are particularly enjoyed, some of the ladies developing a great taste in costuming and arranging. As for audiences, the doctors and attendants exercise their discretion in issuing invitations. As a general thing they know who are to be would be hard to fill her place. Changes, too, are disturbing to the patients, and the death of Dr. Sawyer, the former superintendent, was a great shock to many of them—a thing not to be believed. Walks and drives are a daily diversion for those who can be trusted, and it is seldom that any mischief arises thereby. The grounds are delightful, with their flower beds, tennis and croquet grounds, hot houses, and the lovely picture of the placid, sparkling river in the distance; but the minds clear enough to appreciate its beauties, must also be alive to the fact that they are prisoners without escape, and to the faculties so dulled that they do not realize their bondage the fairest scenes pass unnoted.

Visitors are not shown through the institution. Being a private establishment, the public has, of course, no right to demand admission, and it would be highly unpleasant both to the patients and their friends to have their infirmities made a show. The friends and relatives visiting patients are generally shown to their rooms by us private a way as possible, and altogether the whole establishment affords a happy contrast to the horrors of similar institutions of which we have lately heard so much.

We retrace our way to the car, but of course do not take homeward passage till we have visited the spring, more easy of access than Neutaconkanut's, being, as almost everybody knows, just through the fence and down the path a bit at the horse car's terminus. There, from a very well-ventilated tin cup, which caps a post in a public spirited manner, we drink our fill and return refreshed.

Another institution well worth seeing, interesting in itself, and with delightful surroundings, is Elmhurst, the famous Catholic school on Smith street. It is a short ride in the horse cars from the centre of the city, and the delightful old homesteads with their rambling wooded lawns. The old Eaton place, Bailey's and others are so English in character, so tranquil, quiet and country-like that it seems scarcely possible the rural spot can be a part of bustling modern Providence. Elmhurst itself stands in the grounds of what was formerly the Grosvenor estate, and remodelled from the old mansion is still a striking and picturesque building. Beside the school proper within its walls, patronized by wealthy and refined young ladies from all over the country, a separate life is maintained by the "religeuses," who live here a strictly conventual life. The whole atmosphere of the place is quaint and foreign, and to make the rounds of its tranquil, hushed domains, and meet groups of the bright-faced young pupils in their modest school costumes, chatting volubly in French, the language of the house, is like stepping suddenly into the pages of a foreign boarding school story. Not far from here lie the lovely grounds of the Davis estate, recently made over for park use. And now that Neutaconkanut, with its wild wooded heights, may soon also become a public resort, we shall have parks worthy the growing city's size.

THE CATHEDRAL.

To reach Neutaconkanut, we take a Plainfield street car, pass up Westminster street and by Monument square, with the imposing frontage of the new Y. M. C. A. building, the Doyle monument with the well-known figure looking far away down the sloping highway, the massive and grand Cathedral of Sts. Peter and Paul, beautiful without by night with the moon rising silvery between the two square towers, their high battlements sharply defined against its light, and the shadows black in the arched recesses; beautiful always within, the stranger is fortunate who chances to gain admission on a week day.

On past Christian Hill—a sad misnomer

ally, it is said, and then all along street, of which an exhaustive deion is not perhaps needful. We will say of it that whichever way one along it he is said to go "up High ," and also that it has the pecur of being an extremely charming in the middle and an extremely reeable one at either end. Its easteginning is all groceries and marind its western terminus is all saloons dirty children. Midway lie some of handsomest residences, and the se of the parade one gets at Parade with its graceful elm avenues is a picture.

when their birch wigwams dotted the green and level meadows at its base, which is, to say, The home of the squirrels. And while we are airing our philology we would also say that "squirrel" itself is neither old Saxon nor Indian, as one might guess, for the Indian's squirrel was an "adjidaumo," which is not half so pretty. No, squirrel has the honor of descending by a very roundabout way, one would think, from the Greek skia, shadow, and oura, tail.

Meanwhile we are nearing the cool green hill, clad just now in its delicate misty robes of spring's fairest green. A hundred cloud shadows play along its

OLD MESSER MANSION.

using at Olneyville square for the of denizens of that outer city—as e Providence as if it were not joined by dense acres of dwelling houses— urn down Plainfield street to the left, enter the region of low rents. One get, on almost any of these side s, a very cosy, neat and spacious ient for $8 or $10 monthly that l be double that price farther down . Probably nowhere at an equal ice from the city's centre are s to be rented so cheaply as here. d now, stretching its high green r broadly across our pathway, lies conkanut hill, named by the Indians

many dimpling hollows and rocky sides; and the clustered woods that stand along its base, and climb boldly upward beckon enticingly in the cool breeze. One tree alone upon the summit looks colossal outlined against the sky, and a group of children out maying who come into view for a moment, on the summit seem to be sporting in an elephantine silhouette, and might be Dr. Holmes's fractious young giantesses and the bowlders that dot the hillside below, plums from their rejected dinner as they went

"Screaming and throwing their pudding about,
Acting as they were mad."

Our driver means to give us our money's worth. He goes and goes till the "jumping-off-place" where rails give place to dusty roadway lies only a few feet beyond us, and then the tinkle of bells ceases and we step out. If we were to ask any one of the passers-by what was the name of the hill before us those who did not say Uticognitt would no doubt say Unicognitt, and as for its spelling—well, if ever a spelling match is held that way, and its ranks are hard to reduce, let the name of that hill be put out and they would fall like leaves in an autumn gust. But the preponderance of evidence goes toward Neutaconkanut. and clous raids on garden or orchard, and lowered barways that give escape to cattle. Or we may go around past the little chapel to the right from the car track and take the road hillward that leads by the new nursery.

Persons contemplating extended tours through the mountains this summer would find it excellent practice to come out and ascend Neutaconkanut daily a few times. To the happy man who found he could reach its summit unbreathed, Washington or Pike's Peak would have no terrors. For ourselves, we paused half way and sat down to view the city. From here wrapped in that soft, smoky haze which

ACOTE'S HILL.

at any rate that was what the Indians called it. It is a long, long hill. Go up Atwell's avenue, Manton avenue, the Hartford road, Plainfield street, Roger Williams avenue or Cranston street, and still one may see the sun set behind its long ridge. But here are its local habitation and its name, and here the west wind blows most freely down its breezy sides. We may pass to the south of the hill till we leave the gardens and ploughed fields behind, and then climb via some farmyard way, if we are few in number and modest in port, otherwise we will no doubt be banned as tresspassers; for picnic parties are gaining the ill-will of the hillside dwellers by thoughtless or malicious an accompaniment of spring days and brush fires, it looked vastly picturesque, softened by distance and orientalized by the big red gasometer's dome and the hospital turrets. The many lines of lindens down its distant streets show their green heads among the housetops, and nearer at hand the wood patches and hill pastures on Rocky Hill across the valley seem almost summer-like in their luxuriance of verdure. Roger Williams avenue and its environs are being rapidly built up of late, and houses in white, yellow and brown stand thickly now where a few years ago were only sloping pastures. Silver Lake at this eminence, too, seems more entitled to its name than it does on

des like a veritable
ths. But away in
the fairest scene,
hills lie distant and
pale horizon. One
'e the others, and
only a faint and
epachet's hill called
.nd away still fur-
hose the hills and
incoln, where the
ig the weird, gray
s of the Lime Rock
c know Narragan-
ing sea gulls and
es a-dreaming this
, no Narragansett
t. It has wrapped
antle of haze and

, again to the hill,
h, green sides that
ep down into fruit-
laborers are busy
e plant," we plunge
strewn forest. Tra-
ı spring somewhere
find it. We follow
paths that suddenly
it all, and when at
in a level field on
t very much of a
er all, and it has a
tting in it; but the
old, and we should
ve had anything but
n. But it is some-
t.

p are growing quan-
long-stemmed vio-
s like pansies, and
e came. And when
s of a glistening
to pause and par-
ntaconkanut leaves
. Our course car-
s time around the
hill, and gives us
hat we are in the
we pass the cosy
farm-houses, with
to their eaves, and
and sights of farm-

yard life all about. Forty minutes take
us again to our starting point.

Another pleasant suburban trip is by
way of the Cranston horse cars to the
vicinity of Dyer's Nursery, the winding
Pocasset, and the very quaint and old-
fashioned homestead of the Dyer family,
midway between the Print Works and
Dyer's Nursery; let us journey thither.
Ask any one to direct you to the old
Dyer Homestead; it is but a few minutes
walk, and it is a little old-fashioned house,
standing so red and so low at the foot of
a giant elm that it reminds one of the red
toadstools that nestle beneath the trees of
the forest.

GNARLED PEAR TREE.

But to make assurance double sure,
look for a grotesquely gnarled and distorted pear tree, and finding it be sure it
is the old Dyer homestead you are contemplating. In the great 1815 gale the
pear tree was a lithe young sapling,
wrung and twisted so thoroughly by the

fierce whirlwind that it found it easier to continue growing after that eccentric pattern than to untwist itself and stand upright. So there it stands, capped with a sparse unfruitful crown of leafage, a melancholy warning to giddy youth disposed to scoff at the ancient adage of "as the twig is bent the tree is inclined."

Across the road long years ago stood once an even more eccentric old pear tree, which preferred the horizontal to the perpendicular process; but that is long since dust and ashes, mostly the latter.

Charles Dyer, the builder and his capable workmen wrought with their own hands all the framework, the finishing and the furnishing of this interesting little cottage. Look at the latches on the doors, rough-hewn things of iron; they, too, were home made. And when, not many years ago, some repairs were necessary, the workmen complained of the difficulty they found in drawing out the old nails, they found they were the original old rough iron nails of home manufacture at which they were tugging. Step into what was

OLD DYRE HOMESTEAD.

Draw near to the brown front door, and above the four green bottle-glass tiles, considered highly ornamental in their day, read, faintly showing still beneath modern paint, the ancient date: "1726." That is when the house was built by Charles Dyer, a worthy descendant of the ancient Dyers of Wales, and the youngest son of William and Mary Dyer, the historic Mary hanged on Boston Common. Seven generations have been born within this timeworn but still staunch little red house, have grown up, married and died, and been laid away in the quiet little graveyard over on the peaceful hillside.

in days of yore the "best room," perverted, alas! to the prosaic use of a potato bin—see if it was not a sumptuous apartment in its day, with its solid wall of panelled red cedar, polished and glittering once; and the space from door and window frame to ceiling a solid panel likewise. Veritable eighteenth century windows are they all, tall and narrow, and with eight panes of glass where two would now be placed.

Fireplaces—hardly a room in the cosy little house but has its own; wide and cavernous, though the country-folk are said to have shaken heads ominously in he days of their bu'lding, and prophesied hat they "couldn't draw" on account of heir and the chimney's small size—foureet aperture. The chimney was another wonder, too, in those days, being a reckless extravagance in the way of imported brick; all the chimneys round about had been of native stone.

Out of the parlor opened the "best bedroom," a small square room finished in red cedar, but now ruthlessly painted over an æsthetic green by vandal tenants, who evidently didn't relish the labor of polishing the natural wood. Curious little cupboards open everywhere about the turns and corners of the old chimney; look at the heavy kitchen door. A solid and enduring framework still, but so "punky," as the boys say, that one would think a stone slung vigorously at it might go right through.

The house is no longer inhabited, except by farm hands belonging to the great white-pillared house hard by, the heart of the farm nowadays. The little red cottage makes an admirable storage place for the miscellaneous junk that collects about a farm, and among it is a great umbering chair as big as a sleigh, said to have been brought over from England by some remote ancestor. But it certainly didn't come in the Mayflower; in that much-crowded vessel it would have swamped them all.

In this quaint and cosy little homestead Charles Dyre, having finished his labors, abode in peace and satisfaction, reared his family, and finally his son John inaugurated his wedding day. It was on his auspicious morning, one hundred and forty years ago, that he planted the elm, now towering proudly aloft, and bidding fair to stand for as many years more. As was the custom in those ancient days, John and his blushing bride and a goodly company beside, set out from beside this old front door for their wedding journey, which was to be an all day's trip on horseback. At home, good Mistress Dyre—for the name was thus spelled till the present century came in—Mistress Dyre and her coadjutors bustled about to have the wedding supper in readiness on their return. It was a bounteous repast; and though family history has not chronicled the menu in its entirety, it is recorded that the chief dish at the banquet was an immense pewter platter heaped high with rye doughnuts.

When the first Charles Dyer took possession of this goodly land, the Pocasset river, that now in its windings makes almost an island of the picturesque peninsula, was but a trickling thread of water in the valley, over which one carelessly stepped in a short cut to the city, and primeval savages dwelt in wigwams hard by. Resenting the invasion of the pale faces, most of them betook themselves to the remnant of their tribes down in the Narragansett county, but one young girl, becoming attached to the Dyers, remained, dwelling in her wigwam and performing a part of their household labors. Among the Dyers departed, in the graveyard on the hillside, her gravestone stands, gray with moss that has been accumulating since the last century. Larch trees wave their lacy boughs, and drop their graceful brown cones all about the mossy ground, and the blue stars of myrtle bloom cover all the mounds in spring time. Down beyond it is the spreading marsh, sometimes a goodly lake, and again a green and fern-bordered marsh alone, picturesque, but malarial, according to the needs of the Print Works, far below.

It was over across the fair and undulating meadow that Amasa Sprague was shot down with a bullet from a hidden ambush. The last Dyer who dwelt in the little red house, standing by the old mossy well, heard the fatal shot fired, but did not so much as glance that way, supposing it to have been sent by one of the frequent gunners, and it was only hours later, when the news of the murder spread abroad, that he recognized its fatal import.

Between the well and the old kitchen door are traces yet of the original flagging that made a pavement like a floor.

It is a remarkably peaceful and lovely spot, even now, about the quaint, little old-time homestead. Hardly a home so near the city seems to be so in the heart of the real country, and, stretching its high and dark green ramparts all along from south to north, lies the distant hill of Neutaconkanut. Dyer's Nursery, hard by, lovely as it is, is too well known a spot to call for description here; and, if one wants still more of a jaunt for his outing, he may discard the city-bound car from the Print Works, turn homeward in the other direction, past the nursery along the lovely river road, lined with beech and other forest trees, cross the bridge over the leisurely Pocasset, and journey to the horse car barn over Arlington Heights, with its few fine dwellings, its magnificent avenue, lined with trees that the desecrating hands of "curbing committees" are soon to lay bare, to everybody's indignation, and the finest view of Neutaconkanut to be had from any vantage ground.

Over beyond East Providence lies another haunt of artists, picnickers and lovers of nature generally—Hunt's Mills. One reaches it by way of an omnibus starting from the Arcade, with a short walk still further eastward after alighting at the terminus. In the middle of a flat, barren and generally unattractive land, one comes upon the romantic little nook with double surprise; down through a rocky glen, a wild, wide and babbling brook rushes under green forest trees, with a foamy tinkling fall and a rush over countless rapids. Hard by rise the gray and picturesque ruins of an old mill that gives the place its name. It is but the merest little corner, but its every view is a picture, and the wild little spot has always its devotees. It is an idyllic nook in which to spend a summer day.

RUIN OF HUNT'S MILL.

A huge pine grove lies not far beyond, down the same road, and its sombre and murmuring green depths make a cool and secluded resting place. Once upon a time trailing arbutus grew here, and does now in a faint-hearted and despondent fashion, but too sparingly to warrant a jaunt therefor.

To east, west, north and south, Providence has its inviting outskirts, but those briefly sketched here are among the best known, most accessible and attractive.

Perhaps the pretty village of Oak Lawn

s not to be considered a suburb of Providence, but as it is but three miles beyond the city's terminus, and its business life is wholly within the city, a description of it here, with its famous May Breakfast, may not be out of place.

First of all, bear in mind it is Oak Lawn, with a respectful double capital. Nothing so fills the soul of the patriotic resident with a sense of injury and insult as to receive his letters addressed to 'Oaklawn,' with a little "l." On old maps there will not be found any Oak Lawn, but from years remote there has been a Searle's Corner. The new name came in in 1875, with the post office, established in a corner of the neat little station, whose floors and stove and lamp and lamp chimneys are the pride of the road for glistening neatness. The descendants of the original Richard Searle, who occupied the oldest farm, and gave the place name (though it was Sarle in those days), yet constitute the chief population; and it is a puzzle with which the new comer ineffectually grapples, to straighten the tangles of the complicated relationships of the resident Searles, which the old folks so glibly recite.

The old home of the village's founder on the huge farm now largely divided into house lots, still attracts admiring notice as the fairest old homestead of the place. On the road leading west from the railroad and now known as the Turner farm, its giant elms are a landmark for a long distance, on the lawn stretching down from the old yellow farmhouse, draped with climbing wisteria and trumpet vine. It was some 250 years ago that occupancy was definitely chronicled here, and the oldest elms date back to the same time. On the hillside of the four oaks, which alone justify the name of the village, is a cluster of graves marked by rough stone slabs, whither one by one were borne the bodies of ancient servitors from the old farm house, when negro slavery flourished in Rhode Island. It is along this hillside and from the oak summit that strangers are eagerly led by the beauty loving residents, for a view of wild rolling hillocks, distant wooded hilltops, and the meandering course of the leisurely Moshanticut, a typical brook of delight to the summer boarders and strollers of leisure, as it ripples in picturesque bends and broadenings down from Ralph's pond, in the heart of the dark and silent cedar swamps. Moshanticut was the ancient name of the sheltered brook valley, and aside from records and traditions, there are constant evidences of the old Indian occupancy in the arrow heads and other implements found on the old farms, and the symmetrical oval mound rising from the western bank, said to have been modelled by the encamping tribes.

As near the city as this dreamy little village lies—but three miles from Cranston Print Works—there is many a Providence resident who can only reply in an uncertain way if you mention its name, "Oak Lawn, Oak Lawn—that's where they have the May breakfast, isn't it?" Though this annual festivity is by no means its only celebrity, it is what has made Oak Lawn's name familiar through all the country side. A feast growing in popularity and success since its founding in 1868, it was in '92 a special occasion, for it celebrated its 25th anniversary and commemorated the season by a souvenir booklet, prepared wholly by residents, with a history of the Breakfast, the town and the old Quaker church, one of the oldest in the country, where the festive meal has been spread since its founding. A lady greatly interested in the local town history, who has for years been gathering up the bits of curious old-time fact and story, prepared for the little booklet an admirable article, which fills even the oldest inhabitants with a new sense of respect for their ancient abode.

From 6:30 in the morning till noon the event of the year keeps everybody flying. Scarcely a villager who has had no share in the preparation or contribution of viands, and the first installment of hungry banqueters is apt to be a flock of the farmers' children, eager to spend with rejoicing the pennies hoarded for weeks for the occasion, and invariably ordering, as the preliminary article on a lengthy menu, ice cream! Mrs. Roby

ON THE MOSHANTICUT.

Wilbur, the founder and chief executor of the original repast, was a renowned concocter of the May day biscuit, and those of her coadjutors who still live and assist yet at the banquet, affirm that one May day she exhausted a barrel and a bag of flour in their preparation for the hungry multitude. The day is the great reunion for kinsfolk and acquaintance, however widely scattered. All other vocations are for the day suspended, and Oak Lawn keeps open house to all returning children.

Until a year ago the breakfast was

held in the somewhat cramped quarters of the original Quaker meeting house, but a recent addition gives double room. The old people recall the days when team after team came over the quiet roads on Sunday mornings, bearing Friends to services in the old house now disused and set back of the new and neat little Baptist Church. The date of the old meeting house's founding was 1729; there are but three older in the country. The old-fashioned and lovable faith of the Friends had formerly many adherents here, but they have removed, died, or adopted new religions and the Earles are now the only family in the neighborhood. The old Quaker burying ground shows its mossy slabs close by the gray church.

Beside the old meeting house, Oak Lawn has many relics of former days and uses; there is the famous old Ore Bed, opposite the Comley farm, its shaft now abandoned and closed, but early in the 1700's a flourishing place, and furnishing metal for one of the cannon that helped to make Perry a victor on Lake Erie. There is the ruin, not far distant, of the queer little house that old Chloe Cesar, a solitary negro herb woman, erected with her own hands, and fought successfully against its downfall, decrepit old woman as she then was, in the great 1815 gale. There is the Potter estate, with the many stories of the three eccentric old maid sisters, by whose abode the timorous children fleetly sped, and whose horror of mankind was so extreme that one of them dragged herself home with a broken hip rather than accept masculine succor, and refused all subsequent surgical aid. There is the Gorton Arnold estate, on the road to Natick, known far and wide in former days as a hostelry, and destroyed by fire but a few years ago. There are the old homes of Olney Arnold, Dr. Hudson, Lodowick and Samuel Brayton, and other well-known men yet resident. Between this station and Knightsville is the pleasant home of John M. Dean, on whose estate a chimney stands solitary on the eastern rise, a landmark from carriage or car window. It belonged to an old, old house, once honored, it is said, by the brief presence of the father of his country.

Later, old residents recall its occupancy by the eccentric female members of an English family—the traditional " poor and proud." This praiseworthy household, it is said, used to draw their curtains and lie abed all day, rather than reveal the poverty of their wardrobe, or the slenderness of their household furnishings. They would not dig; to beg they were ashamed, and one by one they wisely departed this life.

There is the picturesque Furnace Brook, the best known of Oak Lawn's pleasant nooks to Providence artists and fishermen, with its leaping cascade and the crumbling walls of the old Furnace rising high and gray beside it. Another and prettier fall lies up the stream, with more ruins, and two little gems of ponds hidden among wooded hills. The lower mill and Furnace, beside the road, have had a varied career, and served in almost every capacity which a mill stream could further, but they are good for nothing any more, but to look picturesque and figure in photographs; and the loitering pedestrian is warned to "stand from under" in a high wind, for the gray and battered walls are leaning toward the road. Frederic Fuller and Stephen Olney were the earliest proprietors of the veteran building, figuring first of all as a braid mill.

Hospitable old homes of the resident farmers dot all the roadways, and the drive by the Rivulet farm is a pleasant one, along the base of the Congdon hill. The village proper is small, but a scant three dozen houses, occupied almost wholly, strangely enough now, by dwellers of old New England descent. The occupations of most are in the city, and night and morning they take the trip in and out. There is no local industry, and the loyal citizens hope there never will be, with its attendant ills. They have a store, a post office, a church and a school house and cater thus to all the real necessities of man's physical, mental and spiritual nature. Social restrictions are few, and the ladies wear sun-bonnets if they like, in morning calls. What would one more?

A scant half mile up the wooded road to the eastward from the little station stands the Oak Lawn School for Girls, silent in the green woods, approached from the road by a winding avenue, through whose oak and chestnut borders the sun glints down on myriad ranks of spreading ferns whose carpet runs through all the grove. In a little clearing behind the house is the adjoining garden, and on the lawn before it is the tennis court; otherwise the scene is strictly rural.

It is ten years that the school has occupied its present site, its inmates increasing sensibly in number since its removal from the old Tockwotton House and its co-existence with the boys' school. This is not probably because bad girls are more numerous, but by reason of the better care that can be given the girls in their new quarters, making it plainly the best home for a wayward girl. The same matron, Mrs R. S. Butterworth, has ruled here since the change, with three under teachers. The order of the week day is unvarying. 6 o'clock is the rising hour, 7 the breakfast, and the forenoon is filled with the home work, performed wholly by the girls and their supervisors, and divided into the kitchen, hall, laundry and sewing work. Every few months the work is differently divided, until the girls get a pretty thorough knowledge of all domestic labor, fitting them for the capable housemaids many of them in after years become. A tour through the sweet-smelling, tidy and absolutely spotless domains shows that heaven's first law of order at least is rigidly insisted upon. As if awaiting its christening, each room, pantry, store room, laundry and kitchen, shines in immaculate splendor, pitchers, pots and pans in glistening rank and file, and the dining room, in its cool gray and white with its half dozen tables, is decked out with truly military precision, the neat little handmaiden whose special charge and pride this room is, having ranged knife, fork and napkin beside each plate with severest rigor, and constructed a silver tulip of spoons in each holder. In the pantry, a baking of bread for a day alone runs the whole length of the ample shelf.

But quite the prettiest room in the whole house is the great sewing room. This is everybody's favorite nook, as sewing is the favorite employment, and it is the rendezvous for the festive season of the year, the Christmas holidays, when it is a huge bower of green, and amid songs and delight the Christmas tree is despoiled of the pathetic little gifts the children have wrought with much mystery for their teachers and friends. No cardboard and worsted will these advanced young misses brook, but request crochet patterns, outline and crazy work, and an abundance of material is furnished by the matron. After tea is the time of leisure for the children, for with the end of the morning's duties comes dinner, then the preparing for school, the afternoon session lasting until 5:30, and tea soon after. The trustworthy girls, in the care of a monitor, are allowed the range of the berry fields now and then in morning hours, and return with praiseworthy promptness within reasonable bounds. There are between 30 and 40 girls in the school at present, 44 having been the highest number, while in the old school the limit was 26. Of course the proportion of girls to boys is very small, 200 or so occupying the Sockanosset boys' school.

Though a girl is discharged from the school whenever it is thought expedient by the matron and Board, yet, as the State claims them as its property until 21, they are rarely returned to their parents, who are almost without exception wholly unfit for their charge; instead, they are placed in families where they often remain until they make in many cases respectable and happy marriages. Of course, there are now and then girls of whom all instructors despair, and whom no good influence seems to touch; but it is a pleasant thing to see the magic often wrought on these wild or ignorant natures by refined surroundings and sympathetic interest.

Proper behavior insures kind treatment, and though firm hands are necessarily at the reins, escapades are few, though opportunity is frequent. At 8 years girls are received into the school, and may remain until 21, though very rarely. How much the fact of a Reform School minority may affect their future is something that cannot well be judged; to narrow-minded and uncharitable natures the mere fact would doubtless serve as a brand to preclude a girl from their service, but the true woman who looks straight into the heart of life and puts forth a hand only to help will feel her sympathies even more warmly enlisted toward these homeless waifs of girlhood whom circumstances, rather than evil natures, have made what they are.

Step into the school room of an afternoon. The girls are only too glad to sing for a chance visitor. These girls have been well trained; their enunciation is singularly good in recitation as well, and they sing rounds capitally and with spirit. "Kittie," says the teacher, presently, "can you remember your last song?" And Kittie rises in her place, and with hands clasped before her lifts her pure girlish voice in tones whose sweetness brings tears to more than one pair of eyes. There is a pathos in it outside the song; in the singer herself, and the deep hush of her listeners, for Kittie is a prime favorite and has aspirations. She once confided to the writer, in a berryfield chat, her intention of some day writing a Book.

The girls have little intercourse with outsiders, this being a necessary precaution; home visitors they are allowed to see only in the presence of a teacher, and, of course, never visit home. There is an excellent library adjoining the school room, its list of authors of juvenile books being among the very best. This is indeed well, for their silent influence is often the strongest.

An especially gratifying feature of the building is the score of tiny little dainty single rooms, with the narrow oak bed, spotless white frilled sham, and toilet table and glass. The matron would prefer the system of open dormitories wholly done away with, as has been the odious uniform system since her advent. The girls dress simply, but neatly, in print and gingham gowns through the summer, in whose making they have largely had a hand, and there is nothing bizarre or with a stamp of an institution on either these or their woolen winter raiment. This fashion has much to do with preserving the self-respect of these young girls, who will need all the kindness an over-cold world has to show when they again go forth into its temptations.

WEST GREENWICH, COVENTRY, EXETER AND BEACH POND.

[To Beach Pond from Providence, Hartford Railroad to Greene, or Stonington Railroad to Hope Valley. Thence by carriage to pond.]

EVEN the brief railroad trip of an hour from Providence to Greene station, our nearest approach to Beach Pond, showed us violent contrasts between the crowding villages of the Pawtuxet Valley, where the huge mills of Natick, Pontiac, River Point and all the rest seem to make a solid rampart along the line—and the lessening civilization as we sped on into Coventry and paused at Washington, Coventry Centre and finally Greene, with its scant two dozen houses, and the green wilderness all about, and blue, low hills hemming in the township. To the southeast lie Week's Hill, Big Grass and Little Grass Pond, that are acres of flourishing cranberry bogs; to the north is Bowen's Hill, in which region was once won, in the administration of Jefferson, a medal awarded to one Madison, a native there, for the best cheese made in the United States; a distinction of which the Coventry folk are to this day justly proud. A mile or two to the northwest of the little farming village rises Carbuncle Hill, with the famous pond of similar name nestling at its foot. Carbuncle Pond has a remarkable history, whose truth it would not do to question in the presence of certain old folk of the region who are nearer its origin than the giddy skeptics of the rising generation. It has a fervid, tropical flavor quite foreign to Rhode Island, and was heard with interest. Before ever the invading white man coveted Coventry and introduced whiskey and civilization, the tribe of Indians whose wigwams graced the green sides of Carbuncle Hill, and whose canoes glided along the green banks of Carbuncle Pond—then named in a forgotten Indian tongue—the tribal treasure was a huge and glistening gem, which had been found set neatly in the head of an enormous serpent, slain after a long and exciting battle by Coventry's most valiant warriors. No electric light system was coveted at Carbuncle Hill, for the radiance of the gem was such that it lit up the greater part of the township, and local pride burned high in the bosoms of the dusky possessors. All was peace till the invading white men entered the land and heard of the wondrous carbuncle. All negotiations for its purchase were fruitless, for aside from its remarkable beauty and lustre it had a most obliging disposition, and was in the habit of informing the tribe by chameleon changes of color, when war or danger menaced. The white men resorted to force and arms; but, in the midst of the melee, when defeat for the red men was imminent, Sachem Strong Arm seized the radiant carbuncle and flung it far from him into the middle depths of Carbuncle Pond, and there it lies to this very hour, with its glory faintly shining up through the waves from its hidden resting place. We questioned concerning this phenomenon of Greene's one litterateur, who is a bit of scientist as well, and he said that it was undoubtedly a fact that in the centre of Carbuncle Pond was an unusual radiance and clearness of the water, making even the smallest pebbles down below clearly visible; but as the same appearance was to be found in less degree in one or two spots nearer shore, he was inclined to think it rose from the head springs that fed the lake, and its outlet to the Moosup. But this the ancient believers laugh to scorn. Away south of the track the distant blue rise over the West Greenwich line indicates Nooseneck Hill, a desolate and abandoned farm region, given over to solitude and the preying tooth of time.

Rice City lies beside Carbuncle Hill, and it is a fact not generally known that it is the oldest city in Rhode Island, for it had its established name and Post Office ninety years ago, though its charter seems to have been unluckily mislaid. The little Moosup that wanders through the section is thought to have taken its name from a veritable moose

years ago. For many years he tilled with success the not over fruitful acres of West Coventry, and there established the well-known old country tavern at the foot of Carbuncle Hill, on the old Hartford turnpike, a veritable "half way house," between Norwich and Providence. Countless are the stages and country wagons that have halted in their day before the old roomy, big-chimneyed house of entertainment, with hoary lilacs nestling thickly at its either end. The Col. John, Jr., who succeeded to the name of the old Revolutionary patriot (who commanded a Plainfield company at Bunker Hill, Flat Bush, and the guard over Maj. Andre,) was major of the 9th Regiment

NOOSENECK HILL.

valley, for by tradition and scant relics the Coventry naturalists think there is no question but in ancient days the moose fed here. A pretty bit of the Moosup river is just here at what is known as Spencer's Rocks; a high, foamy fall drops down on an abrupt descent of some fifteen feet to a huge flat rock nearly 100 feet long, and on its banks, now removed from the wear of water, is the famous Indian kettle, a round hollowed stone, scooped deeply out with perfect symmetry, and said to be the work of the ancient tribes; but some believe it to be the work of the falling water which in former days dropped directly upon it.

The family of Mr. McGregor are among the local celebrities here, the grandfather of the only survivor, John McGregor, having settled here from Scotland some 130

in the war of 1812, and held many important town offices. In the peaceful old country tavern he passed the few last idle years of his long and useful life, dying at the age of ninety-six. His two sons were, John and Jeremiah, and Dr. John McGregor will be easily recalled of Providence people, entering early on a career in which he excelled, and being called from place to place as his reputation grew, and leaving an extensive practice in Thompson, Conn., to follow in the steps of his ancestors and depart again to war in the Rebellion. His fortunes here were peculiarly exciting, and he, had the opportunity of comparing prison life in Libby, Charleston, Columbus, Libby again, and Salisbury. He was at length left ill and destitute by his captors in the wildernesses of the James river, but survived and eventually reached home. It was soon after this that he settled in Providence as a practitioner, and two years later he met his death by the peculiar accident that those familiar with his name will recall. On his way to visit a patient, his horse took fright, backing between a dummy engine and the street cars, the doctor was thrown out and his arm fearfully crushed, and the loss of blood attending its amputation at the hospital, caused his death. The surviving brother, Jeremiah, still remained at the old tavern homestead, farming in a small way, and contributing local history to several papers. He is vastly loyal to his native county and told us much of interest as we lingered at Greene, in the roadside cottage that he occupies, for the old tavern, alas! with its hundred interesting relics, is no more. Only last November, on an unlucky day, when all the able-bodied men of the neighborhood were attending a distant auction, a wandering spark fell on the high roof, between the two big chimneys, and in two hours nothing was left of the quaint old place but a smouldering heap of ruins. The lofty upper hall of the tavern had been full of interesting relics, the collection begun in the days of the eldest John. The very wall was papered with ancient documents and valuable autograph letters, Washington's, General Putnam's, Major Andre's, and others. Ancient crockery, silver, and the old style mahogany furniture, that were heirlooms of both Mr. and Mrs. McGregor, went up in smoke, and files of many old newspapers, from their first number, the Journal included. A large collection of minerals, too, was among the lost; few articles were rescued, but among them was the old Revolutionary sword that had passed unscathed through its third baptism of fire and smoke, and we fingered it reverentially. It was a hard thing, indeed, to begin life anew from this devastation; we listened sympathetically while sweet-faced Mrs. McGregor told us how, in her excitement, she bore out from the ruins her heavy old sewing machine, almost worthless, and left valuable papers and silver to perish. Queer things seem to happen in this neighborhood; it was from this very house, that not long ago, on an extremely dark night, two couples drove hurriedly away, hoping to reach home before rain fell. The first party, having started much the earlier, forgot some article, and returning for it, encountered the second vehicle driving swiftly in the opposite direction; the two horses, neither seeing nor hearing, struck their heads squarely together with terrific violence and dropped dead in their tracks. This would seem an almost incredible occurrence, if truthful Coventry were not prepared to vouch for it.

All this and more we heard as we wandered about Greene, feeling, in this strange country, a hundred miles away from home; but Beach Pond was our goal, and we sought and found a charioteer. Daniel Tillinghast, a native and patriarch of Coventry, the father of Lloyd and Mason Tillinghast, and the other Providence brothers, now that years have unfitted him for the active duties of farming, lingers at Greene's Station and conducts arriving strangers to the bourne where they would be. Our request for Beach Pond even, which was to involve 25 miles of driving, over all manner of roads, did not stagger this worthy old gentleman, and in fifteen minutes our prancing steed was before the door.

Leading southwest, our road lay between stony pastures and wood-bound valleys, toward and through Hopkins's Hollow, and first we passed a jewel of a pond, ruffled by the stiff breeze, and populated by one bit of a shanty close to its shore, like a miniature wigwam of Nokomis by the shores of Gitchee Gumee. It is the trout pond of the younger Tillinghasts, and the little shanty is their sometimes summer camp, and we thought it must be great fun. Hopkins's Hollow is situated, as its name would indicate, in a sheltered vale, between the low ranges of wooded hills. It is a scattered lot of little black houses, a store, a blacksmith's shop, and a grist mill by the small stream that meanders along like a child sent on an errand it is in no haste to fulfill. Just beyond it on a cross road are the old school house and the little graveyard, nore populous than the settlement, for he palmy days of Hopkins's Hollow seem iver, like those of the whole desolate region through which we were to pass.

Many were the little family burying grounds we saw in lonely fields, or even grown roundabout to woods, where even a vestige of what was once the old homestead was lacking. The way grew lonelier, the roads bumpier, as we journeyed, and ever and anon our charioteer cheerfully assured us it was nothing to what we would come to presently.

our own surprised little mare, Dolly. Our guide alighted, and in a tangle of whip lash and flying heels this fiend of a horse at length galloped away, and cavorted up a green lane that led before us to a tumble-down cottage among hoary apple trees. Here, too, we passed a family of the tiniest, pinkest little piglets, in a wayside pen, we have ever beheld. They were far from haunts of men, and only a question as to whether we could keep them contentedly seated in our laps during an all day's drive de-

A WEST GREENWICH ROAD.

No travellers met us in these grassy and pine-perfumed ways, nor, what was more lucky, in the occasional cross cuts our guide made through newly hewn woods, where there was no possible passing, as the hills grew higher and the hollows hollower. Only once was our way contended, by an astonished horse, who was doubtless accustomed to feel himself monarch of all he surveyed, as he browsed along the highway. Squarely in the roadway he planted himself before us and refused to budge; a menace of the whip set his ears lying flat and his eyes showing white, and he flourished his heels uncomfortably near the gentle brown eyes of

terred us from bearing one each away then and there. Dahlias bloomed everywhere, in every dooryard; they were redeeming bits of splendor in a forsaken land.

We passed "Old Warwick Corner," a spot bounded by the four townships of Sterling, Coventry, West Greenwich and Voluntown, and, passing a stone post with an R on one side and a C on the other, found ourselves over the border and in Connecticut, hard by Bailey pond, which, like Beach, is a boundary lake. It lay far down below at our right, winding about the low hills, so that we saw and lost it again, and the slender maples that leaned over to its mirroring waters, were flaming with red and gold, against the sombre green behind it. The nearer waters bristled with the harsh reeds of the water grass. Opposite lay a long, rich green meadow, a sight to feast one's eyes after the acres of sterile, rocky soil; it is known as Bailey's flats, and was pointed out to us with much approval.

Presently we entered the "Bitgood neighborhood," erroneously suggestive of civilization, albeit scant; but the neighborhood was as destitute of dwellings as the outer wilds. But one farmhouse on an eminence came to view, with a cider press in full blast, whereat we paused and drank our fill, while the one surviving Bitgood exchanged the neighborhood courtesies with Mr. Tillinghast, and lamented, as a hard way to get a living, his necessity for cutting and carting a load of wood for the small sum of $2.75 to Voluntown, three miles distant. Oneco, on the railroad, would pay more, but Oneco was eight miles away. Meanwhile the mistress of the Bitgood homestead at the open door stood smiling hospitably, enjoying a rare glimpse of passing sisterhood. This was the only Bitgood family that comprised the neighborhood, though in their father's day there were four or five, now dead and gone.

Six miles of Connecticut we traversed before we came to the long, steep hill road which any mountain might have owned with pride, leading down to the valley where wild Beach Pond lies slumbering. The wide east end of the pond is in Rhode Island and the long narrowing tail of its two-mile length is in Connecticut, where its waters pour out and form the Pachaug river—a name that a frog must have originated in some frenzied leap. At the foot of the lake where the slender stream goes, rushing out between its stony borders, stands a little cottage, where tables were spread in profusion under a canopy of dry oak boughs. Here two gentlemen leisurely reclined and ate apples as we halted at what we learned was Avery Stanton's place. The tables had had their day two weeks before at a grange picnic of 300 from Hope Valley, our two informants said. Our guide knew them, hailed them familiarly, and introduced them in the Coventry vernacular as John Tahnner and John Stahnton, and the former owned a peripatetic steam saw mill, at present located on Beach Pond shores. Mr. Tillinghast had known these two possessors of the land ever since they were born, he declared, and was proceeding to favor us with a lengthy biography of each—the two meanwhile continuing to pare apples with unabashed serenity—when we reminded him that time was flying, and we journeyed on. At the very tail of the pond is a saw mill, and opposite are two or three little old houses together, a crowded "neighborhood." One is the Douglas place, where a Bassett formerly lived, and here is where most of the visiting fishermen hire their boats, as they come from far and wide for the bass, pickerel and other fish for which Beach Pond is famed. A dark-eyed young lad with a frank and manly face, who was tending the saw mill came and conversed with us. Boats were also to be had of Lewis & Briggs, he said; as a rule fishermen stayed only one day. Where did they come from? Oh, everywhere; Connecticut rather than Rhode Island—Norwich, Moosup, Voluntown. Now and then they came from Providence—a party of campers had been staying up to Phillips. Yes, he thought fishing had been up to the usual mark this year, though the pond being low had made a difference. The other end of the pond was the place, and our road would take us all along the southern shore, and with thanks we sped on, noting as we passed the remaining cottage a sign in its small window of "Yankey" notions. For a mile we lost the pond and drove through the woods, and we passed the houses of the Lewis Bros., where wagons are mended and carpets woven, and there we spied, high on a rocky pasture, that slanted to the water, a little black, windowless, forsaken house, with huge stone chimney. We got out to peep in at a probable fire-place, and as we flattened our faces against one of the remaining panes, we beheld a bed, a pair of shoes and a hat, and beat a horrified retreat, falling over the owner, placidly chewing tobacco on the front door steps.

s oxen were stabled in the cellar; he
d another farm hand boarded themselves
the old house. So he told us with a
gthened drawl, as he chewed and spat.
 was the first wholly unbeauteous
uth we had seen in Connecticut, we
ised as we returned to our waiting car-
ge. By and by the woods parted, and
ld Beach Pond in all its placid width
 before us, rippling now on Rhode
and shores. The reason for its name
is plain. All around its eastern curve,
tween woods and water, lay a wide
ite shore of sand, fine and pebbleless,
certainly, and we had taken it for a slip
of the pen, but here it was stretching
across the water to right and left, a made
road, with a bridge for ebb and flow as
the pond rose. What a queer ride it was!
The pond is low, as we had heard, and
east of the road is a submerged stump
forest. In its state of drought this section was laid bare, and was like a scene
of the Dante's Inferno, this weird and
melancholy multitude of soggy black
stumps and network of snaky roots, with
great patches here and there of matted
watergrass as scant clothing, in faded

OLD MILL, EXETER.

 water crystal clear, as we looked
wn into it. Races used to be run here
 olden times. South and west the wood-
hills rise, east and north the wooded
rels, and not a habitation is in sight
 one looks south to where a wooded
int juts sharply down and terminates
 a great overhanging ledge, under which
e may almost row his boat.
And now a puzzling feature of the new
ological map of the township was made
in, the map we had consulted at every
rn of the road thus far, and not found
nting. On the map the road home lay
ross the pond. This looked puzzling,
yellows and sunburnt russet. Dark, still
pools lay here and there close to the
road, and the lapping waves the other side
of the road leaped and coaxed them out
in vain. Off to the left was the sunny
green of the untouched forest, and the
vivid colors of the frost-smitten maples
and tender shrubs, reflected in a waving
band of brightness in the sparkling water.
It was a most effective contrast. On
this water road we encountered our second team; the first had been a tin ped-
dler's cart, with the most ebony of
drivers, straying somewhere in the Connecticut wilds; this was a load of hay,

with two pairs of oxen harnessed thereto, and all four lying comfortably prostrate on the hard highway awaiting the movements of their driver, standing absorbed with rod over the silent pools, hard at it fishing. There he was likely to stand till the sun set, as the oxen well knew, wisely reclining. No, he hadn't got nothin' to-day, he shouted, though he got a pretty likely one yesterday—five and a half—and labst week one 't weighed eight afore 'twas dressed. Pond looked so 'twas fished pretty hard, but he was tryin' to git that twenty-five-pounder that got away from Cummings. And still trying vainly, we left him. The rough road leading east through Exeter up to West Greenwich is known as the "Ten-rod road," though ten feet come nearer its present clearing. It passes a grove where from time immemorial the neighboring populace have been wont to celebrate what is always called the "Last Saturday in June," by repairing to the pond, ostensibly for rifle sand, but long years agone simply for an annual good time and picnic. The custom and the patrons degenerated, and it became the yearly rendezvous for all the roughs roundabout, who lay about and drank the livelong day, and raced horses for rum. But for two or three years back this annual glorification has happily languished, and the campers and the fishermen celebrate more decorously.

Further on is the neat little homestead of Barber Wilcox, with a front yard all ablaze with the omnipresent dahlias. The wife of Barber Wilcox takes summer boarders, and we longed to tarry; it was a charming summer home in the wilderness. We did alight, in fact, with the assurance of a cup of tea, but found no one at home but a lame man and a collie dog of exuberant spirits. We were hospitably bidden to enter, but declined, and as Mr. Tillinghast regretfully aided us again within the carriage he remarked that she was a plaguey smart woman—wished she'd been there. Unsolaced by tea, we journeyed on through Exeter and up to West Greenwich, lunching leisurely. In Exeter we remember nothing of note but a wide and dreary cranberry bog, In its midst an aged man and an aged woman she with a red cloak and a peaked hat, witch-like with her white locks, who stolidly picked and stared. Presently we passed their tumble-down hovel, with the ruins of a great outside stone chimney.

The long rough h'll we now climbed in West Greenwich was spoken of as "'East Cake," or so it sounded to our untutored ears, but reference to the map showed it Escoheag. Up the hill Easkig then, to speak as do the natives, we climbed and climbed, and off to the right a distant blue hill journeyed beside us, across the forests of the valley. Pine Plains, our guide called it, and Raccoon Hill and Bald Hill and Vaughn Hill were all in view. Escoheag has a long, long summit. On it is the oldest house in the region, the John Hazard house, square and gray and huge and forsaken. We passed in at its portals, under the falling piazza, and roamed about its big rooms and climbed to its empty garret. Here the wind whistled shrill and wild'y, and a new hilltop came to view, rising off to the left among the unbroken forest. Penny Hill, our guide said, when we returned. On the hillside were the ruins of what was pronounced the "Abel Rathbone mansion," looking anything but a mansion now, in its tumbled black heap. Hazard Grove is a noted spot on Escoh ag's summit; a land mark for many, many miles, and a magnificent grove. Escoheag's Post Office is here, too, and the valley dwellers must be anxious for mail who would climb here after it. As to getting down, we had our choice of going by "an awful hill, or another one not quite so bad." We chose the awful hill, and—we got it; but like all things else, it had an end. A grist mill lay in the village, also the birthplace of the resolute Beach Pond fisherman, and the lawless little Liberty Brook we crossed and re crossed. Liberty Farm we passed, the thriving home of an eccentric man, whose tomb, cheerfully painted red, looms up in a pleasant meadow hard by and contains two neatly made coffins, one for himself, one for his wife, but neither as yet occupied. In this region, too, lives a man who believes witches—perhaps he, too, has met the d lady of the cranberry bog—and makes figies in his yard and shoots and burns em, in the pleasing conviction that he destroying a witch with each. Here, o, lived the far-famed Elder Slocum, ng since gathered to his fathers, who id a congregation of thousands assembled to hear his funeral sermon, preached, s is not usually the case, by the eccenic elder himself, from his housetop, ith all the fitting accompaniments. It as not till he descended and set fire to is haystacks and burnt up most of the nounce that the inmates were now away at this place or that, and small wonder. Only one who is in love with nature and finds happiness and company in the great out-door world of small things could have the true home feeling of contentment on these isolated old farms. On this wild West Greenwich road we saw but one cottage modern and tasteful, a bit of a thing, likewise closed and silent—a Boston man had built it for a summer home, but his wife couldn't endure the solitude and now he had shut it up and gone and could neither sell nor rent it.

OLD CHURCHYARD, EXETER.

irm's outbuildings that he was universally pronounced insane.

In this wild and desolate land of hills nd valleys, far from social interests and any human ties, it is a wonder that the w discontented lingerers are not all inne. "Dead and gone" was the melanholy summary of the histories of the unders of all the abandoned, decaying ld homesteads we passed. Often we assed furnished homesteads, but with urtains down and a general look of absence, and Mr. Tillinghast, giving us ames and brief biographies, would an-

An old-fashioned square school house stands on this road; through the windows we saw a dozen or so bobbing heads, and there entered at the door, after a frank stare at us, a rusty, shabby elderly man in a long, loose coat, a saw in one hand, an axe in the other, whom our guide indicated as the schoolmaster. It was like an illustration of an old-time story.

Our way homeward led through the fertile acres of the old Tillinghast homestead, with its especially pretty cottages and well-kept farm, and brought us at length out once more at its confluence at

Hopkins's Hollow, and so back to Greene, before either night or the threatening rain fell, and in an hour we were in Providence. It had been a trip unique in our Rhode Island experiences, and its most vivid memories are now of hosts of glittering dahlias, multitudes of forsaken farms, the odor of the "fever wood," or spice wood, that filled the forest, and a poignant regret that we could have brought home with us neither a pine nor a pig.

But Coventry had a hold on our affections that would not let go; when vacation time drew near it beckoned more strongly. Could we not pitch our autumn tent there in the wilderness? At the thought a brighter idea came to us, and we cried in unison, "Let us camp out in an abandoned farm house!" Cheerfully, then, we undertook the quest, not a difficult one, for old farms and new, little ones and big, lay up this road and down that. But the ideal campground presented itself presently.

It lay, approached by a winding cart-path through the woods, a scant mile from the station—what station it matters not. As vague boundary lines, the ghost-haunted pine woods lay somewhere to the east of us; the wind-swept hills of

IN CRANBERRY TIME.

Foster, dotted with gray farms and grayer and more populous graveyards, somewhere to the north; the rippling and winding Buckshorn somewhere to the west, and the Big Grass and Little Grass Ponds— the quaking cranberry bogs with the hundreds of white rabbits tenanting their laurel jungle—somewhere to the south. The house itself—a collection of rambling ells and adjuncts to a primitive gambrel cottage—rose above its ascending orchards on a slight eminence, all the rolling, breeze-sweet, wild country before and below it, and a silent pine grove behind, dropping to a moist and echoing glen, where a spring, roofed and sheltered, made a haunt for the wild birds and a fountain for all the fearless furry folk of the silent forest. Among the feathery young pines and the moss carpet glistening with checkerberries, grew rank and tall and rich with fruit, the swamp huckleberry and the purple blue globes of the dangleberry, abundant still, though summer had passed. We entered into our brief kingdom by way of a winding cartroad through the forest, enthroned on a mattress and a couple of trunks, while two very small dogs, each tightly holding a very large bone presented them by a dog lover at the little station, sat beside and completed the startling picture that drew the good folk of the quiet village hastily to front windows to see us rattle by and disappear in the forest. A mile of delight was our jolting progress between huge balsamic pines and by brook beds glowing like crimson ribbons with clustered ranks of the Indian cardinal, and out from the woods over a stony rise the road issued, the big, gray barnyard gate swung hospitably open, and we entered with all the joy of explorers on our wide domains.

Two attics, two kitchens and two cellars this generous house boasted; and in the farthest and most remote kitchen lodged a wood-chopper for the season; a quiet and inoffensive solitary man, who never said that the enjoyment of his pensive evening pipe was lessened by sounds of hilarity about the hitherto echoing premises. Most abandoned farms are deserted once for all, with no precaution against fire or marauders, but ours had been so recently remodelled and renovated, its outbuildings were all so staunch and serviceable, that its owner had still hope of its sale at a good price, and guarded accordingly against disaster. A pump stood just outside the kitchen door and an old-fashioned well with time-worn sweep lay, according to the good old custom, a Sabbath day's journey distant down the slopng meadow by the railroad track; for he great farm of three hundred acres had een split by the single track railroad ome forty years before, and the wealth f the former owner had come through his means. So inoffensive and infrequent vere the modest trains that sped through ur farm that we bore no grudge against heir transit, but hailed their passing as he only exciting episodes of the day, s they sped by below us along the brook lats, and disappeared in the forest.

It was not long before our landlord, garrulous, hospitable and jovial, visited us and proceeded to seek out any hidden wants or discomforts, after the kindly fashion of the dwellers in that land, whose like we have never seen paralleled. He believed there was an air-tight up in the attic—he would get it down and bring some pipe from home next time he came; we might find it handy if the evenings came chill. A broom, too— we couldn't sweep with that old stub; he would and did bring a broom. Men were digging potatoes in the sloping field under the apple trees down across the track; we were to go down there and help ourselves. He would fix up the door knobs and send a man to mow the grass—the weeds were hard to get around in. All these improvements were promptly and cheerfully made; then, before nightfall even, began visits from unknown "friends in the woods."

They came with offering of fruit and vegetables, of pies and puddings even. They greeted us like long-lost brethren. On Sunday we entertained largely and the old place grew festive while we listened to old-time tales from our pleased and smiling neighbors—about the ghost with shining eyes the size of base balls, the legend of the Buckshorn, the snake's head jewel in Carbuncle pond, the rabbit hunting in the brown November days, and the marvellous sums made in pursuit of the coy partridge. We heard about startling events that had taken place "up t' the Greene" and "daown t' the Anthony," and were invited to rise at 4 o'clock and ride 20 miles to the shore with our joyfully expectant next-door neighbors—accessible by a narrow and fragrant footpath through the forest. Here we went with ever new pleasure at milking time for our daily supply. It was an old, old house, of uniform gray tint, huge square chimney, and dying orchards all about it. Everything spoke of decay, desolation and ruin, but its inhabitants. They were lively to the last degree and cheerful with the cheer that

ABANDONED HOMESTEAD ON NOOSENECK HILL.

only an unaspiring life can bestow amid such solitude.

Our landlord had expressed his belief that we could have our milk brought daily to our door if we wished, by the hands of a "little devil that shot his grandmother." Naturally distrusting this satanic medium, we elected to be our own bearers, and found the resident imp possessed of many redeeming qualities, the shooting to have been purely accidental, and the depraved scion to have numbered at that time only five summers. A rather lovable little imp we found him, hovering perpetually about us in our wanderings about their old, old house, with unremitting offerings of strawberry tomatoes. Seldom did the milk return home. Beans, tomatoes and hot biscuit often accompanied, and our camping out was unprecedentedly luxurious.

Our woodchopper, who was a French Canadian, and who had travelled much throughout the State, told us that he had never, anywhere, seen anything approaching the good will and friendliness that was the ruling spirit of the township. If a man was sick, the neighbors all flocked in and did his harvesting for him, and the women flocked in with medicine and savory dishes.

A prettier testimony came to our ears as we made a neighborhood call on an old lady with whom one of our party had a slight previous acquaintance. All by herself in a tiny white cottage, pine-sheltered and with a garden radiant with flowers, she lived, and we had not been seated many minutes when she brought proudly in from the "best room" a piece of her handiwork, covering years in its execution. It was an ottoman, covered in cloth, its sides gay with clustered flowers appliqued neatly on. The chef-d'oeuvre was its top, a landscape scene, and one could recognize without much difficulty that its model was the little white cottage itself, with the two pines and as much of the detail as was possible. As additional ornament, a huge cornucopia, lavish of contents, was laid neatly on the sky above. We praised and admired the neatness and painstaking character of the work, to the maker's manifest gratification.

Presently she went on to tell us more of her past life and history. For eight years before her husband's death he had been unable to work, and they had been very reduced in means. With an invalid's despondency, the husband had doubted and dreaded from day to day, for there was no food, no fuel, and the winters were long and cold. But the neighbors had come in from right and left; they had drawn wood, sawed and split it, and furnished supplies, all with the cheerful delight in giving that marks this Arcadian corner. The lonely old people had never been suffered to go to their rest cold or hungry. "And so I told my husband," concluded our old lady, "for I finished the top before he died. 'I'm going to put this horn o' plenty right on top,' says I, 'to remind me how there's always one seemed to hang right over this little cottage.'"

Could there be a more pathetic tribute to the neighborhood spirit of good will? We said our good-bys and looked our last on the little ottoman with a far less critical eye, for sentiment filled all the space that art left vacant.

There was the Greene campmeeting, too, now in progress two miles away, to attend, and the great "Line Picnic" up in Foster, whither most of Coventry's inhabitants, in jovial wagon loads, drove at an early hour, to dissipate mildly and meet all their kinsfolk and acquaintance; and there was the daily excitement of going down the track to the post office and getting mail.

But, though diversion offered on every hand, and friends dropped in from home, we agreed that just the quartet of us alone in this almost primeval solitude, was best of all. How many pictures still flit before our eyes as pleasant memories! The cool and silent sunrisings, the air just tinged with the first frostiness; the camp fire out under the apple trees, with the sizzling salt pork and the aroma of coffee; the crack of the gun in a cedar swamp, and the morsel of a yellow and white spaniel trotting delightedly to its master, with just one twinkling fan of joy over the plump partridge in its careful little mouth; the rising of the round silver moon over the eastern pine forests, with the whispers always in their branches, while the yellow glow paled in the west, and the katydids called on every side as we sat around the flickering camp fire; the sweet hay couches, with bright moonlight making twinkling bands of glory through the old barn's crevices, the infinitesimal crackling and rustling everywhere around, and the measured piping chorus of crickets, broken by the tremolo quivering cry of a plump little owl flitting outside.

Sound slumbers came to us from this balsam-laden air, on our pillows stuffed with hay, hops and pine needles, and it seemed a strange and sad thing when we at last returned to civilized ways, to be obliged to dress after we had risen, or to feel constrained to quaff our morning cups f coffee elsewhere than on the kitchen oor. Sadly we bade good-by to all the indly country folk, even the small imp rith his queer trick of crying "Yonder!" o direct one's attention, leaving him apturous with a gift of hooks and lines o supplant his pins and strings when ext he captured "mommychaubs" at the istant shore. More sadly still we looked ur last on the trim little deserted farm ouse as our train sped by, receiving only emporary diversion from the sight of our next-door neighbor" as the train made short work of the distance between the dwellings, standing amid the sun-drying heaps of nether garments and old shoes, that betokened their recent sportings with old ocean, and brandishing with both arms, with all the energy of her energetic nature, a towel in a last farewell.

Golden days of cloudless weather are they that we look back on, in no wise belying the sunny prophecy of the four-leaved clover that peeped up at us at the very threshold of our September home when first we crossed it.

THE PAWTUXET RIVER.

[Electric cars to Pawtuxet, 5 cents.]

PROVIDENCE citizens are growing more and more appreciative of the attractions of an afternoon row on the Pawtuxet—a river easy of access, and of manifold charms.

The coy little stream flowing windingly across the State is as changeable in its varying moods and phases as the tiny maidchild, growing up through the angular, "awkward age" to blushing, conscious maidenhood and maturity. A dainty nursling in its infancy among the green hills of Scituate, it runs southeastward by the thickly-clustered factories of Hope and Harris and Phenix and the other mile-apart places with a perturbed and languid flow quite at variance with its sparkling infantile purity, fed by a dozen hill-born brooks. It is angular and sullen and unpicturesque. Its own mother would not know it. But taking heart again as it leaves the clustering villages behind, it turns boldly up to the northeast and hastens with joyous laughter to the green woods that beckon a loving welcome. Smiling and dimpling and growing ever more beautiful, with gay adorning of flowers and wreathing vines, it moves on—coyly and waywardly indeed, but still shyly advancing—to fling itself at last into the arms of the salt sea, stretched lovingly up to meet and embrace it.

It is along these last three or four miles that pleasure-seekers most do congregate, taking boat from Rhodes's or Gardiner's, near the car route. Each turn of the river reveals fresh surprises, and seems to frame a fairer picture than the last. Rowboats abound until the first and second rapids are passed—if one has the good fortune to pass them; but above them this river-way seems a primeval wilderness. Delicate birches make slender leaning pillars against the darker green, and the placid water by the shore mirrors the brown banks and bending ferns above, till one can hardly trace the faint water-line. Now level meadows stretch along the banks, and now one looks up, up through the green tangle of a wooded hill-side, till the eye meets only the blending blue sky above. It is pleasant to linger here through the late afternoon, to take picnic lunch on some high green bank, with the sweet, faint fragrance of wild-grape bloom in the air, and drift down the stream again with the glories of a summer sunset flooding the sky and waters, dipping an oar now and then to avoid a sharp turn

SCENE ON THE PAWTUXET.

or a spreading sand-bar—the work of the great freshet. And to one who visited the river in the time when the wild roaring flood spread far over these green meadows, the wonder is that the river ever found its own narrow channel again. These trees that stand high on the green banks were baptized with a rushing torrent, and the drift is lodged even yet among their branches. Tufts of grass

THE PAWTUXET RIVER.

and twigs waved forlornly all the summer from the topmost arch of the high bridge. Boxes and barrels and all manner of lighter drift were hurrying down past the submerged boat-houses, anchored to trees to prevent their being swept down-stream, as was a little house farther up the river. Unpleasant reminders lie all along the river to this day in the shape of pebbly shallows, over which a boat grinds harshly and unexpectedly.

RHODES'S ON THE PAWTUXET.

Two young men rowed up the Pawtuxet one day last summer and went ashore at a favorite point, joyfully bearing a lunch basket, and advancing with pleasurable anticipation toward a grassy nook in the distance. Suddenly, the foremost youth espied, gazing at him with an expression of deadly malice, an enormous dog. He turned about without a word and walked shoreward. His companion, cut short in a remonstrance by the same apparition, did likewise, and they re-embarked and rowed some distance up the stream before the silence was broken.

Then said the first young man nonchalantly, "That wasn't a very good place to lunch in, was it?"

"No," said the other. "It wasn't shady." And they rowed on.

Those learned in Pawtuxet lore know where to look for cold springs that bubble up on the starboard bank; for whether it be east, west, north or south, who shall say, unless he keep his eye turned constantly seaward; they know where to disembark and walk across the fields to the pumping station, where they may view the ponderous great giant with limbs of steel and iron, toiling by night and day for the thirsty folk of Providence; and they may ascend the narrow staircase that twines about the tall tower and view the landscape—if they have steady nerves and are not seized with a sudden fear of the tower's toppling instantly over.

There is one enthusiastic lover of the Pawtuxet who has seen its banks clothed in the sheen of early spring, in the green apparel of mid-summer, in the splendid array of autumnal coloring and in the white mantle of winter; and who, better still, has caught the spirit of its varying phases and reproduced them on canvas with a marvellous fidelity to nature. Mr. Barlow, the artist, has given us many lovely bits of Rhode Island landscape, but among them the Pawtuxet scenes stand foremost. Moshassuck Park in late autumn and in winter moonlight—the winding shore by the Stonington railroad bridge—the shallows of the turbulent rapids.

But no artist could paint the exciting struggles with sand-bar and current, the laborious passage up-stream, or the swift gliding rush downward, that make perpetual excitement about these rapids. Until the big freshet the rapids could be passed with comparative ease, but the sand deposits left by the freshet have made the feat a more difficult one, and not a few valiant rowers have submitted to the alternative of getting out and wading, with the unyielding boat in tow, or

UP STREAM.

remaining below to laugh at other aspiring boatloads.

One Decoration Day, a day when a rather unusual combination of circumstances made hard work for many rowers —and possibly for Messrs. Rhodes and Gardner also—one or two picnics were held at a distance up the river, and the row-boats of both above-mentioned parties were all hired for the day, as late comers learned to their sorrow.

The early morning's violent shower, with perhaps some other unexplained cause, had raised the river nearly a foot, and the picnic parties got above the rapids with little trouble. During the day the water subsided; and when the fleet of boats came down at night, one by one, they grounded on the very spots over which they had glided so merrily in the morning. Above and below, and in the rapids, they stuck fast; our own own boats off the shallows looked on in sceptical admiration. The young man pulled desperately, but made no headway, and his boat was bumped against by a half-dozen others which had freed themselves and were gliding down the rapids with a swift, silent speed. Everybody was talking and issuing orders at once; a little dog in a waiting boat barked wildly. The adventurous young man at last gave up, and swung rapidly down stream again. Across the river, aloof from the struggling throng, a youngster sat in a shell, anchoring himself by clutching the long water-grass on either

PETTACONSETT PUMPING STATION.

party, rowing up stream with a boat procured after two hours waiting, came upon the "Invincible Armada" struggling with wind and current, while the sun went down upon their wrath. It was an exciting scene. All the up-coming boats waited below, not caring for an encounter in the rapids.

"Stay where you are—I'll come up and get you off!" bawled a valiant youth alone in a skiff, to some grounded friends above; and he stripped off his coat and rowed bravely for the rapids, while all the parties not occupied in shoving their side, and sending a shrill and derisive laugh across the water at each new attempt to breast the rapids.

By the time the last boat had freed itself and glided down the babbling stream, the sun had set and the waters were darkening. We lingered on the shore to watch the day die in these green solitudes. A muskrat lifted a cautious head above the water and swam silently across, and a belated bird flew overhead with a sleepy twitter, dark against the crimson sky. The night wind began to stir the trees along the lonely shore, and a faint chorus of frogs rose from some distant swampy hollow. A bat wheeled and circled over the waters, and the mosquitoes, alas! had learned where we were lingering, and joyfully thronged about us. We re-embarked and dropped down stream again in the wake of the departed picnickers. Through the broad arch of the demolished bridge, and between the piers of the railway bridge which require more careful steering, we floated, and the lights of the boat houses twinkled around a distant bend. And making more haste, that we might catch the next city-bound car, we touched at the landing and delivered our boat over to the genial Mr. Rhodes, who received us as hospitably as if we had not been one of fifty similar parties.

Across the pretty pleasure grounds, where an odor of roast clams seemed still to linger, we strolled, and walked Pawtuxet-ward to meet our car.

Down in that quaint little village is a real, genuine egg-plant, such as Grandma Fisher adorned before the "Ark." Its fragile blossoms may not yet have withered. Did its owners originate the idea, or are they readers of "Cape Cod Folks?"

But here is our car, and a forty minutes ride therein brings us home with pleasant memories.

CUMBERLAND HILL AND SNEACH POND.

[Worcester Railroad to Manville, 12 miles north of Providence. Fare, 35 cents. Hotel carriage to Hill, one mile. Highland House, George A. Jenks.

PEOPLE are beginning to realize that Rhode Island in the summer months is something more than Narragansett Bay. Scattered through our northern townships are several wild and beautiful spots, where the lovers of hills and lakes and breezy forests annually take their outing, and one of the chief of these is Cumberland Hill.

Its high, clear air is alone a tonic, without its fair accessories. The highroad that runs from Providence to Worcester traverses here the highest table land in the State, though Diamond, Copper Mine and Beacon Pole Hills all present isolated crags still higher. When one remembers that the Worcester Railroad follows the beautiful winding Blackstone up a gradually ascending slope till the Hill's nearest station, Manville, is reached, he realizes that even the low river tunnel behind the hills, in which he alights, is itself considerably above sea level. And yet, on either side, the green hills lift their long, high outlines against the sky, on the left, the white highway leading over the Lincoln hill to Lime Rock, opposite Ashton and Berkeley; on the right, the way turning by a still steeper route to Cumberland Hill.

If one is going as a guest to the Highland House, or is expected by friends, he will no doubt be met at the station and be borne buoyantly up the long incline; but the unexpected stranger must walk, and perhaps it is well, for he will most forcibly realize thereby that it is a hill indeed he is ascending, up and up, past barring rock masses on either hand, on and on over a brief respite, and then up and still up again, till at the far end of the lessening ascent is described the landmark of the road's terminus at the Worcester highway, the Baptist Church, with its four-pronged belfry which balloonists would do well to avoid. Here stretch on either hand the long, hard road, the dwellings, ancient and modern, of old and new residents. There are no side roads to explore; Cumberland Hill stands for review in brave file along this one highway. All along the road, with its narrow beaten footpath, between the wayside grasses and ladies' tobacco bloom the wild flowers of up-country—the snapdragon, daisy and wild parsnip, the yarrow, whose root if one eats he will never more have the heartache, or so the Adirondack folk believe—and over the walls the jewel weed peeps, and the feathery cle-

HIGHLAND HOUSE.

matis tangles itself with wild grapes. Cumberland Hill residents have in the majority ranged themselves on the road's east side, and wisely; for they have before them the changing, varying lights and shadows of the far range of western hill, blue in the forest depths, golden on the parched bare slopes. Quails are whistling and calling happily from right and left, the crickets are trilling cheerily. They, too, have taken an outing at Cumberland Hill, it would seem, for southward their happy little voices are this season strangely silent.

Just at the corner, where an eastern road turns to Diamond Hill, stands the one house of entertainment, the Highland House, keeping open doors the year round, and quite as apt to shelter sleighing parties in winter as city boarders in summer. It is not a pretentious hotel by any means, but just a big, roomy dwelling house, with a long ell. It stands on a grassy lawn in the shade of noble elms, and both it and its next door neighbor belong to Mrs. C. A. B. Weeden, who occupies the second house. The Highland House has usually been managed by George A. Jenks of Pawtucket, but as that gentleman has charge of a hotel in the Bahamas until September, the hill hotel is managed by Mr. and Mrs. Cyrus Taft, whose own beautiful home is but a mile below here, standing lofty on an elevated lawn on the west side of the road. Mrs. Taft boasts the largest number of genuine antiques—china and furniture—of any one in the neighborhood. A descendant of the Providence Earles, the old North Main street homestead fell to her, and she says that from its capacious and well-stored attics she took enough substantial, old-time furnishings to stock this new home at the hill. It is a most enviable collection. Mrs. Weeden has also a multitude of odd chairs, stands, card tables, clocks and china, her own heirlooms, among them a Revolutionary chair owned by the late Mr. Weeden's grandfather.

Two miles above is the famous old Ballou meeting house, a plain, barn-like structure, so old that its exact date of building is not now known, though it is thought to be about 1700. It has a most curious pulpit, but no sounding board, as it has often been said to have—confused, no doubt, with another century-old church farther south, which was some time ago burnt down through the agency of small boys and matches. Cumberland Hill was until quite lately the centre of the township; all gatherings of importance were held here, all travelling entertainments from circuses to Punch and Judy shows, but now growing Woonsocket has usurped this honor, and nothing of the circus pauses here but the gorgeous representations of strange beasts and fairies of the ring, that fresco the walls of the gray little blacksmith shop among the wayside daisies.

Good teams are to be had here, and there are no such beautiful drives in the State as lie westward through Lime Rock, northward over Beacon Pole, eastward to Diamond Hill and the Hill Rocks, and southward about Lonsdale and Quinsnicket. And the jewel of Diamond Hill lies but

WILLIAM WATERMAN HOUSE.

a few rods eastward through the gnarled sloping apple orchard back of the Highland House—Sneach pond, lying silent and lonely among its lilies, its fringing alders and pine woods, and the green, wooded heights that climb still higher eastward to Copper Mine Hill, unspoiled in its wildness by habitation of man. The birds and all wild creatures have it their own way here; no modern improvements except a new ice house erected at the wood's edge by the Woonsocket Company have been introduced, and the cows graze among the gnarled old apple trees that run down to its western edge. Some of the more romantic city boarders have manifested a tendency of late years to rechristen this fair spot "Echo Lake," and allude to it thus in private or even printed letters; but such folly can be only spasmodic and local. Sneach pond it is and will be, a name peculiar to itself, and worth a dozen Echos or Mirrors or Pearls. The full name was an Indian one, how spelt in truth I cannot say, but phonetically it is Sneachkahonk, and said to imitate the cry of the wild goose. It is a bit of presumption in summer guests to rechristen an old stand-by of the kind, to be realized, perhaps, by requesting them to think whether they would take it kindly if our country cousins came to town and insisted on renaming Market Square Jones's Four Corners.

In the quaint little white old-fashioned cottage, vine decked, that stands directly opposite the station road, two huge dead trees draped with woodbine, standing as sentinels, Miss Rachel Sayles of Pawtucket lives. With her is her brother, William R. Sayles, who has tried Cape Cod and vastly prefers Cumberland Hill. Mr. Walter Cook occupies a tall gray pillared house luxuriant with the scarlet and green of a huge trumpet vine and shaded by great elms, which was until recently the old Cumberland bank. Near it is a bit

CUMBERLAND HILL BANK.

of a sloping, gray stone cottage, its end literally buried in ivy with only peep holes of windows showing. This is William Waterman's house. The roomy, picturesque old farm house that stands farthest north is the property of Ornando Vose, now summering at Prudence Park; meanwhile the pleasant old place is let to Mr. Arthur Brown, the Providence lawyer. William H. Ballou of Providence has built one of the prettiest homes here, a long, brown, cosey and cool looking house with deep veranda and bow windows.

By and by when the northeast sends fiercer blasts the country-folk of Cumberland, gathered around a hospitable fire, will, warmed by the exhilarating mug of cider, narrate to open-mouthed youngsters the legends with which the whole town is richly fraught—of the ghost of Poker Hill, perhaps, an eccentric spook which prefers travelling without its head, and which is said to drag perpetually a heavy log by means of a golden chain. A stalwart youth of our acquaintance very nearly saw it one dark night. He heard it, stumbling over the quartz bowlders and groping through the tangled undergrowth, as he walked timorously by. He even recognized the dull thud of the log thumping heavily behind, and—oh, horrors! the clank of the golden chain. Had he fled then the episode would have been charming; but alas! the ghost gave one wild leap into the road directly before him, and slowly materialized into an old horse, dragging its moorings behind it. This anecdote must not detract from the authenticity of the real ghost, however. Then there is the tale of the weird old woman who lived alone in the little black house, and told fortunes that came true. She wore a red kerchief round her head, which concealed quite a formidable gray beard, and she was thought to be a witch. The juvenile population were quite prepared to vouch for her occasional headers into space on the witch's conventional steed—a broomstick. But the poor old woman is gone now, and conjectures are vain.

Then it is well known that buried in the depths of Little Pond lie two golden tables, which are to be drawn from their lurking place only by the united endeavors of an honest farmer and six milk-white steers. The scarcity of milk-white steers has, so far, prevented the attempt from being made.

There is the veracious history of Jemima Wilkinson, the "Second Christ," of Cumberland, who had quite a band of followers, and who, among other miracles, walked on the water, that is, she set out well and "slumped in" only through lack of faith in her adherents.

Mrs. Weeden's mother, who recently died, was the oldest lady in the town, having completed her 97th year. This old lady was familiar with the erratic career of the "second Christ" and recalled hear-ng her own mother relate that she once met at a funeral the eccentric Jemima, whom she unthinkingly addressed by name. Made answer the second Christ, with haughty dignity, "Some calls me Jemima, but I prefer to be called the Comforter." The birthplace of this aspiring being was two or three miles below.

The people at the Hill are quite confident that by another season electric cars will speed from Pawtucket to Woonsocket. This would be an astounding "boom" for the Hill, and those who know it not would then learn what an altogether delightful spot it is.

In our many wanderings about the hill lovely Sneach Pond always drew us as with a magnet, beckoning with force irresistible, and seeming to say, "Abide with me. Tarry for more than a day on my green shores and learn my secrets."

Why should we not? The whole summer was before us; why not spend a week in a real gypsy tent, and live a while with nature undefiled?

To Sneach Pond, therefore, we set our faces, with vague ideas of turning hermit, making morbid and cynical reflections on our fellow-men, and writing a second "Walden." Only we should not call it Walden, but "Sneach," which would be neat, appropriate, and, if brevity be the soul of wit, exceedingly witty. But when our tent arose, white, fair and hospitable, from the rocky promontory jutting out into the lonely little lake, we forgot both cynicism and philosophy. What was there to do but live a life of indolent leisure, a part of the leisurely growing vegetating world around us? We felt the primeval savage stirring within us as we sat before the stone-built fireplace, and tended the sputtering fish—our fish, that our own hands had pulled from their native element but a few short moments since—as their backbones slowly counterfeited a contortion of deadly agony as the fierce heat seized them, and the wild flames, caught by the wandering breeze, soared redly upward. Nay, a vague and evanescent impression seized us, as we tenderly laid a tiny pillow of salt pork under the uneasy head of a slowly browning young pickerel—that sometime, countless ages ago, perhaps, this had been life's normal condition with us, when cities were things unknown. Why does the dog, before retiring to his nightly rest, turn around and around on his cushion or straw-strewn floor, or whatever forms his pallet, before he sinks to repose? Let not the scoffing say he does it to find the head of his bed; no, it is the habit inherited from remote ancestors who trampled down the wiry

J. WILKINSON'S BIRTHPLACE.

grass and brakes of the jungles where their savage lodging lay; so we, in returning to primeval simplicity, felt within us the joy of our savage grandparents, no doubt. Else why, as the days glided by, our growing tendency to discard those utensils of civilization, the knife, fork and napkin, and cluster, an amicable trio about the savory frying pan? And the clearing-up—ah, what a boon to weary housekeepers would such as ours be! Armed with each a tin plate and mug, we formed a procession down to the rippling lake, and with a splash, a dip, and a hanging up to dry, our housework was over. Friendly little servants, too, were the wandering ants, who cheerfully and speedily cleared our green carpet of stray crumbs thrice a day. And as we ate, we gazed upon the glory of sky and forest and shore, and were doubly filled. Even now, we have but to close our eyes, and we see again the marvellous splendor of that first sunset across the darkening water, while the western heavens burned with crimson and gold and threw a brilliant pathway straight down the centre of the dancing lake, while along the far shores lay the dark and unbroken reflections, cool, green and tranquil, of the silent forest. And away to the south, where the dying sun rays pursued and smote the gray wraiths of flying clouds that had but now poured out hasty vials of wrath on the staunch canvas of our little tent, the prismatic colors of a rainbow bent to the horizon, and faintly fading upward to the zenith, framed in our fair picture. It is not every camping party who has a poem written expressly for them by a pen of renown, but we had; for presently, across the yet crimson glory of the fading sunset, flying from the reedy shore to the more remote haunts in the northern swamp, passed a heron, with his shrill cry softened by distance. Was it not for this strange picture in the gloaming that Bryant wrote—

"Whither, midst falling dew,
While glow the heavens with the last steps of day,
Far through their rosy depths, dost thou pursue
Thy solitary way?

Vainly the fowler's eye
Might mark thy distant flight to do thee wrong,
As, darkly painted on the crimson sky,
Thy figure floats along."

Then, as the twilight deepened, a heavy and sombre band began to play beneath the water—a Chinese band, we felt sure, by the nature of the music and the guttural voices of the instruments. No giddy waltz could those sub-aqueous merry makers be treading to the wild and sombre music, but the stately measures of a minuet. We sat on the rocks in the dew and starlight till a tinier and shriller chorus about our ears drove us indoors in despair. We pinned mosquito netting across our door-flaps, seated ourselves on our rude, but inviting, couches, and in the gloom told tales and sang songs till drowsiness bade us seek repose. What a fresh and novel delight was there in lying listening to the manifold voices of the night, breathing in the keen scent that growing herbs exhale at nightfall and feeling, if we flung out a hand from our humble cots, the crisp and growing blades of grass beneath our fingers. The gleaming jewels of Cassiopeia's chair overhung the silent lake and sparkled in our shrouded doorway. It would have been perfect but—oh, these mosquitoes!

It was no use to be silent and tranquil. How could one preserve tranquillity with six vigorous and energetic mosquitoes quarreling for the best place on the tip of one's nose? Our tent resounded with slappings, exasperated sighs and execrations, while a monotonous and incessant chorus, pitched in a very high key, sounded resolutely from everywhere. We heard distant bells, across the ridge, of Cumberland Hill, strike the hours.

"Two o'clock and all's swelled!" we heard somebody mutter in sardonic accents. How we welcomed the dawn that presently reddened the eastern sky, and sent our uncanny visitors fleeing. At last we slept, blissfully and long—how long deponent saith not—but thereafter at twilight four tiny smouldering fires sent up their vigil lights without the four corners of our tent, and mosquitoes attacked us no more.

But what rude awakening was ours, as, lost in oblivion, we sought to make up the needed repose lost in those baleful nightwatches! Were wild and savage beasts still roaming at large in these neighboring jungles? Gigantic footsteps were surely crashing about our tent, as we listened, struggling between waking and sleeping. And, oh, horrors of horrors, a loud and fierce breathing sounded in our very ears, and before our slumber-dimmed eyes was thrust through the insecure fastenings of our western door a gigantic head with staring eyes and menacing horns! It was a—why, what was it?

owly the terrible apparition grew familiar and more inoffensive of aspect. It is a—cow!

Thoroughly awake now, we betook ourselves down to our own particular flat rock, and kneeling at the water's edge, taking a long, refreshing dip downward and letting the breeze seize us full in our faces as we emerged dripping and gasping, we tasted the fresh joy of the summer morning to the full. Was there not, too, a sweet and elusive odor wafted gently to us on the caressing south wind? whence it was borne. There lay the white lake fairies in hundreds in dainty cups of bronze and olive green, and upborne by leathery dull green pads of leaves, which, the wind catching, showed very now and then a glowing crimson from their hidden under-surfaces. How we reveled in lilies through our too brief day. We wore them, we decorated our oars with them, we gave them away, and still, toiling upward unerringly from the mud and slime below, they daily unfurled their gold and white banners to the welcome of sun and wind, and there were enough and to spare. It was no rare sight, as we sculled our little boat in and out among the clinging pads, to see sitting in state high and dry upon some one of their level disks, a melancholy, green specked frog, which did not even condescend to be afraid of us. Dragon flies, too, hovered confidingly about the blue spikes of pickerel weed that grew in straight ranks from the shallow water, bumble bees kicked up their heels in gay abandon in the hearts of wild roses that fringed the bank, and once, as we sat motionless, anchored close to shore, a business-like little weasel came walking briskly down to the water, and beholding us, paused and sat upright with his tiny paws drooping before his white breast in an extremely engaging manner. One sight of us was not enough, either, for after performing his errand, whatever it was, and departing, he as suddenly reappeared again, twice and thrice, and subjected us to the same searching scrutiny. It requires a clear conscience and plenty of time to look a weasel out of countenance.

And now what should we do through these long, bright, care-free days? There was the lake to navigate in the first place, the "Harris rocks" across the water to be explored, the green eastern hill to climb, whose summer woods smiled as serenely down upon the mirroring waters as though its heart were not pierced with a dozen deadly shafts where, in days of old, the copper industry waxed brisk. There were the six oaks on the breezy hillside above us, where swung our hammocks, shut in by the vast rock-walls that stretched across the western approach like the work of some of those phenomenal old-time labor-loving men who carted around rocks just for the fun of it; here we were wont to read a little, talk a little and gaze a good deal more, while the glimmering lake turned gray, white or blue, at the will of the flying clouds, and where, far off to the eastward, the faintly discerned barrel on Beacon Pole Hill rose sturdily and invitingly aloft; Diamond Hill also lay within easy walking distance; who knew what mineral treasures might be unearthed there—since one of us had already found a wee bit of amethyst among the Harris rocks? But when one can go anywhere anytime the desire to do so ceases, and we sat about or went berrying and fishing and mushrooming in our savage and ignorant way, and knew nor cared no more whether the Cove Basin was filled up yet and Grace Church clock set a-going than if we were members of the ——; but someone says hush. Not wholly isolated, either, were we; every now and then came strolling summer guests from the cottages or hotel of Cumberland Hill proper; for a morning row, or a lily-gathering, or a day's fishing they came; they gave us good advice and told us fables about the black bass of Sneach Pond, when, to the best of our knowledge and belief, it contains not a thing but pickerel, perch, bullpout and miserable little roach. There were three or four entertaining boys, whose row boat was moored near our dwelling, and who made the rocky shores their daily resort. Right merry, gallant and frank little lads they were, and we missed them sadly when the weather or other engagements kept them at home.

On Sunday the lake and its borders grew more lively; the working lads and lassies from the mill village now and then found their way up here, and the rocks and hills echoed to other voices than the hoarse bass of the frog and the scream of the wild heron. A happy thing it seemed that this fair and quiet breathing place lay within so easy access of the few who are to be found in every hamlet who really love nature for its own sake. Trophies of wild flowers, water lilies and luscious blackberries they bore away, to brighten other homes with their coming, beside pleasant memories which happily may be borne world-wide. We must not forget a mention of the genial old countryman who was wont to pass our tent daily in some mysterious cross cut, and whose beaming face glowed regularly in upon us with the unvarying salutation, "What be ye all—takin' yer comfort?"

But there came a morning when we looked out upon nothing but a wide, still grayness: when clouds and sky and forest and wind-driven lake were one in hue, and birds were silent and hidden. A chill wind blew a flying mist in our faces as we ventured a first look outside our doors; we went jubilantly down to our bathing rock through the fog and rain-laden grasses, feeling that to-day was all our own. Blue skies and tranquil waters were for transient pleasure-seekers, but this shoreless gray sea that stretched eastward with its wild lapping waves rushing to our feet through the green lances of the sturdy pickerel-weed—this and the wild wet wind that smote our faces were our very own. Like gray, ragged ghosts of the air the battered mist clouds went flying past us inland, catching and shattering in the glistening wet bushes; out in the translucent gray distance, fair white spheres dotted the heaving waters— the dear white faithful lilies, sunny-hearted still. How glad we were of a storm! camping out would have been but a tame affair with only sunny sides. After breakfast, made within-doors this time, we betook ourselves shrouded in ghostly gossamers down to our waiting row boat for a morning's fishing. We must have fish, rain or no rain, and the clouds were lifting just now. So out into gray space we pushed, and, with lines flung wide, patiently waited. What was this distant muffled roar that presently sounded faintly, like the tramping of hosts down the wild hillside? We listened and wondered, not knowing that in a moment more we should be caught by Kuhleborn. Our eyes pierced the gray veil of mist that hung about us, and as the roar came nearer, we cried with one accord, "Rain!" How thankful we felt to be afloat on a lake, where a deluge, more or less, could not hurt us. We wrapped our protecting mantles tight around us, and bent our heads to the downpour. The whole surface of the lake, as far as we could see, looked as if covered with a raised steel bead-work, with the force of the rebounding rain-drops. We sat it out as long as possible, but there was no diminution, and we "pulled for the shore."

All day long our tent sheltered us and a hundred flies, and a wondering little toad which evidently congratulated itself on having found such a commodious and waterproof toadstool. We read and talked and ate, and speculated on the weather probabilities. At length, late in the evening, the clouds parted, and we stepped rejoicingly out into the moist air for a look at the heavens. But what menacing constellations were these that greeted us! In the north the Great Dipper hung alone, with suggestions of plenty more rain inside. Southward the Little Dipper, upside down and drained dry, showed us where the downpour had come from; and further west, through a rift in the driving clouds, Aquarius, the water bearer, leaned nonchalantly on a cloud-bank, as if only waiting his time to give us particular fits. These alone appeared through rifts in the drifting clouds. Appalled, we fled within doors, and the foreboding constellations fulfilled their promise. Another day of rain dawned upon us, and now a gentle stream from the northeast corner of our tent was trickling gayly within. How we rejoiced now in our gigantic fryingpan, the victim of much ridicule! we slipped it derneath the canvas, and our floor was ved. But before tent-life had fairly lled upon us, the skies cleared as if by igic, and, still high and dry, we and a toad stepped gayly forth into freedom. So the days glided on, in "the land in ich it seemed always afternoon"—and is, mostly—till the sad day came when what had once been our home was only a melancholy hole in the air; when we packed our fryingpan and left our fireplace desolate and returned to civilization. But Sneach Pond is always there, and we shall return. Will not the waves laugh for delight and the green woods wave a welcome? If not, we shall fancy so.

THROUGH THE NORTHERN TOWNSHIPS.

[A two days drive from Providence and back.]

EARLY on a breezy summer morning, a light, but commodious beach wagon drew up before our door, and into it we packed away with pleasurable anticipation, frying-pan and coffee-pot, pork, potatoes, and other kindred supplies, for we were bound for a two days trip, and were to cook our own meals by the wayside. The scene of our wanderings was to be the northern half of Rhode Island.

We had decided to postpone our European tour, and to take this one instead, for we deplored the ignorance of Continental travellers, who knew nothing of their own country; besides, we could be gone only two days, anyway.

Our course lay due north for a time, and we passed the gypsy encampment in the Pawtucket suburbs without a sigh, for were we not to have a taste of wild life for ourselves? Following the Blackstone, our way led past the high bank looking off into the counterfeit presentment of a salt marsh, and over whose then unguarded edge a valuable yoke of oxen once walked to their death, on a dark night years ago. Their owner had tarried too confidently in the rear, and the oxen meekly obeying the command to "Haw," given by a passing team, had stepped over the treacherous edge, and crashed to the bottom, where they were found a few moments later with broken necks.

We passed Scott's pond, a picturesque enlargement of the Blackstone, made famous by its erratic floating island, for which two of us had searched in vain a few weeks before, and lo! there it lay before us now, a green wooded mystery, calm between us and the further shore.

It is of goodly size, large enough to build a house upon, did one wish to trust himself to so fragile a foundation, and it is densely wooded from end to end, a mass of shimmering green. It is said that a young man once lost his life beneath it, having rashly ventured there for a subaqueous view of its structure. It is supposed that he either became entangled among its roots, or lost his way and strangled before he could regain its edge. But the island tells no tales, and tranquilly wanders up and down, at its own sweet will—or that of the winds and current. We passed the spot again at a later day, and our island had come ashore! One could have stepped upon it from the beach. A fragment of it has become detached and roams about likewise, a wandering dot of green.

Through Lonsdale we drove next, most picturesque of mill villages, though lately shorn of the glory of a magnificent grove by the railroad station, displaced to make room for the gigantic new factory.

We halted for a moment to admire the little Episcopal Church in the old village, which, with its lovely setting of green, we one and all declared to be the fairest gem of a church we had yet beheld. The railroad crossed, we passed through Berkeley and Ashton, pretty villages, with the green hills receding from them back to a far horizon. Passing the Ashton graveyard, we paused to read the inscription on a great black headstone that bounds five graves. "One fate surprised them and one grave received them," reads the heading, and below, "Sacred to the memory of Hopestill, wife of Russell Jenks, who, with her four children, was unfortunately drowned in Scott's pond." Then follow the names and ages of the four little daughters, all under eleven years of age. The poor mother, it is said, was insane, and drove into the pond with her wagon, and made sure that every child was drowned before she released her own hold. Poor "Hopestill!" did the fair promise of her name lure her on to a dream of rest beneath these engulfing waters?

And now we turn sharply eastward, and leave the river and the railroad behind us, as we begin to climb a long, wild hill. The morning breeze blows freshly from its sloping stretches, and the quail are whistling and calling across its lonely pastures. Now and then we pass a wandering brook, winding leisurely down the meadows, its course marked by the heavenly blue of the wild iris, guarded by the shining lances of

"The rushes, the green yeomen of its manor,
The outlaws of the sun."

Somewhere about here is the historical spot called the "Nine men's misery," where perished a scouting party in Revolutionary times—nine brave men who, surprised by the Indians, stood dauntlessly up before a protecting rock and returned the hostile fire till the last survivor, standing bravely alone amid his fallen comrades, felt his own heart pierced by a fatal arrow. A great cairn of stones is said to mark the spot, and off in a distant field we saw such an one. It may have been it, or—an equine grave. And now by the wayside, holding their dainty heads defiantly up before our gladdened eyes, what should we espy but a cluster of maiden's hair fern. What were these lonely little pilgrims doing in Rhode Island, in a spot where one of us, who had roamed these hills for years, had never before beheld one? We gathered one spray for a memento and left the rest, but we shall not tell where they are. Presently, before a wayside cottage, a rockery gleamed upon us, dazzling in the sun. We all alighted and proceeded to examine the beautiful crystal masses, found at Diamond Hill, two or three miles beyond. It seemed rather an unsafe place to rear such a tempting structure, and there is no knowing how much of it would have been left when we drove on, had not a woman come opportunely around the corner, and begun a pleasant chat with us. She gave us roses and information, but she did not pull down her rockery for us, though we were extravagant in our admiration. At parting she presented us each with an enormous crimson peony which we bore about rather helplessly until the bright idea occurred to us of adorning our vehicle with them. We stuck one in each of its four corners, where we could admire them unrestrained.

Arrived at the summit of the great wild hill, we alighted once more, tied our horse and followed a cart path up a rocky pasture leading to an ancient rock thick with moss-grown impressions of naked footprints, becoming yearly less discernible. Here also in the distant ages when this unyielding granite was softest clay, the devil, wearied with going up and down the earth as an itinerant preacher—which he must have done, judging by his various pulpits scattered broadcast through the country—sat him down to rest, and laid by his side his stout walking stick and his frying-pan—whatever he was doing with that.

This legend we know to be true, for we saw the impression of both cane and pan in the solid rock.

Descending presently from this airy outlook, we found ourselves in the wildest and most primeval nook which we ever visited, in Rhode Island or elsewhere. A great ledge of rock, wild and jagged, rose to one side, great masses of clinging ivy and shrubs rioting about it, and set in a frame of gigantic forest trees. Round about it lay tumbled bowlders, and beyond it were shaded dells and wooded hillocks and locust groves—it was a combination of nature's wildest and most beautiful forms. We lingered here entranced, till the mounting sun warned us we had scant time to reach Sneach pond for our noonday camp, then went reluctantly on. A short drive brought us to the wood road that leads to the lonely, hill-bound lake and jolting over the pasture stones, we drew up at length under an enormous oak on the green slope overlooking the lake.

Now was our hour of bliss. We would make a fire and cook our dinner. Joyfully we essayed and dismayed we waited. The wood didn't burn. There was smoke, though. Plenty of it blew in our faces as we set the table on the grass, and watched the ants and spiders skip joyfully over our viands. We were to have coffee, and we hung a tin pail of water on a long stick over the fire to heat. Presently the fire waxed hot and burnt the stick and we took it hastily away and arranged another out of harm's way, and patiently waited. We were very hungry, but the potatoes were already in the ashes, roasting.

Crash! hiss! splutter! what was that? the handle of the pail melted off, and pail and contents in the fire. In despair we took out our alcohol lamp, "a small, slight thing the pressure of a finger might have crushed," and meekly made coffee on it. It wasn't the way the gypsies would have done, but we would do differently at supper time. We had plenty of tinned meats, and enjoyed dinner immensely. The potatoes were not quite done when we finished, and we left them. Our hunger appeased, we had leisure to enjoy the view before us—the lonely, lovely lake, with the green silent woods stretching down to meet it, and the cloud-shadows making fantastic changes across its rippling surface. It might have been one of the little silver gems sprinkled so plentifully through the Adirondacks, so far as appearances went. Surely, this was not the Rhode Island scenery to which we were accustomed. We lingered happily here for several hours, then we turned our course to Diamond Hill. We would have visited the old copper mines near the pond, but knew not where they were, and there was no one of whom to make inquiry. Diamond Hill loomed up before us soon, lifting a scarred, bristling front against the sky. In the shadow of it we halted and made a hasty excursion up its side for a little space, in search of "specimens." Not only beautiful masses of white and rose quartz crystal have been found here, but more valuable varieties—even a rare amethyst geode being occasionally opened. But it is probable that other excursionists had searched in the same spot we chose, and we found nothing better to reward us than an occasional jasper vein in a rock or an isolated crystal in an inaccessible cavity. A long ride was before us still, and our evening meal must be prepared and eaten before we should reach our lodging place, Woonsocket, for we were headed westward now, and were to drive along the high range of the Cumberland Hills, becoming of late years very popular as a summer resort. A portion of the way led through a section somewhat demolished by the spring floods, and low and swampy at its best. Laborers were at work here with spades and shovels, the first people we had met since noon. And here, amid the mud and mire, were growing plants, perhaps familiar enough to botanists, but rare to us, perfect calla lilies in form and color, except that the pistil was rather greenish than golden. We dug some of these carefully up, and bore them about until the next day, when—but we anticipate. The sun was setting when we drove into a little wood path and prepared for supper. The mosquitoes were beginning to be inquisitive, and we agreed that it would be better not to build a fire to-night for our pork and potatoes—they would taste so much better in the morning. We abandoned the idea reluctantly, for it had been the greatest feature of our hopes—a wayside fire and meals cooked thereat. But we brought the tiny lamp into requisition again, and had hot tea with our other eatables. One of us, rambling through the shadowy roads at the banquet's close, started a brood, flock, covey—which is it? of young quail, which fled in rustling terror through the brush.

It was quite dusk when we turned back on the main road again, and we looked off from the long hill-road, over which we merrily sped, only into misty distance below, studded with the evanescent flash of fireflies—the gleam of diamonds in the night-queen's gossamer robes.

The lights of Woonsocket gleamed cheerily through the gloom at last, and we drew up presently before the Monument House, where some itinerant vendor had evidently just finished a lecture to a departing throng; he was packing away his goods in solitude by his flickering torches.

We were pleasantly and commodiously stowed away for the night in adjoining rooms, and fell happily asleep, well content with our first day's trip.

We arose betimes—a word of vague meaning, but sounding well—and drove away, leaving the landlord obviously astonished at our having refused both supper and breakfast.

Fried pork and johnny cakes we were firmly resolved to have this morning, as soon as we were well out of the Woonsocket suburbs. We drove west, for we were to explore the unknown wilds of Burrillville and Glocester, which looked so tempting on the map. But we had not travelled far upon the broad highway before we saw it furnished no suitable camping ground, so we turned northward up a side road, which led, a guide-board said, to "Blackstone, two miles." We took our callas from the water pail and hid them among the bushes till we should return, for we needed the pail; then on we went. Up and up, amid stones and gravel and deep ruts and a narrowing road and wayside trees that slapped our faces, looking vainly the while for a pair of bars. We jolted and scrambled, and still climbed on, waxing wroth and hungry at each moment. Our horse rebelled, and we got out and walked. But there was "no backward path; ah! no returning!" the road was too narrow to turn in, and we couldn't back a mile. We came to a little clearing presently, by an old barn, and here we stopped in despair and began making preparations for a fire. But the wind was strong and we feared to set the barn afire, so after some discussion we repacked, got in the carriage and drove away, after having taken the precaution to fill our pail at the well. We drove

GROUP OF SCITUATE HOUSES.

and drove. Not a cart path was to be found or a secluded nook anywhere. How cross we were! the male members of the party, that is. It always makes men cross to be hungry.

We arrived at Blackstone at last, and in spite of ill-temper, were soothed by the lovely view from the hill top—fair meadows and uplands, and distant hills lying blue all about the horizon, the little village lying cosily among them like a nest. After divers turnings, we found ourselves driving back again, on a road parallel to our ascent of the Hill Difficulty. But there was no good place to camp. We wanted a good place, now that we had come all this distance for one, and we one and all declared we would go till we found one. We drove for about two hours, and came to a lovely nook in a great white pine grove down a sheltered cart path, and alighted in great joy. But it was too late now to build a gypsy fire, so we made coffee with the lamp, and ate tinned meats and crackers and fruits, and after a half hour's rest drove on. Words fail me to describe that Burrillville wilderness. Sand and dust and hills, and great stretches of red and white clover fields, and now and then a house. And if ever we stopped at one for water the inmates invariably came out and told us their well was the best in that part of the country, and never went dry. More sand, more hills—not picturesque hills, to look at, but sandy ones in the road, to climb, and sometimes a meeting house or a school house. One would think the "chief pursuits" were education and religion, instead of agriculture, as the geography says.

We are told of the crowded condition of New England, and we know that Rhode Island is the most densely populated State in the Union, but surely there is room for all Rhode Island's inhabitants to come and stand in these up-and-down Burrillville clover fields; if they want to, that is. Once was enough for us.

By and by a suspicion seized us that we were going the wrong way, and were heading north instead of west, as we were following the Springfield railroad. A glance at the map would have set us straight, but we had scorned such guidance. We quarrelled vigorously for some time, partly for diversion and partly because opinion was divided. The sun being overhead, it might have risen from any quarter of the heavens for all we knew. At length we met two men and a woman. They told us we were within two miles of Pascoag, approaching Mapleville, and thus relieved we pressed forward. Just beyond a road led southward, and we turned gladly into it, for we wished soon to see Glocester scenery. Prospecting for dinner, one of us alighted and advanced to a house set back from the roadside, in whose yard cows were browsing, and knocking at the door, proffered a mild request for milk. He was met by an individual in scant raiment, consisting of a single garment, and who answered shortly, "We ain't got no milk!" and slammed the door in his face.

LAPHAM INSTITUTE.

Thus repulsed, we continued our course till we came to a beautiful sheet of water lying at the foot of a sloping pasture, and which we decided, from our limited geographical lore, must be Herring Pond. We took dinner there, but we made no fire, because we thought we would not have time. We gave some potatoes to two cows, who liked them quite as well raw.

After dinner, resuming our ride, we drove for some distance along the shores of the pond, which we were surprised to find of so great extent, and had hardly left it behind us when we were confronted by an institution we had deemed well-nigh obsolete in Rhode Island—an old-fashioned toll gate. The toll keeper was a garrulous old man and entertained us with a long account of how the Glocester folks wouldn't take the road, and so on. He was curious to hear the news from Providence, but as he took a daily paper—however he got it—he had heard from there more recently than ourselves. He also set us right as to our whereabouts. We were in the southern part of Glocester, having traversed that township without knowing it, and our Herring Pond was the Waterman Reservoir!

Having paid our toll, we drove down to North Scituate for a glimpse of the lake and the old Lapham Institute, afterward metamorphosed into the Moswansicut Hotel, and then deserted to await an unknown fate. Poor old Lapham! Your stately, white pillared heights look no more down upon merry groups of studious youths and maidens, such as thronged here in your palmy days, before the seats of learning lay in cities; but you made a most charming hotel, with accessories of grove and sparkling lake, and deserved a long future in that capacity.

We drove down to the lake, which, pretty little sheet of water that it is, compared but poorly with wild Sneach Pond among the northern hills.

Then we supped for the last time on a secluded hillside not far from the village, and made cracker toast and coffee by the little alcohol lamp. It did not seem worth while to make a fire so near home, we remarked pensively.

On the homeward ride from thence we had been speaking of the peculiar "cluck" of the whip-poor-will, which only one of us had ever been near enough to hear, when by one of those frequent strange coincidences, a whip-poor-will lighted upon a bush by the roadside and piped his best for our benefit: "Whip-poor-will! (cluck) whip-poor-will! (cluck)," and so on—an odd sound.

Driving eastward through Johnston, the electric lights of Providence shone at last upon us and our tour was ended. We had seen the townships of Providence, Pawtucket, Lincoln, Cumberland, Woonsocket, North Smithfield, Burrillville, Glocester, Scituate and Johnston, and felt that we had gained a fair idea of northern Rhode Island geography.

Some day we shall take the southern section and camp out and have johnny-cakes and roast potatoes; but perhaps it will be well to take an alcohol lamp also.

DIAMOND HILL.

[New York and New England Railroad, 14 miles from Providence. Fare, 35 cents; 40 minutes ride.]

LURED by the magnificence of the title—the suggestion of glistening crags and dazzling peaks, as well as by the oft-told legends of the mineral wealth exhumed from the crags of Cumberland, we prepared to spend a day at Diamond Hill.

It is but a forty minutes ride from Providence by the trains of the N. Y. and N. E. road, yet the contrast of the scenery through which we sped could scarcely be greater in our little State; from the flat, hot pine barrens of the Seekonk plains, desolate with heat and dreary with the never ending wail of the wind in the ranks of pine woods, to the towering hills, the abrupt ravines, the singing brooks and daisied uplands of the wildest, loftiest corner of our thrice-blessed Rhode Island. The gods have surely smiled on our fair little State, which is not an island, as our ignorant cousins across seas will insist. With the crown of enduring hills on her brow and the heaving Atlantic laving her feet, she offers endless variety to the growing host of summer pilgrims. To the lovers of the hills and forest the region of Diamond Hill is a consoling substitute for foregone mountain joys. The hills hemmed us in as we stepped from the train and looked about us: Beacon Pole, Copper Mine, Cumberland and the dominant crag in the foreground we had journeyed to behold, but gleaming with no radiance, alas! save the glance of the sun on the leaves of its forests. Away sped the train through the woods to the north and left us alone in the wilderness, a scant half-dozen houses in sight, as we boxed the compass in a hasty circular glance. We would step in at the station and see about return trains. We stepped in, but lo! only an empty room well frescoed with pencil autographs, its only occupant a pile of wood in a corner, reminiscent of last winter or anticipating next. We learned on inquiry at the nearest homestead hard by, that this was the station's chronic condition; and, indeed, a station master installed here, would soon be driven to suicide in a fit of ennui. But how, then, were we to get a train? for trains paused here only by flagging. We were to flag our own train, we were told. That is, on its approach, we were to stand well out on the platform in an expectant attitude, and the train would pause. On no account must we take seats in the station, as strangers sometimes did, leaving the train to thunder by unwitting. Forewarned was forearmed, and we dismissed care. Now, all about the hill if you please, madam; and the pleasant-faced mother of the household gave us information, while a beautiful Irish setter and a pert imp of a bull terrier "showed off" around the yard, begged, crept, rolled over and retrieved in a state of high delight and consciousness of our divided approbation. Up the winding hill to the left was the old granite quarry, now idle; to it belonged the queer little cluster of red cottages our train had passed in the valley below. There was the little school house close by to the east; no, there was no church building, Arnold's Mills was the nearest place to go. And wouldn't that old abandoned black cottage across the way be a delightful place to camp out? Well, perhaps, but it was full of fertilizer just now, and we hastily dismissed the idea.

Where was the man we had heard of, who had a collection of minerals here?

He was close by and we were directed there. There was also a beautiful building, with a crystal front, somewhere in the neighborhood; where was that? Well, that was the gatehouse of the Pawtucket Water Works, and we were directed there likewise. With thanks and adieux we passed on, pausing to admire a beautiful rockery of nature's own handiwork in the yard, in whose crannies grew ferns and vines and iris in brown and yellow. Our way to the home of Charles Fisher, the collector,* was through the woods, cool, shady, and filled with a thousand nameless floating odors of the wild growing things, and brown cart-paths down which we longed to wander, invited to still cooler and greener depths.

It was Saturday morning and baking day, but the daughter of Mr. Fisher was hospitable and did the honors of the little white cottage as amiably as if we were the first rather than the last of a long line of inquisitive visitors. On a table in the sitting room glittered a collection of brilliant minerals that quite atoned for the ordinary green of the crag that loomed without. Not all were gathered from the hill, but there were some magnificent specimens there. Mr. Fisher is now an old man, and he has been an ardent enthusiast in minerals for seventy-five years, he says, since, when a little boy, he remembers his elder brother coming home with a huge piece of crystal unearthed from the crag. Among the treasures Diamond Hill has produced were splendid pieces of jasper, red, green, blue and yellow, most of those exhibited being polished to a rich lustre, chalcedony, porphyry, agate—and there was one banded piece here in glowing red and yellow that we specially coveted, iron, and the most abundant quartz crystal which gives the region name. Masses of it were here crystallized in every form from opaque white masses like petrified cocoanut to the long, pendent, clear crystals that caught the sun's rays on their sharp angles like veritable diamonds. Pink, yellow and white, the various specimens showed, and the largest and handsomest was one found by Mrs. Bartlett herself, Mr. Fisher's daughter, at the root of a tree. There was a great agate slab, so curiously marked in queer dark colors, black and brown blended with the red and yellow, as to look like two quaint figures in Japanese inlaid work. The granite quarry has turned out some prizes also, one of the loveliest things we saw being a long thin slab of hornblende crystal in quartz, a watery clear foundation stone with the faintest hint of translucence, and shot all through wth the tiny black arrows of hornblende, lapping and overlapping. It resembled almost exactly the magnified dust of a black miller's wing which we prepared recently for a microscope slide. Mrs. Bartlett lamented the geological knowledge that died not long ago with her brother, Mr. Frank Fisher, but the lady herself is no superficial student of stones, and talked of cleavage, fracture and crystallization with a fluency that shamed our hazy memories of schoolday mineralogy. Mr. Fisher has attained a more than local reputation as a collector, and as our enthusiasm grew, the old gentleman and his daughter brought forth from hidden nooks more and more beauties and curiosities for our inspection, exchanges, many of them, from lapidaries and mineralogists. There were beautiful polished minerals, cut gems, fossils, and all sorts of petrifactions, flexible sandstone, phantom crystals, resurrection plants and other curios innumerable. We passed a most enjoyable morning, and at length set forth in search of the far-famed gate-house, lying at the southern end of the new reservoir. For this lovely valley, the undulating, silent hills lying greenly all about it with glimpses of more distant grays and blues between, no one would have dreamed the fair little lake was not expressly made, it nestles there so cosily and happily, but four years ago it was only a leisurely winding meadow brook. One may see it now, dropping down below the road on the other side of the gate-house and pursuing its way through the rich marshy green bordered with iris and daisies and musical with the

---

*Mr. Fisher has died since the above sketch was written.

tinkling music of bobolinks, apparently quite unconscious that its upper course has, so to speak,

> "Suffered a sea-change
> Into something rich and strange."

It is the spreading reservoir of the Pawtucket Water Works Company, and in the centre of the long white-walled boulevard that borders its southern shore rises that unique little gem of a gate-house that is the embodiment of what Diamond Hill can do in the way of minerals. Built of granite stone from the native quarry, in a massive but graceful design, across the middle front springs a crescent in darker polished granite, bearing its name and date of founding—1887. In horizontal panels on either hand, the width of the building, are set thickly tiles and blocks of the native treasures of the hill-polished agate, glowing banded jasper, dark porphyry and the blocks of yellow, pink and white quartz crystal that gleam with their own radiance. Down the tower front run perpendicular bands of ornament, rough-hewn and projecting masses of dazzling crystal; and when the sun shines on all this mass of crystals and sparkles many-hued from their shining prisms, it is indeed a sight worth coming far to see.

Beyond and up the lake a little distance, perched on a picturesque rough rock, vine and shrub decked, is a pavilion of polished wood, set on pillars of more mineral wonders. Picnic parties come here, dine and dance and enjoy the prospect. It was erected also by the philanthropists of the Water Works Co., and solely for the public good. As we gained this inviting eminence overlooking the breezy lake, and opened our lunch boxes, we began to take exception to a statement old Mr. Fisher had made. He thought that a certain Prof. Jackson, in a report of the Franklin Society, had been much mistaken in recording apatite as a product of the hill. We now concluded that the worthy professor had been quite right and that only his spelling was at fault.

Rested and refreshed, we presently strolled back up the lake shore to get the direction of the old Fisher homestead, the oldest house at the hill. We paused for a drink of water at our white cottage again—this time observing the little pewee's nest over the front door, packed full of babies—and were rewarded by the most beautiful sight in the form of a well we have ever beheld. It was lined thickly as a nest on the cold, damp stones with the beautiful, fern-like, twinkling moss that never grows anywhere but in a well; great ferns grew in clusters in every cranny, and the few vacant spaces were filled with the queer growth called lungwort—a composite of fern, moss and lichen. Above were bigger clusters still of ferns, and a columbine bent to peep at its scarlet trumpets reflected in the round black mirror below. It would have been sacrilege to supply this well with anything but old-fashioned sweep and oaken bucket; we drank deep draughts with satisfaction. A great iron pot on four little legs stood among the flowers, itself painted red and converted into a flower pot. It is an old, old heirloom, the great-great-grandmother of Mrs. Bartlett used to swing it from the fire, filled with the boiled dinner. We saw other heirlooms, among them a still older pewter platter, hacked with the steel knives of many generations. By a delightful cross-cut through the woods, we departed for the Fisher homestead, bearing bouquets of pansies and roses, picked by the hospitable hand of our morning hostess. The great square, unpainted house, black with age, stands at the foot of a gently sloping hill, green and cool with woods and tumbled rocks, and with the looming crag of Diamond Hill frowning across the way. Its interior has all its old-time simplicity, low-ceiled rooms, with the huge framework guilelessly in sight overhead, and the broad fireplaces and cranes that are always a source of fascination and envy. This was the old home of Darius Fisher, the oldest place at the hill, and now occupied by a son. Next door, built by the son, who is dead, is a neat white cottage, now standing with closed shutters in the midst of a view that ought daily to gladden the hearts of appreciative occupants.

In both door-yards were small rockeries heaped with glistening crystal fragments from the crag; indeed, if all the specimens from Diamond Hill could be gathered from the various Cumberland door-yards they would make a fair-sized hill by themselves. The hill has been pretty thoroughly ransacked now, and we were assured that it would be no use to climb and try our luck without picks and drills and other suitable implements. It was rather sad to come so far to see Diamond Hill, and yet leave its pinnacle untrodden, but consolation told us it was far more beautiful to stand at the foot and look up than to reverse the process.

Therefore, we flagged our train successfully and journeyed south; but when at night we closed our eyes it was not to see flashing before our vision like Wordsworth's daffodils the gleaming stones, the peaceful lake or glancing brook, or the wild green wood, or lofty crag—it was to recall what seemed now the loveliest memory of all—a broad waving field of blossomed grass, soft, fawn-tinted and billowy like the sea, its waves breaking at our very feet, and far beyond it a looming pine forest standing mute and silent.

QUINSNICKET.

[Two miles west of Lonsdale. Worcester Railroad, 7 miles from Providence.]

A SHORT article appearing not long ago in the Providence Journal kindled in us the desire to behold Quinsnicket, and on a sunny day late in May we set forth, knowing only vaguely that the desired goal was said to be "somewhere near Lonsdale." Inquiry of the officials at the station produced only mirth and not information. Why Quinsnicket should be any funnier than Shawomet, Sockanosset or Chepiwanoxet it is hard to say, but ticket agents will sell you tickets for those places without a transient gleam of hilarity, whereas it seemed difficult to compose their features sufficiently to say they hadn't any idea where Quinsnicket was. We embarked, therefore, for Lonsdale on one of those trains whose terminus is one's own goal, and in which the conductor reverses all the seats but one's own and the one before, a station or two before the journey's end, making one feel apologetic for defiantly continuing to journey in an opposite direction, and wonder whether it is best to also reverse, or to offer an apology and remain seated. The conductor looked friendly, and we ventured to say as we proffered our tickets, "Can you tell us where Quinsnicket is?"

"Wh-what?" said he, recoiling.

"Quinsnicket."

"What line is it on?"

No line, we thought. It was an Indian place in the woods somewhere near the Butterfly factory, we believed. Oh, yes. Well, Lonsdale was the nearest point to the Butterfly factory, and that was past old Lonsdale—well, our best course was to cross the bridge at Lonsdale and inquire at the first house at the left of Magoon, the boss farmer, who would doubtless tell us all about it. The Butterfly factory was a long way distant, though—two miles or more. Thanking him, we disembarked and turned bridgeward.

There is no lovelier point along the Blackstone's shores than the bend of the river just here at Lonsdale. It curves away like a winding water road between the great bending elms, and verdant islands, little and big, dot its surface; beyond stretch emerald green meadows away over to where the ancient village sleeps shrouded in green. Years ago the east side of the track was equally picturesque, and it is only of late years that the magnificent grove by the station was sacrificed to the needs of the last and hugest factory of Lonsdale's eight—the mammoth "Ann and Hope," or, in the common parlance of the English laborers therein, the "Hannanope." Two hundred great windows front the track: one can see the glass tremble and vibrate to the jarring of the great engine pulse that moves the myriad wheels. It is not at all a bad looking throng that pours out at its gates noon and night, and there is in it a pleasing absence of over-young folk. The villages of the old "Brown & Ives" firm, now called the Lonsdale Company, are models of their kind, and there is nothing in the appearance of the homeward hastening crowd to cause quotation of the "Cry of the Children," or recall the harrowing English tales of mill operatives.

Notice the girls and women passing; it is factory fashion to wear a white apron home from work; and a connoisseur of hand-made edgings would find every pattern under heavens adorning their hems. These immaculate starched aprons are by no means worn within, but hung religiously up with outer wraps and exchanged for gingham or print, the garb of toil. Among the men there seems to be also an unwritten law of uniform in most mills—overalls and cotton shirts for the ordinary laborers, black raiment, vest, but no coat or section and second hands, complete black suit for overseers. This is not an infallible rule, but it is a pretty general one.

In the old days, when many haughty dames who now own their carriages and request their poor relatives not to mention that they ever worked in a factory—in the days when they acknowledged the simple fact and were not ashamed—Lonsdale's mills were standing then, the old No. 1 and 2 over the river, and what different things they were from the giant Ann and Hope and her modern improvements! Nice New England girls were at the loom and the spinning frame then—cleaned their looms in the morning, and in the afternoon came in fresh and dainty with muslin gowns on! The web drawers, who now with a steel hook toss out the ends of the white warp with skilled speed, three or four to the second, used then in place of the steel hook to employ a small boy, who sat behind the warp and handed out the ends to the operator with guileless leisure, amid affable conversation. Still life was not the feverish whirl it now is. Those were the days of the "Lowell Offering," as remarkable a specimen of the people's literature as our continent has to offer. What sort of a "Lowell Offering" could be produced now, I wonder? For the sake of comparison it would be worth while for the philanthropic man of letters to offer prizes for literary products of the Lowell laborers.

But we are lingering too long upon our bridge in meditation. Let us pass on. Old Lonsdale, with her time-worn stone houses, and long tree-shaded streets, with ancient wood cottages, is to my mind far more attractive than new Lonsdale across the river, with her spick and span brick cottages, and imposing row of modern mansions for overseers, bookkeepers, superintendent and so on. A prettier little church than the ivy-shrouded Episcopal chapel, amid its picturesque setting, with the soft red of its arches and the mellow light of its stained glass, is scarcely to be found in Rhode Island, and as for "the first house on the left," the enviable home of boss farmer Magoon, it is simply the most charming house in Lonsdale, with its quaint design, its gray shingled walls and ivied foundations. Magoon's men, when questioned of Quinsnicket, were happily not mirthful, but communicative. It was a plain way: Turn down the hill at the church, cross the bridge over Scott's pond and keep straight on to the factory. It was a pretty smart mile and a half, they added. It was, indeed, the smartest mile and a half we ever travelled, and succeeded in convincing us it was at least a mile more than it really was, though every step of the way was fair, over the graceful stone bridge, where the wooded hillside sloped so temptingly down to the lovely lake, where rowboats were lazily rocking, and where, not far below, is roaming the erratic and treacherous floating island, broken again from its moorings.

Fairly out of Lonsdale proper, the most peaceful and picturesque rural homes dot the way. We wondered at them all. Homesteads of peace and plenty they looked to be. Were they ancestral homes of Lonsdale's ancient settlers, or the more recent acquisition of retired and thrifty mill operatives, enjoying well-earned rest? Flower gardens, chicken yards, bee farms, all manner of delightful pastoral pursuits, greeted the eye. An air of free-and-easy comfort was everywhere in the glad May air, and a wild desire came over us to stay here always, and "visit round" and never go home any more. We rested by a typical "babbling brook" in the shade of a deserted saw mill by the roadside, and ate oranges to the tinkling drip of the foamy, useless dam, regarded with breathless interest by a windowfull of bobbing heads in a cottage across the stream, whence the murmuring hum of many bees came fitfully. At last at our left rose the Butterfly factory, an anachronous old building, its original walls of vari-colored quarried stone, a long extension built for tanning purposes of more recent wood, and an extremely new and pert-looking brick chimney towering obtrusively aloft. We spied, or thought we did, the butterfly on the end wall, and sneered at the imagination that thought the resemblance worth the distinctive name, but passing the front we looked up again, and lo! here was the butterfly indeed in dark steel gray on the lighter walls, its mammoth wings made from one great split stone, set turned apart in the wall, and therefore, of course, exactly corresponding. Light seams through the dark gray add to the resemblance as veinings in the wings.

Idle stands the old factory, as it has been at intervals since the day of its building; used for various purposes—shoddy making, tanning, cotton carding, and at present idle altogether, it has not had a particularly useful career, but it looks staunch enough to be put to any purpose. From its situation, remote from anywhere in particular except its own little laughing Moshassuck, it will be long before it becomes a hard worker.

Right opposite is the old gray stone house, with its towering portion and lofty white pillars, built also of the same huge mottled stone from the Quinsnicket quarry, and by the same owner, Stephen H. Smith, long since passed to his rest. More carefully chosen is this stone front, and it is a pleasure to look at the soft harmonies of its red brown, its shaded grays and steel blues set skillfully together like a huge design in "crazy work," and softened by the tender green on the great trees on the lawn before it. Now the property of Daniel Meader, its twenty great rooms echo but to the footsteps of the worthy couple who alone occupy it.

Through winding paths, bridging the little Moshassuck again, the hostess kindly accompanied us through the forest mazes to Quinsnicket. Its approach is through a dense jungle, up the steep hillside, along the banks of a fern-bordered ravine, down which a wee stream trickles like its far away prototypes in similar glens among the mountains. Magnificent boxwood trees flare densely white in their pale green setting across the pathway, and solemn white pines murmur perpetually amid the silence. At last it is reached—a natural amphitheatre, rock-walled and tree-sheltered, a valley in the wild hillside, and through it a small stream flowing, with a grove of huge pines and hemlocks on its banks. This was the winter camp of the Narragansetts in far-off days, and opinion is divided as to whether its name Quinsnicket signifies "winter quarters," or, according to latest authority, "the place of many stone houses."

The remains of stone houses are here plainly enough in the scattered bowlders and hewn rocks; and until lately the stone wigwam, known as "Queen Mary's," was still standing till overthrown by a stupid workman sent up for stone for a wall. A huge honey locust, planted by the fallen stones years ago to further mark the spot, towers skyward, and up high on the sheltering hillside towers the stupendous mass of pulpit rock, whence King Philip harangued the warriors on the level below, among their stone houses by the brook beneath the pines.

Two caves are yet well defined in the jutting masses of Pulpit Rock; one easy of approach, the other now submerged; for the little jewel of a lake that flashes on one when the rock mass is climbed, is growing yearly deeper, and Pulpit Rock's overhanging masses bathe deeper in its laughing waters, shut in everywhere by the silent woods. Table Rock is the highest crag of all, and everywhere one turns the view seems lovelier.

The goldfish, with which the ancient owner stocked the lake, sparkle here still, and down in the Indian camp a few solitary garden flowers peep among the wild growth—vanishing relics of a once blooming garden in the forest. Old Stephen Smith was a passionate flower lover, and when he changed his abode from the stone house to the little cottage down by the stream, whose quaint grounds still bear traces of his adorning, folk came from far and near to behold the wilderness of bloom about it.

Private property until now, wild Quinsnicket is about to pass by will from Ruth Smith, a niece of the old owner, in-

the hands of Lawyer Tillinghast of
s city, to be held for the public enjoy-
nt; a worthy gift, but the place can
rcely be more public than it has been
de by picnic parties for years back,
the ruins of many a camp fire, more
dern than King Philip's, will attest.
d, indeed, a faint and shadowy memory stole over me, as I threaded the yawning ways of vast Pulpit Rock, and looked
out with surprised delight on the bit of
a shimmering lake, that in far-off school
days I had climbed that very way with a
party of schoolmates, that someone had
said, "There's goldfish in that pond," and
that I had laughed the idea to scorn.

FOSTER AND SCITUATE.

[No railroad in Foster. Danielsonville stage runs through Scituate and Northern Foster.]

A FARM in Foster. This is a term which in Rhode Island has grown to be synonymous with the acme of barrenness and sterility. Summit, where the train halts last before you get there, looks not so exalted as its name sounds, but it is on very high table land, nevertheless, and the map shows it to be the water-shed for all the small streams about. Near Summit, itself a region of stones, is a curious isolated collection of round bowlders, smooth and round and containing no signs of mica, as the surrounding stones do. They cover a space of some 50 acres, and can hardly have been placed together by man; and, as a Coventry native indignantly and unanswerably demanded of us, "If the Almighty put 'em there, what in the name of common sense did He do it for?"

South of the present railroad runs the old "seven and 'ten line" of the former one, called so both in legal and common parlance still from the fact that it was owned by seventeen men, seven of whom owned on one side and ten on the other.

The present line divides the township as nearly in halves as may be, and from the car windows one looks easily north into Foster and south into West Greenwich, between the wooded hills. Along with the train runs the Flat river beside it, named from the fact that for seven miles here it has an average fall of but seven inches to the mile. Away down to the southeast, just over the border, lies Mishnock Pond, about whose wild borders lives a scant population in as wild and primitive style as Rhode Island can show. Here came once, when covered carriages were new to these regions, a young couple in one of these resplendent vehicles, to seek the resident clergyman and be wed. The few natives hastily repaired thither—not to attend the wedding, but to see the carriage. But, alas! during the ceremony a gale arose, that stylish top was hurled off and blown into Mishnock Pond, and went sailing away in the darkness, and the new-married pair, after having paid the minister in a bag of white beans, were obliged to drive home like ordinary mortals.

Two miles south of Greene lies Coventry's chief source of wealth outside the wood lots and the farm lands—the great cranberry bog of 400 acres, black and treacherous with "pot holes," shut in by dense jungles of deer laurel, and surrounded by wooded hills. When the quaking bog freezes numberless cartloads of sand will be distributed all over its surface, to suit the perverted tastes of the little amphibious berry. There are lively times at the bog in the picking season, when 200 pickers are employed, and sometimes 2500 barrels of the red and white fruit go into the great cranberry house by the grass pond's edge. There they are sifted down inclined sieves, over which the big berries speed nimbly, while the little ones drop through, to be sold as inferior quality. The bog is anything but safe, for even where the pot holes are not, the matted carpet of vines overlies a spongy substructure. The pickers, as they bend on their knees, gradually sink deeper and deeper on their frail mats, and when they arise it is from a deep, moist hollow. Only last season a woman sank into a bog hole up to her neck and was rescued with difficulty. The bog is the bane of hunters, for all wild

atures know the place as a safe and
ckless haven, and in among the dense
:r laurel the dogs and the quarry dis-
pear and are seen no more till it pleases
:m to come forth.
A breed of great white rabbits have
ir homes about this bog, and there live
peace and multiply. They are mottled
l reddish in warm weather, but by mid-
iter become snowy white; and some
nter of the wild and uncanny ought
catch them at their concourse in win-
moonlight.
To Foster the road lies due north from
eene, past Rice City and Coventry's
ist interesting section.
The little Buckshorn is crossed, named
m the ancient discovery in the brook-
l of two pairs of buck's antlers and
ills, firmly interlocked in what was

running through it, two huge elms towering over the whole place, before the big
square, southward facing house known
as the Hutchinson place, birthplace of
Judge Matteson. The little white church
here was known for years as the Christian
Church, and here old Elder Burlingame,
the first licensed State temperance lec-
turer, preached for 65 years. It was this
church that the old slave attended who
is remembered still in the walled field
known as the "Jack lot." Jack was a
slave kidnapped in the old fashion when
the slave trade most flourished, brought
direct to Warren from the Guinea coast
with a young girl companion. He was
brought to Foster where he proved a faithful and willing servant, though he never
mastered but two words of the English language, which were, singularly enough,

MOUNT VERNON.

)bably a death struggle. A depression
the earth, a few huge crumbling stones,
se by the road, near the brook, show
.ere once stood the home of "Sheriff
rdan," a terror to tramps and evil
ers, and wielder of the town whip in
 still remembered days when a whip-
ig post was a necessary part of the ju-
ial armament. Another ruin stands
ther on, across the way, the old chim-
y of what was the birthplace of the
stress of the well-known Fiske home-
ad of Cumberland. A strange fact
own of this road past Rice City is that
e dwellers upon it committed suicide—
ck. Bly, Andrew Knox, Fairbanks and
ittison, and that three of them are
ried here in one small graveyard.
Rice City, wee hamlet as it is, makes
pretty picture as one comes upon it over
 rising road, the hard, level turnpike

the two unmanageable ones for a foreigner's tongue, January and February.
Jack had a deeply religious nature, and
managed to convey the idea of his wish
to join the church, for he was an adept
in his invented sign language. Being ex-
amined by the church worthies, he gave
them to understand that his religious
beliefs were similar to those of Richard
Waterman, a leading citizen. This was
satisfactory, and the old slave was admitted, and thereafter took part in the
conference meetings with great enjoyment, rising and repeating "January,
February, January, February," numberless times with much solemnity and satisfaction. Jack worked hard, saved money,
bought himself and his kidnapped companion, married her and ended his days
in a bit of a home in the old Jack lot.
The road which one traverses now for

a space before getting into Foster is the old Norwich and Providence turnpike, the old residents along which can yet remember when in lieu of the humming telegraph lines, dispatches were sent on the backs of slender boys, mounted on swift horses, while the old stages, lumbering along at a four-mile-an-hour gait, brought up the rear with detailed information. Here, a trifle west of Rice City, stood the famous old "half-way house," the McGregor tavern, where a scant two years ago the most interesting private collection of old relics in the State went up in flames and smoke. Just east of Rice City, to the left as we journey Fosterward, is the chimney of another old tavern, the Carpenter tavern. It rises sharply and staunch on the rocky rise close to the road, huge fireplace, brick oven and rusty crane all open to the daylight, and a lightning rod swaying forlornly above it.

Two miles east is the decaying old Walker house, marking the spot where the old turnpike gate used to swing. The Walker family had this post for 80 years. The old house is still inhabited by an aged and solitary member of the departed family. The old man has relatives with whom he might live, but prefers the solitude of his old home. Enormous quantities of "creeping Jenny" are found along here, and Alfred Cahoon, who lives near the line, is keeping the neighboring youth busy procuring and twining it into ropes for shipment during the holiday season. New York is the chief market, and Mr. Cahoon has already promised 30,-000 yards. Over across a marshy pasture, among the stones at the hill-foot, is a spring, known as Lafayette's ever since, in 1825, the Marquis paused there to drink.

Just at the Foster line stood the famous "great chestnut" and a school house of the same name at its foot. In the hollow of this famed old tree it is said one could turn a fence rail around in a circle unhampered. The old tree has been dead for years, and the school house, whose master once eluded the sheriff by skipping jauntily over the boundary line running through its precincts, is gone, too. Now one may take a road straight north to Foster Centre, more commonly "Hemlock," or northeast to Mt. Vernon, a quaint little hamlet, still known as the seat of the old Mt. Vernon Bank, estab-

SITE OF THE OLD BANK, MT. VERNON.

lished in 1823, when the mouldering homesteads were then the centre of a thriving little village. Even now its dwellings rise superior, in a look of thrift and substantial architecture, to most of Foster's settlements. "Cannon Rock" is an old-time relic still pointed out with enjoyment by old farmers—a huge rock hollow without a crack, in whose egg-shaped concavity used to be fired the explosive gunpowder blasts that heralded any especial festivity of the hamlet, with a roar that reverberated round the country side. Mt. Vernon's old residents will tell you tales by the hour of the eccentric school master alluded to above. It was about 1840 when the bank was abandoned, and the little village began the day of decadence. Still, on its breezy heights here is more charm yet in its air of abandonment than in its most prosperous days.

There are no more substantial farm houses in the town, with evidences of former prosperity, than two or three roomy, rambling old places on Mt. Vernon, where Mrs. Dorrance now holds sole

MT. VERNON POST OFFICE.

way as Postmistress for the neighborhood, and dispenses the mail from a wall cupboard.

Between here and the north road lies the old home of Dr. Thomas O. H. Carpenter. The ruins of the home are here, and in a more modern cottage on the estate a grandson lives. Judging from old ledgers, the doctor's fees were modest and his practice extensive. Most curious of all the old doctor's history is his graveyard, all by itself, down on the edge of lonely swamp. The doctor married a second wife, but when he came to die he expressed a desire that none but his first wife should be buried near him. To effect this wish he directed the construction of the unique enclosure. It stands among the leafless hazels and alders close to a lonely cross road, and is like a huge stone box, without a cover. It is composed of four mammoth stone slabs, planted on edge, each 10 feet long, four feet high, and some six inches in thickness. These four enormous granite slabs are firmly riveted together by ponderous iron bolts, and will stand as long as the township does. Inside are the two gravestones, side by side, each with a carved weeping willow at the top, one recording the doctor's death in 1839 at the age of 62, the other of Henrietta, his wife, in 1827, aged 20 years. Rank green moss grows thickly in the moist soil of the enclosure, and a pine is starting up on the doctor's grave.

Far away to the northwest is the Arcadian Mount Hygeia, where the Hon. Theodore Foster, from whom the township's name comes, came with a bosom friend to realize a youthful and romantic dream. A college classmate, afterward botanist in Brown, Solomon Drowne, joined hazards with him a quarter of a century after their young agreement was made, and here on these heights they built their ideal farm homes, improved the land, laid out a broad highway, christened the "Appian Way," and gave classic names to all the region. It was a quaint fancy, harmoniously executed, and a pretty bit of

FOR HIMSELF AND FIRST WIFE.

romance to come upon in this depopulated silent country. In 1820 the small township numbered 3000 souls; now it has a scant half that number, and the homesteads are widely scattered, many falling to decay.

Southwest from Mount Hygeia, just on the Connecticut border, is a beautiful great grove, hard by where the well-known "Line store" once stood, but now burned down. Here every summer or early autumn has been held for long years the annual Foster picnic, when all the 1500 inhabitants turn out to a man, and great is the festivity. It is the occasion of the year. On Fenner Hill stands the Foster Asylum, with some eight or ten inmates. A pleasant place it is, too; a roomy, gray, rambling old farmhouse, once the Obadiah Fenner homestead, with its barns and sheds sloping down the abrupt drop of the gnarled old orchard to the winding Moosup, with huge elms drooping over its gray roof, and the old Fenner graveyard across the way, enclosed in a massive, square stone wall, and filled with tall, slender spruces.

Pleasure driving in Foster is not the chief amusement. We met one team and overtook one in our 20-mile circuit, and encountered one patriarchal pedestrian, trudging down a wood-bordered cross-road. Howard Hill was the home of the seven Howard brothers, the tales of whose stature and prowess recall the "fierce Doones of Exmoor." All the way from six feet to seven were their various heights said to be, corroborated by the length of the graves in the walled enclosure out in a stony and swampy field. Of one of these Howards, Richard, it is related that he set out one morning to take the stage to Providence, but walked on till it should overtake him. He had got down into Scituate when it came along, and thinking as he had got so far on foot he might as well continue, he walked on into Providence, arriving some 15 minutes behind the stage.

The few old-fashioned farms we passed seemed in their day to have been more opulent and prosperous than those of southern Coventry and West Greenwich; there the little homes were sprinkled more thickly, but were less pretentious in character. The old Hopkins place was among the finest we saw in Foster, with a most beautiful distant view from its level heights. The Hopkinses, the Howards and the Aylesworths were the earliest settlers in the township, and several of their descendants are to be found there still.

More hills, more woods, always more stones, and by and by the neat little settlement of Foster Centre in the Hemlock district dawns on us like a positive joy, so refreshing is the contrast of modern and prosperous humanity to the mouldering look of antiquity that lies even over the face of Nature herself in southern Foster. So gray and old were all her unhewn forests, so rock-strewn the hoary pas-

tures that it was sometimes difficult to tell where stone wall left off and pasture began. The old graveyards were most numerous and most populous of all the settlements; but among their varying mortuary lore there was nothing that proclaimed the tide of poesy at so low an ebb as the doggerel rhymes we had spied back in the Mt. Vernon burying ground.

Candis
Wife of
Amaziah Blackmar,
Died Feb. 13, 1816,
Aged 65 years.

Candis Blackmar is my name,
America is my nation,
Foster is my native place,
And Christ is my salvation.

When I am dead and gone,
And all my bones are rotten,
Jesus Christ will think of me,
When I am quite forgotten.

Northern Foster is seen most agreeably by means of the old stage-coach route that passes through it and Scituate; it is a most agreeable all day's trip, in propitious weather.

In these days of rapid transit, it is a

are experience to travel over the same route as did one's grandparents, by the same mode of conveyance, and with the self-same driver. All these may one do if he bespeaks passage to Danielsonville at the old city stage office, for the quaint, lumbering coaches are running yet, with good patronage, and the veteran of the road, John W. Richards, reigns on the box seat still, and will tell you, with a touch of pardonable pride, that he came in in the Administration of Andrew Jackson, 57 years ago. All along the city streets, as the old coach rattles along, picking up passengers, it is stared after with a good degree of interest by passing citizens outside its daily route, and there ston elm" by the highway, towering and stately, but it is nothing to the giant that died here of old age a few years since, of national repute, and which Holmes, the tree-lover, came searching over this very route long years ago. Our fallen monarch he pronounces "a grand old elm for size of trunk, spread of limbs, and muscular development—one of the first, perhaps the first, of the first class of New England elms." Of those who saw it in its green cloud of glory, his description will almost make the heart leap as did his in the finding.

"As I rode along the pleasant way, watching eagerly for the object of my journey, the rounded tops of the elms rose from time to time at

DANIELSONVILLE STAGE.

are many who gaze after it with a retrospective fondness, and a memory of the days when Smithfield Seminary was in its glory, and the jolly stage ride out was the event of the term.

Inside the coach the old-time decorations prevail yet, the age-blackened leather, the faded velvet upholstery, the confronting seats with the always avoided "middle," and the swaying straps that are great comfort on the hardest roads. It is 10 a. m. when the stage leaves the down-town office, anywhere from 10:30 to 11 when it makes its first halt at Olneyville square, and rattles on, its four horses fresh and mildly hilarious now, toward the Elm House and the Johnston suburbs beyond. There is still a beautiful "John-

the roadside. Wherever one looked taller and fuller than the rest, I asked myself: 'Is this it?' But as I drew nearer they grew smaller, or it proved, perhaps, that two standing in a line had looked like one, and so deceived me. At last, all at once, when I was not thinking of it—I declare to you it makes my flesh creep when I think of it now—all at once I saw a great green cloud swelling in the horizon, so vast, so symmetrical, of such Olympian majesty and imperial supremacy among the lesser forest-growths, that my heart stopped short, then jumped at my ribs as a hunter springs at a five-barred gate, and I felt all through me, without need of uttering the words: 'This is It!' "

Over beyond, as the land grows higher and the June air sweeter, lies to the left beside a small school house, a bit of a graveyard, conspicuous in which is the King monument in memory of the Governor contemporary with the Dorr War. Far away, too, Acote's Hill, another memory, looks across serenely from blue distance on the quiet graveyard. Up in a corner is the tomb, now guarded by iron doors, whose copper ones were a few years ago so mysteriously stolen and disposed of, that no trace has ever yet been obtained of them. Where the tracks ceased at the roadside the clue ceased too. Neutaconkanut's long green rampart dwindles and ceases at the left, with but small likeness to its imposing height at the Plainfield car terminus, and, on the other hand, away beyond the mass of

JOHN W. RICHARDS, THE VETERAN DRIVER.

swaying forest tree tops lies the famous Snake Den, with its tumble of rocks and slippery ledges, and the cascade that most observers pronounce a perfect miniature of Niagara. From the Snake Den on, the road lies through a tract once dreaded of solitary travellers, Waterman's Woods, where more than one vehicle has been held up and despoiled. It is as lonely and untenanted now as in the days when highway robbery flourished, but most of the heavy forest growth is cut down, and the remaining woods are a younger generation of birch and chestnut.

Stump reservoir sparkles cheerily beyond it presently, and at its far end across the boggy pastures, is "The little dam school house," title innocent enough in itself, but provocative of severe displeasure on the part of some of the stage occupants when inquired for with equal innocence by the prospective school ma'am.

It is high noon when the stately evergreen grove and lofty white-pillared walls, rising still higher behind the woods, show where deserted Lapham stands silent, but queenly yet, even in her solitude. The pleasant pastures and stone-strewed old orchards about North Scituate are passed, the quaint little Quaker meeting house by the roadside whose scattered worshippers hold now but yearly service, and then to preserve their title; Moswansicut Lake, silent and lovely among the enshrouding woods, the old-time delight of hundreds of young men and maidens when the boarding school across the fields was a fact instead of a memory. In a clearing of the grove by the water is now the pleasant camp-ground of the family of Henry T. Root, who have for some time made this pleasant spot their summer rendezvous. On and into the quiet little village, past one of the oldest of old homesteads, the Bowen house with its brown walls and two huge chimneys, the village academy, the long tree-bordered West avenue, up which the stage used to merrily lumber with its load of anticipative pupils. Two present stagers, with memories yet warm, grow retrospective and exchange many "Do you remembers?" concerning the oak-tree seat, the Friday night socials in the hall, the cupolas scribbled full of pencil names and sentiments, the "connecting blocks" with the jingling old pianos still in the music rooms, and the pranks of departed pupils. Many people are of opinion that with suitable facilities for travel, Lapham Institute might yet come again to the fore in its old capacity. There is no more peaceful and charming spot in our State for an institute of learning; but at present it is used occasionally by the Masons as an assembly hall, and occupied

r a family or two to prevent the decay
hich solitude hastens. The seminary
ays made the life of the village; since
en the quaint little Four Corners has
own sleepier and quieter, and the grassy
ads seem almost deserted. There is a
ore, a Post Office, where a Quakeress
igned for many long years, a tavern, the
hillips stand, where the stage halts for a
oment, exchanges mail bags also at the
tle office, and jolts on again through

CHOPMIST POST OFFICE.

e shaded main street of the village
ith its well-kept, tree-bordered home-
eads, where all through the warm sum-
er afternoons the main diversion is, as
has been for the last 25 years, playing
oquet.
Just beyond North Scituate the stages
eet; the drivers collect each their fares
presence of the other, to avoid blunder-
g, the news of the day is exchanged
d the various commissions, back starts
e coach toward the city, and the new
iver mounts and starts us on for Daniel-
nville. Although Mr. Stone is much
unger than his uncle, Mr. Richards,
, too, may be classed as a veteran of
e road, for he has driven for 25 years,
d, unlike most old stagers, is still
alive to the beauties of the road as his
ost enthusiastic passenger. On the brow
Chopmist, Scituate's western and high-
t hill, he halts the stage and calls at-
ntion to the wide and spreading view,
ding southward with a faint, pale
impse of blue ocean, down Narragan-
tt Pier way, and showing, ahead of
the wild, rolling and wooded wilder-
ss of Foster's deserted township. We
ve passed the old Angell tavern stand,
id to have been honored—as what old-
me hostelry is not—with fleeting visits
Washington and Lafayette. Just be-

hind us lies the old Stephen Hopkins
place, or more modern title, the West
homestead, where all manner of scape-
grace tales are told of a certain Archi-
bald West, descendant of the Governor;
among others, his fondness for firing at
a mark and taking on one occasion the
spreading border of his wife's Quaker cap
for his target. Naturally objecting, the
lady fled, shrieking up through the
house, emerging in her alarm through
the roof scuttle and running around the
square huge chimney that rises solidly yet
to adorn the tale—a feat which the gazer
thinks the much-tried wife would have
hesitated to attempt in her calmer
moments on the sharply sloping roof.
The house is full of relics of olden time,
and just beyond lies the family burying
ground, with names yet older than the
present house, for the original Stephen
Hopkins house crumbled to its fall on this
same site.
Chopmist's long hill is climbed, the
western descent begins. Why Chopmist?
And the driver thinks because this hill
ridge is a literal "chopmist." He has
noticed, he says, hundreds of times, the
morning fog rolling and tossing heavily
down the valleys on either hand, while
the hill highway lies in clear air, and
perhaps there is no one living to confute
this theory. Chopmist has a Post Office,

GOV. WEST HOMESTEAD.

a neat little white cottage on the summit, with its sign in an old lilac bush,
and the Postmistress leaves her croquet
game in the shady orchard to run hastily
in and come out with the leather bag.
It is surprising to see the amount of
mail that comes and goes along these
lonely roads—papers and magazines, that
is. The stage sometimes delivers four

sacks of printed matter at one trip. Everybody is on the lookout for the stage and the mail bag, and a temporary excitement attends the whole route. Parcels and packages fly through the air at the scattered homes; the natives run out with letters in their hands, and the family dogs come trotting with joyously wagging tails to get their newspapers. "Jack," a tawny mastiff, is one of the most faithful customers, and will manage to spring even up to the high box seat for his bundle in case the driver forgets or neglects him.

It is easy to tell where Scituate ceases and Foster begins; bad roads and stony pastures mark the change at once, though the northern part of the township, through which the stage line runs, is nothing to the rocky wilderness farther south in the region of Hemlock. The houses grow fewer, the woods denser. Now and then the driver points out the old homestead of man or woman well known to his Providence passengers, for many of its notable citizens are of Foster origin. Queer door-yard decorations strike the eye before the isolated farms and cottages, a favorite being a sewing machine body and a box top on which gay flowers and vines disport. One lady of an inventive turn of mind stands among a parterre of flower-bedecked furniture, where the hastening stage party catch a fleeting glimpse of bedposts, chairs and an old lounge rejoicing beneath a wealth of bloom. Every little house has its flourishing garden patch—a matter almost of necessity at this distance from market, and scarecrows are more frequent than their original models.

At South Foster Post Office—locally known as Hopkins Mills—there is a longer halt. Horses and stage, too, are changed, and a lighter wagon goes the last half of the trip. In the barn are all the varieties of the coach family, even the huge sleighs for winter use—arks like the primitive coaches themselves, only on runners. The three styles of stage coach for summer travel are, first, the huge, curve-bottomed vehicle called distinctively the "coach," and hung on high jacks; second, a similar but lighter vehicle, straight of bottom and hung on thoroughbrace leather, called the "stage wagon," and third, the passenger wagon, in which the way now lies to Danielsonville, the ordinary modern stage seen elsewhere, merely a roomy covered express wagon. Ancient as the quaint old-style coaches are, it is predicted that they will hold their ground for many years yet over routes where no railway runs, as there is yet to be invented any vehicle combining passenger space and comfort with baggage and express facilities so well as does the swaying, non-capsizable old coach, one of the few remaining last century vehicles. There is an old, old piece of sheet music, coarse of print and of obsolete type, entitled "Trip to Pawtucket," whose title-page is adorned with a fac-simile of this oldest coach.

Long ago, when the stock companies owned the road, the coaches were given names. The father of the present driver drove the "General Washington"; there was an "Excel," also, and the winter coaches went by number. Stage coaches are rather costly things at first hand, a first quality costing $800, though there is naturally little demand for a second-hand one, and the traveller sees them mouldering away their latter days in deserted, weed-grown fields. As a whole, stage traffic keeps up its numbers, though on this road the abandoning of the seminary, of course, took off half its patronage, and the fact that the large coach no longer goes the whole trip debars some picnic parties from trips just for the novelty of the thing. Still, there is even now an average of thirty or more passengers a week, and expressing brings in an equal sum. During warm weather excursionists swell the number, and small picnic parties take trips to some of the many beautiful groves and streams of Foster, and are picked up on the return three hours or so later. There is no more accommodating public conveyance in the State. Does a passenger desire a tempting flower by the wayside, a snap-shot at picturesque ruin, a visit to an old burying ground, there is always time and to spare; and if the stage is late into Danielsonville at night nobody cares.

The one important point is, imperatively, that the stage trip must be made, whether slowly or speedily. As a mail carrier, it must stop for no weather. The wildest snow storms and the biggest drifts —and Foster snow drifts are something appalling—do not keep the faithful coach at home. The rule of the road is imperative, "Keep going." Through snow and gale, with helpers along the populated roadway, without in the loneliest bits, the driver gets out and shovels and treads a way through the deepest blockades, and the horses, too, imbued, apparently, through long service, with a sense of their responsibility, struggle heroically, and it is a hard day indeed when the old coach does not at last pull through. When this rarely happens there are cordial shelters anywhere on the route, the driver merely lending his efforts to finding a sufficient one for the horses.

North Foster, or Foster Post Office proper, is the next stop, and it is claimed to be the oldest post office in the State. It looks it, surely, and the same family have had it in charge for more than a half century. It is a long, low, gray building, looking most like a blacksmith shop, and hollows and holes are worn through the floor, the threshold and door steps. The family all live within, though some years ago the Postmaster built next door the most pretentious house of the place; but when completed the heart of his wife failed her, and they stuck to the old home.

The mail exchanged, and the oldest inhabitants gratified with a long and guileless survey of the coach and passengers, Foster Post Office is left behind and the ascending road leads to Mount Hygeia, the seat of an idyl of Rhode Island quite worthy a pastoral poem. All the hills have names; there was Dolly Coles, way back in Scituate, and here is School House, with its namesake half way up its long limb. The seats of learning are but sparsely patronized now in Foster; the Mount Hygeia school has seven members enrolled for the current year, with an average attendance of three.

Mount Hygeia itself was named by the Damon and Pythias who founded the charming home here, now almost a century ago. It is seldom that two men of mature years carry out the enthusiastic dreams of early college days, but these two did— Dr. Solomon Drown and the Hon. Theodore Foster, for whom the township was named. With their taste for nature and pastoral pursuits still unmarred by social and professional success, they jointly established in this remote, wild and breezy nook the farm and home which they gave its present name; they broadened the then narrow and neglected road, renamed it the Appian Way, established quaint nooks about the dreamy old home—Virgil's Retreat and others—planted the old-fashioned garden whose traces are yet lingering, set out the thorn locusts and tulip trees that make the dropping, shady lane leading down to the wood-enclosed house from the stage road even now a path of delight, and had all things in common.

MOUNT HYGEIA.

The end of this charming departed pastoral comes upon one suddenly, on the mossy gray headstone among the silent graves in the fragrant old orchard just beyond:

SOLOMON DROWN, M. D.

Was born in Providence in 1753, graduated in Rhode Island College '73; studied medicine in Providence and Philadelphia; commenced practice in his native place; served as surgeon in the army of the Revolution; visited the hospitals and medical schools of Europe, '85; was present at the first settlement of Marietta, '88; moved to Pennsylvania, '92; returned to New England 1801; settled in this place; was appointed Professor of Botany and Materia Medica in Brown University, and continued the practice of medicine till his death, which occurred Feb. 5, 1834, in his 81st year.

The old farmhouse is square, white and hospitable looking, with old-fashioned fan light, but an illustration gives little idea of its romantic situation, or the many quaint and delightful nooks about it, and the old garden, with its ancient box borders. During a part of the year it is occupied by the family of Thomas L. Drown of Providence, a descendant of the original owner. Many public improvements were made by the first owner, notably in the highways, which the present population might emulate to advantage.

It is getting towards sunset when the Rhode Island line is crossed, and prospects brighten, for the roads grow speedily and perceptibly smoother. The way is enlivened by a home where dwell the happy parents of thirty-six children, most of them disporting in the door yard as we pass; the little Whetstone brook dips down into a sheltered valley; and the scenery on either hand grows lovely. We are loyal to our native State, but it certainly is a refreshing change as we penetrate farther into Connecticut. Factories line the Whetstone Valley, the brook empties into the Five-Mile river, that in turn flows into the Quinebaug, and on the Quinebaug is our terminus. The sun sinks behind the distant dreamy hills, the lakelets by the way and the foamy mill stream that follows the roadway glow in the gold and crimson light; East Killingly, the last Post Office, is reached and passed, and at last a broad suburban avenue lined with pleasant residences, a public park, monuments and fountains tell us we are approaching at last a real town. Before we get fairly into Danielsonville it has grown really dark; the stage halts once more at the Post Office and draws up at last with a flourish before the Attawangan House. We descend with pride from our all day's journey. To be sure, we have not gotten over the four hundred miles modern improvements would have made in that time, but we are travelling after last century models, and feel that to have come all the way through from Providence to Danielsonville without pausing is to have accomplished a most creditable feat.

LINCOLN AND NORTH SMITHFIELD.

[Worcester Division N. Y., N. H. and H. skirts Lincoln's eastern boundary. North Smithfield's tations are on Springfield Branch of N. Y. and N. E. Primrose Station, 15 miles from Providence. 'are, 50 cents.]

UST to the westward of Albion, where the Blackstone, recovering from its fall over the foamy dam, glides between high ledges and fringing woods, a oad leads past the plush factory and by pleasant old homestead distinguished y having had the scene of two books aid in its generous domains. While either has attained more than a local elebrity, there are few old families bout Lincoln and Cumberland who have not read "Three Holes in the Chimney," r "Rhoda Thornton." In the pleasant ld homestead now known as the Ieader place lived, in the early years of his century, a certain Deborah Hill, of vhom many conflicting traditions are ow rife. She once took in, partly out f charity, partly because she needed uch help on her extensive and flourisharm, two orphaned children, Betsey Ann Ray and her brother George. She s said by many to have treated these hildren with extreme cruelty, while the lescendants of her friends strenuously leny it. At all events, when she afterward adopted another child, Rhoda Jrocker, and when a Pawtucket lady, Irs. Pratt, published the book "Rhoda Thornton," which was an account of this hild's life which represented Deborah till in a too favorable light, Betsey Ann Ray prepared her own volume, "Three Ioles in the Chimney; or, a Scattered family," to enlighten a deluded world. Now an elderly woman, married and living outside the State, she is represented s an extremely garrulous person who arries constantly with her a portfolio of rude drawings which represent the various scenes of her childhood's wrongs and who seizes every opportunity for once more relating the more harrowing portions of her youthful tragedy. The book itself is crudely written, garrulous and digressive, though related calmly and with no apparent vindictiveness. Here is her naive portrait of her tyrant:

"Her name was Deborah Gill. Her father was a carpenter, and Samuel Gill was called one of the best of men. He gave his children, 15 in number, a good education, and some of them trades. He lived on a farm one mile northwest of Albion, in an old house which was called the old 'Muzzy House.' It stood down in a lot called 'the meadow,' near the stage road that leads from Woonsocket to Providence, on the Smithfield side of the river. This woman had so many peculiarities that her father used to say he believed 'she was the only child he had which was scarcely worth raising.' She grew all the same to be a strong, muscular woman, although not at all coarse, and in her general appearance and conversation could act the American lady. She was five feet six inches tall, with upright figure, and was perfectly well. She had straight, black hair, sprinkled with gray, low forehead, gray eyes and a nose quite large at the end; thin, compressed lips, straight wrinkles from nose to mouth, long teeth, well filled with gold; these she took great care of, always after eating taking a string and drawing it between them. When the Friends School was first opened in Providence she gave, as an opening offering, her services for three months as a teacher, hoping she might thus help the school and also secure a good situation; but as a parting salute for her numerous chastisements she had inflicted upon the scholars, as she stood upon one of the steps of a building belonging to this institution, a pail of water, not over clean, was unceremoniously turned over her, thus ruining a cloak and a new silk bonnet."

With equal prolixity of detail she describes the homestead where the scenes of these two narratives are laid, on the westward leading road from Manville, a little distance beyond Handy's plush mill, and which, though now modernized and altered, has many of the old landmarks distinguishable, and is one of the most attractive and hospitable-looking old homesteads on the length of the road.

DEBORAH HILL HOMESTEAD.

The "three holes in the chimney," which, without apparent reason, are thus exalted to the dignity of a title, are briefly mentioned thus in various places. "In the centre of the cellar is the chimney; the chimney is a small sheet iron door; if you push this up and look in you will see it is for ashes, thus secure from fire." "The chambers were the same as the rooms down stairs, only in the room over Deborah's sleeping room, behind a large chest in which bedding was kept, there was another little door. This opened into a great chasm, it seemed to be, over the oven in the sitting room." Again, "Half way up the front stairs at the left was a little door opening into a place in the great chimney, prepared for smoking hams, and under the stairs a dark closet."

Of her confinements in this first abode of darkness she writes at length with realistic fervor, and of Miss Deborah's shaking coat sleeves at her from without and growling that she was "old black Henry come to fetch her," without, however, greatly terrifying further the lonely child, who preferred anything to the cold, darkness and ashes within. She was also immured in the ham-smoking hole on the stairway, among the charred corn cobs, but the third hole seems to have failed to immortalize itself, except as counting one. Outside this narrative, however, the hole is historic. In our rambles about the old house, the little chimney door was opened, and it was shown us as having been the hiding place for all the Lime Rock Bank's money and papers during the Dorr war; out of its jurisdiction as the house then was, it certainly seemed a safe and improbable place of search, with the little door concealed and its existence unsuspected.

In its early days the house must have been embowered in more blooming shrubbery than now, judging by what the historian says. Many of its features are still unchanged; the old well still draws with a stubborn resistance that calls for the strong arms of a man; down in the cellar beside the chimney hole is cut the date 1787 in the stone, but whether it represents the house's age no one can say. In the tent-shaped stairway hole the four-pegged posts still rise for ham smoking, with the pan of charred corn cobs on the floor beneath. Out in the broad and tree-shaded yard is the tool house with the cheese room in the rear, where the little Ann once shut in the tramp of evil intent. The rose still grows beneath Miss Deborah's window, where that ancient maiden stealthily crawled in to make herself festive for her older lover, Captain Jenks, who eventually became her husband.

The tale, with all its crudity and the doubt that hangs about its sincerity, has yet something in it that haunts one, as a simple, old-fashioned record of New England life; and if a tenth part of its chronicled cruelties be true, Miss Deborah must have been indeed one of those unlovable females who have never been young.

Here is one instance: "'It would serve thee right,' said Deborah, after her niece had gone, 'not to give thee any dinner, but here are some victuals on Charles's plate that he has left to be wasted. Thee go and bring the swill pail in that stands under the wash bench.' Ann brought the pail covered with swill, sour and filthy. Deborah put the dinner for Ann in the pail and told her to carry it out and set it on one end of the sink drain, and to get down and eat it with her fingers. She was so sore and lame from her whipping she could not get down on her knees as she was told, so Deborah told her to stand in the drain itself, and then she could just reach it out of the pail.

"'None of thy sniffling; thee must eat it.' 'I can't,' said Ann; 'I feel sick to my stomach.' But she had got it to eat, so she shut her eyes that she could not see the pail; but in spite of all she was sick and nearly fainted. Then Deborah told her to get up and go to knitting. 'Here is some salt water to wash thee in; it will make thee tough and well.'"

Again: "Mary John laughed and said, 'When were you baptized?'

"'Perhaps I wasn't, but Aunt Deborah has ducked my head in water ever since I can remember for not getting my stent done and for being a naughty girl.'

"'It don't mean that way at all,' she said. 'A minister tips them backward into the water.'

"'Yes, Aunt Deborah took Capt. John's bathing tub, a great long tin one, big enough for me to lay down in, and had it filled with water and made me get in and lay on my back. I was afraid to, and she pushed me down under the water, and when she pulled me up I didn't know nothing. Aunt Hannah asked me what she done that for. I told her I did not get my stent done on Daniel's stockings and I wished all the men had to go barefoot. So I don't know whether I have been baptized or not, as Aunt Deborah sits in a higher seat than Joseph Smith, and he is a minister.'"

Over and over such tales recur—of perpetual whippings with shingles on hands and feet till the child could not step, once because she was found fondling a gauze kerchief of her mother's, when she had slipped from her bed, of feeding her with cayenne, of keeping her a day without food and setting her impossible tasks whose non-completion met with punishment; of specious promises and fair talk "before folks" and vengeance dire afterward.

The naiveté of the book, however, is often mirth-provoking, as in this statement: "Lydia Haynes, her friend Huldah and others watched her last moments, and they were shocked to hear her last words: 'Have I always given them children enough to eat?' Friends for different motives came to the funeral of this noted woman; some to whom she had been very kind felt sorry to see her laid away in the ground; they would no more receive favors at her expense. One friend prayed over her open grave with great earnestness, and enjoyed one thousand dollars of the dead woman's possessions, also, most of her clothing. Her kind niece, Olive, received a much worn bed quilt. Once more are childish voices heard in this country home, but how different! A kind father is the faithful David Kidder, and the gentle Lois is an affectionate mother. The great holes in the chimney will never hold their little boys."

David Kidder, in reality Daniel Meader, worked for Deborah Jenks in the last years of her life; he was 20 years of age when he came to the farm, and worked there for ten years; to him the farm was left, and it is his children who occupy the old place now. The Meaders disclaim the idea of extreme cruelty on Deborah's part, and say that Ann was a fractious child, who required severe treatment. It may be the truth lies, as it is wont to do, midway between extremes. A parting thrust, perhaps unconscious, lies in one of the closing paragraphs, as the author pictures herself revisiting the scenes of her childhood.

"Again she travels the sandy, lonesome road, now gladdened with dwellings. She stands beside the grave of Deborah; the trees are now large and shadow her resting place. She turns away with a sigh of relief that Deborah now rests from her labors, and her works do follow her."

Two or three miles west from here, over the North Smithfield line, is a house still more interesting in itself.

If the traveller, journeying by road

from Providence to Woonsocket, turn off the main highway to the left, just about where Lincoln ceases and North Smithfield begins, he will find the road gradually begin to ascend the long, long incline of Sayles Hill. Pine forests, oak, birch and chestnut border the silent roadway, where no man has yet built, and where, on snow drifts lingering under the mossy walls, are the tracks of quail, rabbit and fox. Up and up, till at the far away summit in a clearing to the left one sees two empty and abandoned homesteads, and across the way to the right, its entrance way emphasized by an aged ash tree, huge of bough and crumbling to decay, the quaint and curious old Sayles homestead, known far and wide as the "royal house," since the ancestors of the present occupying generation lived and died under the King.

Sufficiently odd in its outer architecture to catch the eye, its interior more than fulfills its promise of quaintness. A square, sloping-roofed central part, with a wee kitchen ell at either end, and all three boasting a separate front door and huge chimney of their own; but the western ell is unique. Scarcely anything but a huge chimney is it, of massive stone foundation, tapering gradually upward and capped by a four-cornered finish of brick;

THE ROYAL HOUSE.

the room around the chimney ingenuously reveals its substructure to the most casual eye, for the massive beams and rafters and the huge chimney itself rise above the mammoth fireplace without the slightest attempt at concealment, and one can step inside the ample hearth at any time and gazing upward view the heavens overhead. Nine feet wide is this colossal fireplace, its only mantel a huge beam 16 inches square, laid solidly across, and blackened and grayed into exquisite tints through the smoke of long years. Two ranges grace this otherwise unused fireplace, and three could be easily accommodated side by side within its ample recesses. The tiny panes of glass in the windows, the primitive latches of the doors, the break-neck stairway that winds about the central chimney, and, above all, the dining room door, are delightfully primitive. For this floor, that of the front room in the central part, instead of adhering to the conventional horizontal line common to doors, sweeps down from the centre in a graceful parabola, so that to gain the centre from the pantry, for instance, one makes an ascent of two decided climbing steps. No trace of irregular warping is there in these broad, hard pine boards of which the floor is laid, and the present occupants are of opinion that the arched floor was intentional, for some reason now never to be known, whether for ease in mopping, sweeping or as a primitive toboggan for the small fry. Passing through the central house by way of the pantry, where one prays as he views the old china, in the wake of the unsuspecting hostess, "Lord, keep my hands from picking and stealing," he emerges into the second kitchen ell, a room bright with the sunlight through its tiny panes, gold and white wall paper, and the cheer of immaculate and spotless housekeeping, and with a quaintness of shape that one discovers presently is due to the fact that this chimney is built cornerwise across one end of the room. A tall old clock ticks solemnly in another corner, splint-bottom, straight-back chairs stand all about the cosy room, and one breaks the 10th commandment again. Overhead, pendent from the low ceiling, are many huge iron hooks, now thriftily utilized as framework for an aerial clothes horse, primarily to hang the old flintlock guns across, in the troublous times of Indian invasion and when the tracks on the snow were of less innocent animals than fox and rabbit.

How old is the old house? Alas, nobody living knows. And as for the kitchen floor, Mr. Ben. Mathewson, who lives here, says he remembers to have heard Welcome Sayles declare at the age of 85 that it was always so as far back as he could remember, and that his father also could remember only the sloping floor in his day. This much is known about the house: Its first occupancy by the Sayles's was in 1720, when a grandson of Roger Williams and his bride took possession; and even then it was an old house. Its walls are not plastered, even at this late day; everything has been religiously preserved as nearly as possible as in the olden time, though wall paper covers the laths and keeps out the cold. Overhead, in the sloping floored rooms, is the huge centre beam, still called the "summer," as old New Englanders named it.

Here, on the bracing and breeze-swept heights of Sayles's Hill, are said to have originated the whole Sayles family far and wide through the Union. The first John Sayles came to this country in 1650, and tradition has it that, being a shipmaster, he came in his own ship. At any rate, he arrived by some means or other, and married Mary, the eldest daughter of Roger Williams. His son John also lived on Sayles's Hill, farther over its brow; he was the father of three boys, John, Richard and William, and it was Richard who, on Thanksgiving Day of 1720, brought his bride to her domain in the old "royal house." Five generations have lived and died there, Mr. and Miss Mathewson being children of a younger daughter of the fifth generation. The first resident Sayles was the first Town Clerk of Smithfield. Descendants of this old family are the Pascoag Sayles's, William R. Sayles of Pawtucket, W. F. and F. C. Sayles of the Saylesville Bleachery, and more than one new Western town bears the name Saylesville in loving remembrance of the old ancestral home.

A wide view over the hilly Cumberland forests, the Smithfield and Lincoln wastes, the distant suburbs of Woonsocket and the crowding villages of the beautiful Blackstone Valley one gets from the sloping meadows that rise still higher about the old house. Over the way and up a little rise is the old family burying ground, with stones ancient and modern. Here the last daughter of the race lingered lovingly and wistfully as she led her guests about, and spoke the words of loyal devotion to her old home that one could but feel amid all these mementoes of bygone ancestors, by the quaint old fireside full of bygone memories, and in the silent, crumbling graveyard where lie one's nearest and dearest.

Such as these are the true New England homes, growing daily fewer under the combined destructiveness of time, climate and progressive ideas. It is worth something to have merely entered one, and breathed, even for a time, its ancient and homelike spirit.

But North Smithfield was to reveal to us a vastly different phase of life in its more remote and wooded wilderness.

A CERTAIN fur dealer of Providence who has, of course, frequent dealings with many Rhode Island trappers, once remarked with a retrospective smile, "There's an old fellow named Owen Dixon that's quite a character, if you could only find him. He's trapped all over the State as long as I can remember, and I believe he lives somewhere in the North Smithfield woods—I don't know just where."

Neither, it transpired, did any one else in that line to whom queries were put; month after month this tempting ignis fatuus of a trapper seemed to dance alluringly before, receding as the searchers advanced. Now and then one had heard of Owen Dixon, or of a Smithfield trapper, but the "just where" was still an unknown quantity. That it is no longer so is a matter of great complacency in the minds of his exploring expedition, who may be designated as the hunter and the guileless one. The hunter was to serve as the "open sesame" to the trapper's heart by a common bond of interest; the guileless one was to remain innocently in the background, with eyes and ears well open and camera in hand.

Equipped for a day's tramp, if needful, the searchers took a morning train up the Springfield road, intending to alight at Field's Station, for their most positive authority believed he had some time seen the ignis fatuus hovering about that spot, and at any rate, some of the residents there might know something about him. This was a doubtful spur, but fortune favors the brave. The genial conductor warmed to the cause, and presently returned beaming from a quest in the smoking car with the welcome intelligence that a brakeman not only knew Owen Dixon by sight, but was also confident that his habit was to take and leave trains at Tarkiln. With Tarkiln prospective then, and Field's discarded, there was mental freedom to gaze upon the narrowing Woonasquatucket valley, with its crowding line of old-fashioned factory villages: Lymansville, Allendale, Centredale, Graniteville—the brakeman rang constant changes on the dales and villes at the mile-apart stations, till Georgiaville, most populous of all, called out most of the few passengers, and the train sped on to Stillwater and the reaches of its spreading reservoir. Nearly every little village has its gambrel-roofed factory cottages, nearly every one the highway leading off across the reservoir and dam. Allendale lay most picturesquely of all, and had a quaint little gem of a stucco church on a wooded rise. From Stillwater up, the stations lessened, ceased to be the home of industries, and dwindled to mere sheds beside the railroad, with a swinging sign overhead, and seats running around the three sheltered sides within. Field's Station announced itself by the long, low-roofed building which was once the most flourishing piggery of the State, but with some of the business now transferred to Smithfield. Far off to the wooded east the conductor pointed out the classic spot where Lannon and Ashton once met in combat. The snow lay deeper as the train sped up the river valley, the pine woods thickened, brooks widened into broad marshes and the habitations of man grew few and far between. Overhead the crows circled, and one could see the forests bowing before the breath of the northwest wind. Tarkiln dawned modestly in view at length—a scant dozen houses clustered round an abandoned mill and a tiny station all by itself on the woods' edge. Did the station master know Owen Dixon? He did. (Intense joy.) Could he tell where he lived? He could. (Breathless anticipation.) Turn up that road through the woods—he lived in the first house to the left. (Entire collapse, and disappointed cries of "Does he live in a house?" to the station agent's vast perplexity.) But that the trail was not a false one, even though it ended in a house, was something, and the explorers pressed on, over crusted snow ankle deep, though a kindly thaw had laid Providence outskirts well-

recent wearers, and spirits revived. He did not live here, then, after all. The hunter advanced and rapped, a string lifted the latch, and a stalwart, elderly six-footer stood within, while about him swarmed a band of infants of tender age, their ablutions apparently in a state of suspense. "Can you tell me where Owen Dixon lives?" cheerfully inquired the hunter.

"That's my name," responded the host. With commendable presence of mind the hunter inquired, after a perceptible start, "You are a trapper, I believe. Have you any furs on hand just now?"

Mr. Dixon had not, but bade them

THE TRAPPER'S HUT.

nigh bare two days before. The breezy North Smithfield hills have a vastly different temperature from that about the bay, and it is the portion of the State most resorted to by invalids of consumptive tendency. That it was decidedly cooler than at home was a fact quickly discoverable, and it was with a shudder that the travellers hastened over a roaring icy trout brook that crossed the road and plunged babbling into the forest. The first house on the left was a small, white, out-of-repair structure standing almost directly on the road; a wash waving on the line indicated a goodly number of small fry as

enter, and engaged the hunter at once in affable conversation on the subject of skins, while the guileless one executed automatic smiles for the lesser infants, and calculated with sinking heart the chances of getting an article out of this material. But what were these welcome words the trapper was presently uttering? "Yes, I've got a hut two and a half miles or so from here in the woods; just come down from there to see my darter."

"Oh, may we go and see it?" cried the guileless one. "We should so much like to go and see where you live in the woods!"

"Why, yes," replied the trapper with a

slow smile. "If you want to. It's awful goin', though. Worst walkin' of the hull winter." As though this mattered! "I'm jest goin' back," resumed Mr. Dixon, getting into his coat, his hat having been all the while donned. "Lucky I be—guess you couldn't never find the way there alone."

The event proved it lucky indeed, for in that wild forest of pine, oak and chestnut, with its dozen of trickling brooks, its hundred hills and hollows, its marshes and its pitfalls, one might hunt the longest day through as vainly as for a needle in a hay stack, for the hidden hut of the man who tramped staunchly and unhesitatingly ahead, threading his way through the thickets, making detours for brook beds, skirting the highest hillsides and striding across the frozen marshes, while his followers, slipping over the crust, stumbling in the frozen footprints, breaking through the snow softened by sunshine, and now and then plunging more than overshoe deep into some hollow deep with ice water, felt doubly sure that it was indeed the worst going of the whole winter. There was exhilaration, though, in the high, bracing air, in the soothing forest odors, in the rushing sweep of the leaping brown trout brooks, the vivid green of the snow-freshened moss on the black, rotten stumps, and even in the vigorous buffetings of the northwest wind on some breezy rise. Here by the brook was a mink track; there a partridge had run, and a fox track lay beside the invisible pathway for some distance.

"I had an otter trap stole out of that culvert," shouted back Mr. Dixon jovially from his commanding eminence, as he toiled ahead up a rocky rise. "An otter travels down this brook every spring, and I'll git him yet."

"There seem to be mink tracks along here, too," observed the hunter.

"Yeup. There's a place up the brook where mink's been running. I set a rabbit's head bait for 'em, an' caught three a runnin'. Mink's going to be high next season. "If 'twant for this pluguey snow a man might make something this winter. I ain't doin' anything now—traps all froze up. I've got a hundred steel traps set, too, here and there, and deadfalls all over the country."

"Whereabouts have you trapped most, Mr. Dixon?" queried the guileless one.

"Oh, all over the State, pretty much, though mostly in the northern townships. I was born near here in Smithfield, but I lived quite a spell in Eastbury, and trapped round a lot o' them Connecticut towns."

Down the wind came a long, high, musical bell note. "Boo-o-o-o-o-oo!" Another chimed in, not a hair's breadth lower. "Boo-o-oooo!" Is there a hunter living whose heart does not leap to the cry of hounds giving tongue on the trail? "Guess Jake and Buck have got into our trail," remarked Mr. Dixon. "You can't get them two old hounds of mine to look at a rabbit track. Fox and raccoon is all the scent they'll notice." The bell tones grew clearer, nearer, the underbrush crackled, and the two dogs, with noses to earth, came plunging through the crusted snow by the brook border, and flung themselves with boisterous rejoicing upon the trapper, gun and all.

"I've seen thirty-four foxes before that hound," continued Mr. Dixon, indicating the younger. "He's a fast one. You see how thin the other one is? Well, they hunt together, and Buck's just run him to death. He wears his flesh all off trying to keep up with Buck."

"Are foxes plenty about here?"

"Well, fairly, though nothing to what they was. I figure I've killed 148 foxes in the Rhode Island woods, first and last."

On and on marched the trapper and his augmented band of followers in Indian file through the faint trail, now and then descending into marsh or ravine, but mainly climbing, until the hunter, suddenly turning to the next in rank, silently raised his hand with the air of a Balboa discovering the Pacific, toward the pilgrims' Mecca.

On a bare round hillock stood the hut, wind-swept and breezy, rising roundly from a silent cedar swamp, and this in turn shut in by the wooded hills of the sighing pine forest. Built some years ago, when a peripatetic steam saw mill occupied the shorn hill, it was diverted to its domestic use by Mr. Dixon some four years ago. A rough structure some 12 feet square, a section of stove pipe protruding through its roof as chimney, one small window facing south and another north, and its front entry opening from the east, and adorned with skunk skins, it stood on the rising hillock unsheltered from the four wild winds of heaven, except by a high banking on the more exposed quarters to keep the structure from rocking too wildly in the north wind's grasp. The sole outer decorations were a saw horse and a rusty stove, which latter was sometimes pressed into summer service as a camp fire. A wee square of comparatively level ground, having an air somewhat less rampantly wild than its surroundings, Mr. Dixon indicated pridefully as the garden, and remarked that he had raised two crops of potatoes last season. He produced a key and flung the one door open for his guests to enter.

"And do you keep house here all by yourself, Mr. Dixon?" asked the guileless one, entering the square fireless room flooded with sunshine.

"Well, no; I've got a wife round here somewheres—guess she's gone down to Tarkiln. Set down, won't ye?"

A Mrs. Dixon, forsooth; this was indeed a bitter blow, and nipped in the bud many pleasing anticipations as to original recipes and other domestic notes masculine. But its pangs were assuaged as the twain gazed with interest about this primitive abode. Rough was its floor, rougher its walls, its cracks ingeniously suppressed under stretching boards here and there, no doubt to be levied upon sometime for their original use. The furniture consisted of two old-fashioned four-poster beds, also neatly mended with a skunk stretcher, a wide and a narrow one, on either side the room, and the narrow one economically pressed into service as the preparatory step to mounting a ladder that led into unexplored upper regions. The single downstairs room, however, held most of the simple Lares and Penates,

and boasted also three chairs, a table, and an open cupboard, where the modest display of stone china, tin and pewter showed the unworldly aspirations of these forest denizens. Under the lowest shelf were a barrel of flour—a flour barrel, rather—a meal keg, vinegar and molasses jugs, and another barrel held invisible contents, afterwards judged to be apples, when a sprightly young grandson took a header therein and emerged with a sample of that fruit triumphantly impaled upon a jack knife. On a swing shelf overhead was a piece of salt pork. A Farmer's Almanac represented the literature, but Mr. Dixon didn't think much of it as a true prophet nowadays, he said later.

THE NORTH SMITHFIELD TRAPPER.

"I'll have a fire for ye in no time," announced Mr. Dixon, seizing a hatchet and departing for the forest, whence he presently returned with several sections of young birch trees. His guests, meanwhile, scrutinized the various mural decorations, consisting of many newspaper cuts, their sombre hues enlivened by an occasional gaudy lithograph, a fox terrier in pasteboard, a tissue paper lady, clothed in raiment of gorgeous hue—a concession, perhaps, to a feminine weakness for surveying fine apparel, which found small gratification in this far-reaching forest—and the whole interspersed with the nail-hung raiment of the occupants, in artless but effective draping, while boots and shoes were thriftily hung up aloft. Everything was put tidily in place, though more than one article evinced the paucity of the water supply, and the truth of the fact that a woman couldn't work much when she wan't feeling smart, as Mrs. Dixon, who appeared later, remarked.

The hunter espied a fiddle bow poised aloft. "Do you play?" he asked.

"Oh, yes. I've played more'n forty year," said the trapper, applying a match. "Used to play down to Buttonwoods twenty-five years ago. Played for the Howard races and the fat woman. Used to sit in the door and fiddle, it didn't matter much what, jest to git the folks in."

"Give us a tune," requested the hunter. Nothing loth, the trapper seated himself on the bed, tuned his festive violin, while columns of smoke rose from the protesting stove, and sawed a sprightly air, waving his bow deprecatingly at the murmured applause, and exclaiming, "Well, they say it takes a fool to make a fire, but I donno but mine's gone out while I been fiddling here."

"Mr. Dixon," now said the guileless one, "I should very much like to have a picture of your little hut, and of you also. Do you mind if I take one?"

"Land, no," replied Mr. Dixon, with alacrity. "Is that your instrument you got with you? How do you want me to look?"

The "instrument" was focussed, the shutter snapped, the hermit immortalized, the hunter afterward reporting to the absorbed operator that the various play of expression and pose on the part of the sitter, as various happy ideas on the subject struck him, were diverting in the extreme. Returning to the house, the fire was now found to be crackling merrily, the two hounds basking beside it, and a gray and white cat curled into a circle and standing on her head in sound slumber on the bed.

"I am afraid your fire is going to make you out a fool, after all, Mr. Dixon," remarked the guileless one.

"Wall, 'twon't be far off the truth if it does," hilariously shouted the trapper, casting on more fuel. "Hallo, here comes my wife now. Thought she'd git round before long to see who'd come. News travels fast in these parts."

An apprehensive and startled look passed over Mrs. Dixon's face as she entered breathlessly, and beheld two strangers in place of the "folks" she had doubtless fondly imagined. Her manner and look were those of one to whom wild-wood life was not, as to her husband, an unmixed joy. She told the guileless one later, somewhat wistfully, as she cast a hasty glance across the room, that it was "kind o' lonesome, sometimes, and they went to bed as early as 7, generally."

Life was not an amusing thing to her; she had th· air of one who rarely smiled, and then under protest. She had been sick, she said; she always had asthma, and getting cold made it worse. She, too, was born in Smithfield, but she hadn't been used to living that way; she'd always lived more among folks. Yes, she got down to the village when she could, but you couldn't in such going. Summers they had some company. Folks come there to pick swamp huckleberries. Lots of them grew round there. These bits of information were sandwiched in, in an undertone, between the trapping talk of the masculine element. All about muskrat, mink, skunk and otter they talked. They lamented the rarer growing otter, and told how Allen Lillibridge had just brought a magnificent one up to town, five feet long. They discussed traps and methods of baiting, and agreed that deadfall traps were best for skunks, as they killed instantly, and did away with the disagreeable work of killing them in the trap. They told how they buried or immersed the skin in running water, to rid them of the scent, and they smiled in a superior manner over the high flown titles under which the mephitic animal masquerades on ladies' raiment.

"The skunk," mused Mr. Dixon, as he relit his pipe with a fragment of twisted paper, "is an ignorant critter." "Well, I don't know about that," returned the hunter. "I know I found one in a

other day, and I was
up with a noose, and
d that noose over his
w poked it off quick
nk I tried it a dozen
he same success. It
ble intelligence, it

: his head. "I've took
same hole," he said.
ant critter." The in-
o from time to time
ily aloft, when the
to wane in interest,
diant and announced,

p of the old block,"
er, with a touch of
settin' figger 4 mice
ret."
mink the topic now
d. North Smithfield
than those caught by
a good many first and
kin and Tarkiln brooks
im think; he'd got a
p there, too, weighed
, and, as a general
the mink caught in a
uld be found dead and
hedges, too, the guile-
Dixon heard about—
ningly constructed of
, in a runway down
in the brook by the
r if there are no signs
Spot where the trap
hang there untouched
. Muskrat, Mr. Dixon
good a bait as any.
traps put? Oh, out
m the bank, or in a
ing water that won't
In March you can
miles and miles along
ist want to be careful
his own door, so to
wn paths.
been taking pictures?"
d Mrs. Dixon at this

e nodded assent.
"
d that they were not

yet on exhibition in the garish light of day, but promises were made that they should be promptly forwarded if satisfactory, and the conversation proceeded.

"When I begun to trap—that was in war time—mink was awful high. I had three skins, and she"—nodding towards his wife—"sold them for $30. I taought trapping was about the thing to go into, and I've followed it up ever since."

"And how old are you now, Mr. Dixon?" queried the guileless one.

"I am in my 69th year," responded Mr. Dixon. "You've seen muskrat houses, I suppose?"

Yes, the hunter had espied and pointed one out to his companions from the train, on the Woonasquatucket; or was it called the Stillwater at this end? It was assuredly called the Stillwater, for Mr. Dixon declared with much firmness that he had never heard of the Woonasquatucket, and didn't know where it was. With this error rectified, the instructive conversation went on to the structure of muskrat houses, now rapidly disappearing from New England, soon to be obsolete like the beaver—sedge covered and skillfully plastered within; even repeated demolitions of portions of it do not daunt the cheerful little toiler within, who patiently and neatly repairs it again. Some premonition of what the coming winter will be has the wise little builder in the eyes of many old trappers, who aver that by the height of his aquatic home can be judged whether high or low water will prevail, and by its thickness whether the winter is to be severe or mild. Trappers often detect his habitat by the presence of uptorn roots and floating grass upon the water, for he feeds on sedge, lily roots, and fresh water clams. "A good many shoot muskrat in the spring," said Mr. Dixon. "Them that know how imitate his call, and when he answers 'em, down him. Jacques from Greenville—he's a great bird hunter—he buys most of my furs. He does as well by me as most city dealers."

"Did you ever have any adventures in trapping, Mr. Dixon—anything exciting?" put in the interrogation point of the party.

"No, I donno's I have," mused Mr. Dixon. "Had a skunk bite me once. Put my hand into the hole and he grabbed and bit me to the bone, but I hauled him out and killed him. Ever get lost? No, I'd be ashamed to get lost in these woods. I know every rod of 'em the darkest night."

"Don't any animals come round 'your hut in the night?" pursued the thirster for knowledge.

"Oh, no; nothin' but foxes and rabbits, and they won't hurt you. The owls you can hear, too, screeching down in the cedar swamp."

The infant grandson, who had been quietly amusing himself by excavating a wasp's nest and offering the inhabitants one by one to the unsuspecting dog, now made more frequent headers into the apple barrel, and his grandmother looked furtively at the clock. It would not do to embarrass the genial host and hostess by remaining to witness their frugal meal, or cause them to suffer too intense pangs of hunger by its postponement. The guests, therefore, having obtained a brief sketch of the shortest route to the nearest station by cross cuts, made their adieux and looked their last upon the lonely wood-bound hut, Mrs. Dixon pausing in an earnest altercation as to whether the station lay two or three miles away, to say hospitably, "Well, call in again, both of you;" and Mr. Dixon to call out lustily, "Say, don't forget them pictures!" and at last, through snow and ice and slush, by the queer old "Samanthy Evans" place, rock-strewn and brook-bordered, with its cellar one huge hollow out of a solid rock—by the singing pines and the rushing rivulet, past the old "Yellow Tavern" of two centuries fame on the Woonsocket road, and down to the tiny little Smithfield station, where passengers flagged their own trains or were left behind, the travellers returned blithely from their successful quest. Though the wee station was post office as well, neither station agent nor postmaster materialized before the coming train, and the only token of previous occupancy was a glowing fire, shining redly in the tiny stove.

Back in the calm shelter of Providence, it seemed dreamlike to picture again, as the wind of the next blizzard howled, the lonely little hut on the forest rise, with the winter moon shining down on the flitting foxes and rabbits, while the little owls hooted from the cedar swamp.

BURRILLVILLE AND HERRING POND.

[Central Division of New York and New England Road terminates at Pascoag, the largest town. Harrisville is nearest Herring Pond.]

BURRILLVILLE is one of our few remote townships which began a flourishing career away back in the early years of the century, and has not since sunk into innocuous desuetude. Forty years ago there were 24 factories within its borders, 451 houses and 287 barns—hinting largely, by the last item, of rural population, after all. The same curious discrepancy obtains in the township to-day. With Pascoag's big machine shop and its six woolen mills, and at least one mill attached to every settlement that dots the course of its half dozen baby rivers, it is yet one of the wildest, craggiest, most densely wooded territories in the State, away from the track of the rivers and railways. There is a charm even in the sound of its hills and swamps and streams—names bestowed long ago by the simple country folk of another generation, or in an earlier century yet by the Nipmuc and Pascoag tribes, its earliest possessors; its woods, the Horsehead, Herring Pond and Pine, its swamps, the Cedar, Mehunganup, Maplesap, Reeds and Pine; its ponds, the Wallum, Herring, Round and Sucker; and its rivers, the Branch, Pascoag, Clear, Chepachet, Tarkiln, Nipmuc, Muddy Brook and Herring Pond Brook. Wilder yet are the suggestions of its hills—Badger Mountain, Buck Hill, Benson's Mountain, Round Top, Eagle Peak, Snake Hill, and so on. Larger game than rabbits now hunted on Buck Hill once roamed these forests, and the huge crag that frowns above the little hamlet of Oakland is called Snake Hill in memory of the clans of rattlesnakes whose fastnesses lay along its jutting gray ledges. When, in Mehunganup swamp, the two-century old cedars were hewn by the dozen to supply modern needs, bullets were often found imbedded in their hearts, perhaps more indicative, in their numbers, of an Indian swamp fight than marksmen's missiles gone astray. In 1836, Capt. Samuel White, excavating for some cause, beneath his woodshed, turned up with his spade the skeleton of a man some eight feet in height, which the old settlers pronounced that of an Indian. Some traces of the old wigwams still exist here and there, where the Pascoags and Mohawks used to exchange friendly visits, and now and then a bundle of arrows comes to light among the arrowheads common to most of our Rhode Island fields.

But Burrillville's old country folk of the present day will relate with more gusto, tales of their own ancestors, and dimly remembered doings of those dear old delightful days of the "good old times" that will never come again for loyal New Englanders; they will tell you of the feats of agility performed by the departed strong men like Esek Phetteplace and Otis Wood, and how a certain Capt. Wm. Rhodes, a once humble youth who rose to comparative opulence among his fellows, did, at the advanced age of 70, lay out a 30-foot length of timber, and "go the length of it at three hops," beside various other kindred exploits that remind the hearer of one of those world-wide Wonderland jingles:

" 'You are old, father William,' the young man said—
'Your locks are besprinkled with white,
And yet you incessantly stand on your head.
Do you think, at your age, it is right?' "

The natives lived longer in the early years of the century than now, the Estens being a large family, notable for longevity,

90 years being about an average life among them.

Some of the old Burrillville school reports show how painfully education was acquired by the country youths, and, even in their meagre outlines, how far from covetable a post was that of country schoolmaster. A teacher in 1840 reports the pay to have been $1 50 weekly and "board around." Schools were held variously in dwellings, corn cribs and shops, and one flourishing school is reported from the house of one Welcome Sayles, east of Pascoag reservoir, where the housewife always came in for one day during the week to bake in the brick oven. The school house proper was a one-story house, with seats on three sides and an open fireplace; and William A. Mowry, who taught in 1847, pictures himself figuring at the age of 18, "in cap and circular cloak," behind a desk one foot wide and 16 inches long. Few girls studied arithmetic in these early years of the town's history, and it was in 1831 that Miss Abby Owen introduced grammar and geography. The names most frequently enrolled among the lists as pupils were Lapham, Wood, Clark, Smith, Harris, Mowry, Steere; they are the predominating names still.

It was in 1806 that Burrillville was separated from Glocester by a line running east and west, and taking half its territory. The Burrillville people found Chepachet too far away to conveniently attend town meeting there, and the Hon. James Burrill, Jr., Senator from 1817 to 1820, had the honor of a namesake in the new northern township. Outside the river valleys the country was one wild, untrodden jungle. When Roger Williams, prospecting for the limits of the Plantation domains, returned to Providence from a quest in this direction, he drew the line at the Burrillville forests, remarking with a confident naivete amusing in the light of later years, that "no one would ever settle beyond there." The pioneer settler of East Burrillville, bearing the somewhat prosaic name of John Smith, crossing streams by means of felled trees, where his axe laid them low, called a halt in the region of the old Tarkiln saw mill, concluded it to be the most favorable spot along the stream for a future settlement, worked away in solitude till his supply of food gave out, then returned for his brother and a few more adventurous pioneers, who made the first homes in the section. Deer were abundant, and meat plentiful in consequence. Before the dams were built the fish came up the streams to spawn, returning in the fall to the sea; sweet wild grapes grew in profusion, as they do to this day in the wild region about Wallum pond, and maple sap was boiled into a drink jocularly known as chocolate, as well as being used to sweeten the universal bean porridge.

Along the Branch river, the town's largest stream, little settlements sprang swiftly, and in 1856, though there was no railway in the town, Waterford being the nearest station, there were seven factories on it. An old-style coach ran to Providence and also to Waterford from Pascoag, though drivers were apt to retire after a brief service, announcing that Burrillville roads were too much for them.

Even now the traveller would best select his time for pleasure driving off the beaten highways; and let him not be deceived by a delusive thaw about Providence in time of snow; arriving at Burrillville he will find some of the northern cross roads well-nigh impassable with drifts, and spring mud lying deep when the southern roads are hard and firm. Spring is about two weeks later in arriving at Burrillville than in making her advent along South County shores. Few farmers wax opulent without some specialty, for the land is poor, the soil rocky, and patriotic residents lament bitterly that the Massachusetts State line did not run a few miles farther north through the rich and arable lands of Douglas.

One who is abroad with only a beauty loving eye and but superficial sympathy with farmers' sorrows, finds only enjoyment, not only in drives about the lonely hills and wood-roads, but in the railway journey to the township, up the Woonasquatucket valley; factory villages though they are, along the southern half of the trip, they are such quaint, sleepy, woodbound little hamlets, nestling so cosily in the lap of the valley, that one is not disposed to find fault with any of them; and as the train speeds on to the northwest and the view broadens, and the white pines grow denser, the villages cease, and only flag stations announce the "centre" for some sparse farming region. Pascoag is the road's terminus, the most populous of all Burrillville's villages, and with more hotels than anything else, apparently. Pascoag supports two newspapers, the Burrillville Democrat and Pascoag Herald, while a third, the Burrillville News-Gazette, is published in Harrisville. Unlike the factories on our other rivers, these of the Woonasquatucket valley, even through Burrillville, are owned by several different corporations and individuals, the Inmans, Fisks and Sayles having chief sway in Pascoag. Every few minutes, as one drives along, through the township's central section that follows the railway, he comes upon the little cluster of cottages, painted a uniform tint, that belong to the mill hard by. Out beyond Pascoag's crowded streets stands what is left of the "White Mill," now owned by Mr. Fred Arnold and Mr. Perkins. Though half the mill was destroyed by fire, business still goes briskly on in the remaining portion, and the goods are shipped for their finishing to Nasonville. Graniteville has an attractive looking factory, with two imposing towers, and Harrisville's mill stands near a pleasant grove, and with the road crossing so close to the foaming dam that the spray flies in one's face in crossing. Irish and French operatives make up most of the employes, where English were once predominant; as a consequence the churches are changing about, and the Episcopal Church at Harrisville is now converted into a temperance hall, while the Catholic and Universalist have come to the fore. Across the river in Harrisville, the grounds of the superintendent and owner lie in pleasant groves, and the road that leads east from here to Glendale is one of the fairest in the town. One may meet here the mail coach, drawing up with a flourish at the little Oakland station, and bearing on its side this inscrutable legend, "U. S. Mail. Newport and Tiverton."

In Harrisville proper, a neat little village, there are but few pretentious houses, that of Mr. De Witt Remington the most attractive and homelike; in the cool and well-kept precincts of the chief grocery store some of the garrulous old mill hands drop in at the noon hour and entertain each other with varied lore till the clang of the bell calls them off, then the little street is silent again. Says one, as the listeners pause here a moment, "Yes, Johnny he vowed he wouldn't drink no more water till the bluebirds come, 'n this morning there was about twenty on the band stand, 'n some one says, 'Johnny, come up and see the bluebirds.' By George, you ought to see him start!" And the mill bell cuts in upon a possible explanation of some strange Lenten sacrifice.

But there are pleasanter pastimes in Burrillville than following up mill villages, and it is a very easy thing to leave them all behind. The most popular wild wood rendezvous is Herring Pond, easily accessible from all the villages, and the local Rocky Point. Here are held most of the township's summer festivities—picnics, clambakes, boating and bathing parties, for this small but charming sheet of water affords facilities for all. Only a mile or so in a walk across lots from Harrisville, and a three or four-mile drive by a more roundabout way, it lies among sloping pastures and a magnificent grove of pine, chestnut and oak at its north and favorite end. On the cross road one passes a little old black house by the roadside, scarcely more than a hut; it is the house where Lydia Phetteplace murdered her husband some thirty years ago—the crowning stroke in the tragic family history, which a local editorial thus sketches:

Many years ago James Harris and wife lived in Herring Pond woods. Harris was found dead in a shanty near what is now Tarkiln station. He had been on a protracted debauch, and the cause of his death was plainly evident. He left four children, George, Stephen, Louis and Lydia. George was killed on the railroad near Fox Point, Providence. Stephen fell into a coal pit and burned both legs so that he was a cripple to the day of his death. Louis shot himself in the woods just above Glendale, placing the muzzle of the gun to his breast and pressing the trigger with a forked stick. This was in 1845. Lydia married Stephen Tourtellott in 1836, and on July 3, 1837, Stephen went into a neighbor's barn and hung himself with a leather whip lash. He was discovered, cut down, resuscitated and driven away. He went directly into another neighbor's (Stephen Bartlett) barn and hung himself with a stake chain and ' when discovered was dead. His widow (Lydia) married Ziba Phetteplace in 1838. She lived with him until 1860, in which year, Phetteplace, who was addicted to strong drink, came home one day, and, after giving his wife a terrible beating, lay down on the kitchen floor and went to sleep. He never awoke. Lydia, raging under the cruel treatment, took a keen, heavy axe, and as her husband lay asleep she struck one, two, fierce blows, and the sharp steel, driven by every ounce of power in her sinewy arms, sunk deep into Phetteplace's bared neck, nearly severing his head from his body. After the bloody deed she dragged the dead body, by the feet, across the floor, down the steps, through the yard into the orchard. She then went back, cleaned up the house, sat down and awaited arrest. It soon came, and she was sentenced to imprisonment for life for the crime. She died in the Rhode Island Insane Hospital in 1886. In that same year (1886) her son Harris, who as a boy had witnessed the crime that made him fatherless, left his home, which was near where his father had been killed, walked into the woods with his gun and shot himself in almost the identical manner and very close to the place where his uncle Louis killed himself forty-one years before.

From here on, the way leads over a pasture road, and terminates at the old farm house where Mr. Mosely, an English operative, dwells in the solitude of the woods and fields. A few weeks ago, as old Mr. Mosely sat alone by his evening's fire, he was astonished by the wholly unlooked-for appearance of a still more elderly brother, his wife and three children, who had with difficulty conquered some appalling snow drifts between there and the station as they arrived unannounced and unexpected, from England! The two old men had not met since boyhood days, and the family had crossed the ocean in hope of better luck in America.

Another dwelling stands not far from Herring Pond—that of Arnold Comstock, who caters to the picnic parties in summer. Otherwise, the sloping grove that runs to the water's edge stands in its pristine fairness, and the waves ripple against a marvelous white sand beach that makes bathing a delight. The lake, only a mile or so in extent, lies north and south, and as the south wind is summer's prevailing one, picknickers may be sure of air here in the green woods by the dancing lake, if a breeze is stirring anywhere. Regular clambakes are served here, with all the salt water accompaniments, and down at the south end of the lake Mr. Putnam does not confine himself to summer patronage, but gets a weekly dinner the winter through for the male patrons, with an occasional " ladies' day." On a bit of an island not far out from shore some of the Burrillville youth have constituted themselves a sort of fresh water Squantum Club, built a shanty, and have mysterious good times all by themselves. Herring Pond is not the only scene of summer camps, however; take the road that runs west along the shores of the Pascoag reservoir—a wild and romantic road, bordered on one side by the masses of splintered gray stone of the Pascoag ledge, and on the other by the long, winding sheet of water whose jutting wooded promontories and low boundary hills make it a gem indeed in its fair setting. In the beautiful great pine grove that slopes down to the water at its farthest and wildest bend, the Sayles family have founded a delightful summer house, and with a few congenial friends camp and keep house here and live delightful out-door lives the season through. Not far from the point lies an island the trees of whose sloping orchard are visible still from the farthest shores; it was planted years ago by an old man named Page, who had this solitary water-bound farm all to himself, and in consequence carried matters with a high hand, ill-treating his stock and starving his cattle, it is said, and who was finally removed to mainland jurisdiction.

venturesome explorers, climbing along the perilous narrow passes of its face, will come upon a cave hidden in the heart of the rock, in which small-boy romance of to-day loves to revel, and reconstruct many a possible tale of the past. Cooper's den is the name this gruesome spot is known by. Forger's Cave has an authentic history of once lawless doings within its black recesses. This lies far to the west, on the banks of Round Pond in

SAWMILL IN BURRILLVILLE WOODS.

Although the migratory steam saw mills that pervade the forest have their haunt in Burrillville, too, it will be many a long year before the wide tracts of woodland have disappeared before them; and they add a not ineffective touch, in their camp accoutrements, to the wildwood pictures one sees along the lonely forest drives.

On the road from Glendale to the Stephen Cooper place rises the highest ledge of all the region round, and the

Buck Hill woods; an underground cavern whose entrance, when it was in use, lay behind a huge tree with the cavity covered by a stone. Here Spanish milled dollars were counterfeited, and the gang of forgers wrought undiscovered for some time till one of their number got drunk and too freely spent in a neighboring village his bright silver coins of the same date. Arrests and a trial followed, but the leaders of the gang shrewdly implicated several of the neighboring citizens and proceedings were indefinitely stayed. Some of the old people remember a singular apparition peculiar to their childhood days—a mysterious yearly visitant clothed in wine-colored vestments, who made his way through the township on some strange, far-off pilgrimage, and who was locally known as the "darned man." In rain or shine the bent, shabby figure had yearly passed over the quiet country byways, as regularly returning year after year. Those who learnt his history said that his mind had given way under the shock of finding his love faithless on his marriage eve long years before, and that the raiment of peculiar hue which he so cherished in its growing shabbiness was his wedding outfit. At the few houses where he paused he requested needle and thread, and finding the proper hue, proceeded to patiently and neatly repair the growing rents of wear and tear—hence his sobriquet. Queer local characters abounded, too, in the backwoods, and do to this day; hermits, hunters and clannish tribes of the wilderness, chief of the latter being a gregarious company known as the Badger Mountain tribe, and whose home was on the heights of Eagle Peak. A lawless and wildwood-loving life lived these outcasts—their family originally the Rankins, but a certain William Inman and a band of Moffits joining fortunes with these, later. Uncertain in their sojourns, predatory in their habits, they herded together in clannish comradery, now and then driving down to the nearest village, a hilarious wagon load, the feminine contingent powdered and painted to the last degree. William Inman married the beauty of the tribe, who afterward died a most miserable death. The physician called to attend her in her illness says that her bed was merely of hay covered with feed meal sacks. But the Badger Mountain tribe has of late hied itself out of Burrillville domains and betaken itself to fresh woods and pastures new.

Far in the west of Burrillville the country lies still fresh and new, and unspoiled as when first from its Maker's hands. Wallum Pond, with its white sand beach, its grape jungles and its wooded northern summit looking far away to vague and distant blue western hills, is still the haunt of wild beasts and birds, and unspoiled by touch of man; and in these regions lies still the densest and most primeval forest region of our State. Even on many of the old country roads one may journey mile after mile and see only the sleepy old farmhouses, lying comfortably down grassy lanes, and meet only strolling and isolated types of the old-fashioned New England civilization. Here, among the many dancing brown brooks, and along the upper reaches of Clear river flowing fresh and undefiled from the wonderful crystalline waters of Wallum Pond, the lover of upland and forest may feel that he is in truth "near to nature's heart."

LIME ROCK.

[Worcester Railroad, 9 miles from Providence. Carriages from Ashton or Berkeley, one mile.]

"LIME ROCK."

ONLY the long ridge of western hills which, following the Blackstone from north to south, marks the dividing line between Lincoln and Cumberland separated us from a sight of the picturesque little bit of country whose name sends scraps of the gay old dancing tune floating into mind; to whose lively measures, the country folk say, used to wax nimble the feet of the old kiln-tenders by the red glow of their fierce fires on winter nights. Yet it was with the air of pilgrims entering a strange land that we, on one of our few fair October days, climbed the long, brown and russet slopes beyond the yellow-grass plains, where cows were placidly feeding, and shaped our course for the quaint old roofs that sparsely showed among the clustering orchards. A bit of genuine, old-fashioned country settlement is Lime Rock, rare to find nestled among the crowding factory villages of modern Rhode Island. Hardly a dwelling among the old hospitable farm houses set comfortably down amid towering elms and fruitful orchards but boasted its enormous double chimneys or still more enormous single one, its happy-go-lucky windows of varying sizes to suit the growing members of the family, and its quaint door ornaments. The iron scrapers by the door stones, the shining knockers, the worn stone steps inserted in terraced walls, the turnstiles here and there, the farmer lads, lustily singing as they drove barnward with loads of golden corn, with here and there a coveted "red ear" of husking time peeping through—all seemed to send our fancy roving among pages of those delightful, prosy old New England novels whose heroines are so exceedingly limp and useless, and whose heroes so blusteringly dramatic, but whose bits of description, grudgingly inserted, touch us with the same vague and delightful thrill as does the scent of lavender, or the sight of a sprig of caraway freshly culled. For all these have power to send us back to our earliest church-going days, when we sat solemnly erect between our elders and contemplated our horizontal shining shoes, which completed the painful right angle which we represented like an illustrated letter L. All this did Lime Rock for us as we strolled among its winding roads; here and there a hill-summit giving us a glimpse of far and distant heights stretching in tender purple mystery, faint and fair in the afternoon shadows and sunshine; of the sparkle and glow of hundreds of sunlit windows and clouds of faint hovering smoke over the cities far southward—Pawtucket and Providence, and Fall River even, with the yellow sunlight strong on the great white front of a towering factory, easily recognizable to the naked eye. Then down again into valleys which are yet far above the river level, with new and fairer pictures greeting us at every turn; a sloping cornfield, with its grotesque corn stalk statues, in fluttering rank and file, accented by the mellow golden glow of ruddy pumpkins; a rushing brook crossing the road with a musical drop of its hurrying cascade among the glistening white limestones; a group of ancient oaks in a meadow; a towering rock with scarred sides strong in the sunlight, and a barberry bush lending its crimson pendants to the cold gray; a placid pond by the roadside, lying so unruffled in its sheltered bed that we at first mistake its green reflections for solid land, until a hovering bird, lighting on the sere ranks of bending rushes, ruffles its still surface with a dip of flashing wings in a hasty bath; a quaint old house, with one end pretentiously started in stone, and meagrely finished in wood by ambition-losing

OLD KILN IN THE WOODS.

builders; and last of all the kilns and the quarries, and the pond holes, which are Lime Rock's chief attraction. And has no artist entered this fair harvest field to catch and hold its beauties? Yes, there has; we have found him out, thanks to an extremely conversational old kiln-tender; and I dare say he has kept very quiet about his find, and does not mean to let anyone know where Lime Rock is, that he may paint it all to himself; but he is betrayed, and now all the artists in the State are at liberty to enter and possess the land. How do you get there? why, climb right over the hill, as I said. If you start from either Berkeley, Ashton or Albion, strangely enough it will still be only a few minutes walk.

There are plenty of cows and massive oaks on windy hillsides for Mr. Bannister; there are towering ledges and reflecting lakes for Elmrich Rein; there are floating clouds and woodland paths for Mr. Barlow; there are plenty of mysterious, incomprehensible and suggestive things, all red, yellow and sage-green, and full of meaning, for our impressionists of the new school, and I daresay a neat little group of pumpkins, cabbages and a little drapery could be arranged for Mr. Leavitt; while as for Mr. Whittaker—well, he has no doubt found out for himself before this what he liked best.

As one ascends the road westward through this delightful scenery, the increasing quantity of bits of white limestone along the way, and the faint and muffled clang of the pick, show that the quarries are being neared. Off to the left a white and glistening pile of rock and the slowly ascending cloud of blue smoke through rocky rifts in the top of a grassy mound, mark the spot where the great lime oven is in active operation; while to the right there rises suddenly, cut sharp and crude against the clear sky, an enormous rock pinnacle, whose jagged sides and broken angles in cold slate-gray and dazzling white the sparse and clinging shrubbery makes faint attempt to soften. Across the rocky, yawning chasm from which this huge rock monster rises in lonely grandeur a second mass towers skyward, but the dazzle of its glittering marble-white is broken by no soft and tender gray; crude, un-

A MODERN KILN.

shadowed and unbearably white it lifts its face westward across the hollow space, and the eye turns hastily away. Far down below, at the foot of the sheer precipice that lies black in western shadow, lies the deep quarry-pool, with light puffs of the breeze that is blowing up aloft just ruffling its calm green surface. And about the shores of this abysmal pool, the sound of their profanity coming faintly up to our ears as they address their tugging horses, the workmen are loading teams with the quarried rock, which has been blasted in every sense of the word, no doubt.

Among the strange white soil and splintered rock are growing sturdy barberry bushes, and their scarlet splendor completes the rich coloring of a picture which, it is safe to say, cannot be equalled in the State. But for the most effective view of this weird scene one must pass around to the north of the great guarding peak, so that its giant gray shoulder may form the foreground for the chasm and the silent pond and the black western hill, with the twin white peak and its scarlet foliage rising in sharp contrast across the silent space; here might one linger for hours, could he have provided himself, like thoughtful Ulysses of old, with wax for the ears, to exclude the siren-like voices of the quarry laborers, who still shout and yell and call down imprecations on the heads of their hapless steeds.

We retrace our steps and, crossing the road, visit the kilns, less picturesque than of old, when the charm of the glowing fires that kindled the black night into splendor failed to offset the prosaic fact that they consumed five times the amount of fuel that the patent ones in present operation require. Here, among the roofed structures at the base of the great oven, where rows of white-dusted barrels stretched off into space, we found the presiding genius of the place, a communicative old fellow with a humorous mouth and twinkling eyes, who pounded the burnt lime in his intervals of fire-tending, and packed it away into barrels, and as he pounded offered us bits of information. Twenty-five barrels a day, he said, the kiln was turning out on an average, each barrel valued at over two dollars. But we reflected that three cords of wood were daily consumed in this one great roaring furnace, and we also bethought us of the workmen busy across the way, and ventured a remark as to the doubtful profit of the business.

"Oh, there's money in it," our informant hastily answered. "The lime business is always good, and there ain't much expense besides the fuel. We keep going here night and day; night and day them fires is never out. The fellow that owns this business come here poor when he first started out, but, Lord, he's got independent rich now!" and he shook his head with pensive envy.

AT THE TOP OF A KILN.

"Want to see the fire?" he continued. "Come round here and I'll show it to you," and he led the way to the great iron door, which, being flung open, disclosed a mass of glowing cord-wood gleaming red like fiery serpents, and moreover sent out such a sudden blast of hot air that we were glad to step aside. The old kiln-tender, stepping to a pile of timber near at hand, began thrusting on log after log to the glowing mass, whose flames, kindled into new fury, leaped wildly out at the open door, and faintly fading into blue smoke, went soaring and vanishing up the great expanse of lime-washed chimney, which age and smoke had faded to a tender gray. And now we thought that this was a picture more effective than the last,—the mammoth chimney, blackened about the open door, the lurid depths of leaping fire, the stooping figure of the old man as he thrust on fresh logs, and the cosy corner in the gloom where a great barrel-chair stood invitingly in the warmth.

A fire that never perished night and day! It ought to engender salamanders, and we were about to inquire if it did so, but our conductor was now taking us out to view the disused and picturesque old kilns outside. Fearless little ferns and vines and other tiny growing things— tions of Hawthorne in his wild romance of "Ethan Brand." Into the once yawning top of a raging fire here one could fancy a man casting himself in sudden frenzied despair, and we could picture the dismay of the old kiln-tender on discovering the bones of a skeleton lying in ghastly white outline on the burning mass; but the patent kilns are destructive

THE JOINTY ROCK HOLE.

how they shunned that other too tropical lurking place!—had climbed its sides and nestled in its crannies, and a brilliant and effective panel was made by a long spray of nightshade, whose clusters of translucent scarlet berries had flung themselves across the white background of the open oven door. Here was a kiln which one could fancy peopled by the weird creations to romance. Before a man could slip and wriggle through the oven door into which the logs of wood so blithely glide, he would no doubt, by the preliminary scorchings and chokings, have grown heartily sick of his bargain, and chosen some more poetic form of death. "We chuck it in at the top," said the kiln-tender, blithely interrupting our musings, d poke it out at the bottom, you see. It's put in to-day won't come out for reek."

And how do you know how much to ? out? How can you tell when it is ned enough?" we queried.

he kiln-tender shook his head with sage air born of experience. "We w," he said.

resently. "Lots of company we get cold evenings, too," he continued. amps now—they like to put up here rate, and if they can put up with lodgings, why, they're welcome. Can't ? much lime away in their pockets. n'? well, look round there further n the road and you'll find some more s that ain't going now." Which we ordingly did, much to our enjoyment. ther up the road, beyond where the sent quarry is being worked, lies what hance passer would take for a natural d; but it is a worked-out quarry, d up with water, and it adds a charm- feature to the rocky hills that lie ut it. Only those who knew it in the days, when it was a prosperous quarry, yielding a superior quality of lime, which seems now to be exhausted, would dream that the tranquil lakelet's expanse was but the surface of a tremendous chasm, beside which the quarry now in operation sinks into nothingness. The suicide within this pond would find a deep grave.

Meanwhile the sun sinks and the great white pinnacle across the way flushes from golden to rose red, and then softly glides into tender gray and awaits the moonlight. The quarry men turn homeward, and the teams come winding out from the gathering darkness below.

Only the kiln fires leap up fitfully through the gloom as the doors swing open and the great billets of wood are flung on; and behind the old kiln-tender a grotesque shadow, sharp against the white-dusted floor, seems in the flickering firelight to dance to the measures of the merry old tune:

THE END.

www.ingramcontent.com/pod-product-compliance
Lightning Source LLC
Chambersburg PA
CBHW020909230426

43666CB00008B/1385